- Revised Paperback Edition -

ROVER

P4

1½-litre GP Racing 1961-1965 (Whitelock)
AC Two-litre Saloons & Buckland Sportscars (Archibald)
Alfa Romeo 155/156/147 Competition Touring Cars (Collins)
Alfa Romeo Giulia Coupé GT & GTA (Tipler)
Alfa Romeo Montreal – The dream car that came true (Taylor)
Alfa Romeo Montreal – The Essential Companion (Classic Reprint of 500 copies) (Taylor)
Alfa Tipo 33 (McDonough & Collins)
Alpine & Renault – The Development of the Revolutionary Turbo F1 Car 1968 to 1979 (Smith)
Alpine & Renault – The Sports Prototypes 1963 to 1969 (Smith)
Alpine & Renault – The Sports Prototypes 1973 to 1978 (Smith)
An Austin Anthology (Stringer)
An Incredible Journey (Falls & Reisch)
Anatomy of the Classic Mini (Huthert & Ely)
Anatomy of the Works Minis (Moylan)
Armstrong-Siddeley (Smith)
Art Deco and British Car Design (Down)
Austin Cars 1948 to 1990 – A Pictorial History (Rowe)
Autodrome (Collins & Ireland)
Automotive A-Z, Lane's Dictionary of Automotive Terms (Lane)
Automotive Mascots (Kay & Springate)
Bahamas Speed Weeks, The (O'Neil)
Bentley Continental, Corniche and Azure (Bennett)
Bentley MkVI, Rolls-Royce Silver Wraith, Dawn & Cloud/Bentley R & S-Series (Nutland)
Bluebird CN7 (Stevens)
BMC Competitions Department Secrets (Turner, Chambers & Browning)
BMW 5-Series (Cranswick)
BMW Z-Cars (Taylor)
BMW Boxer Twins 1970-1995 Bible, The (Falloon)
BMW Cafe Racers (Cloesen)
BMW Classic 5 Series 1972 to 2003 (Cranswick)
BMW Custom Motorcycles – Choppers, Cruisers, Bobbers, Trikes & Quads (Cloesen)
Bonjour – Is this Italy? (Turner)
British 250cc Racing Motorcycles (Pereira)
British at Indianapolis, The (Wagstaff)
British Café Racers (Cloesen)
British Cars, The Complete Catalogue of, 1895-1975 (Culshaw & Horrobin)
British Custom Motorcycles – The Brit Chop – choppers, cruisers, bobbers & trikes (Cloesen)
BRM – A Mechanic's Tale (Salmon)
BRM V16 (Ludvigsen)
BSA Bantam Bible, The (Henshaw)
BSA Motorcycles – the final evolution (Jones)
Bugatti – The 8-cylinder Touring Cars 1920-34 (Price & Arbey)
Bugatti Type 40 (Price)
Bugatti 46/50 Updated Edition (Price & Arbey)
Bugatti T44 & T49 (Price & Arbey)
Bugatti 57 2nd Edition (Price)
Bugatti Type 57 Grand Prix – A Celebration (Tomlinson)
Caravan, Improve & Modify Your (Porter)
Caravans, The Illustrated History 1919-1959 (Jenkinson)
Caravans, The Illustrated History From 1960 (Jenkinson)
Carrera Panamericana, La (Tipler)
Car-tastrophes – 80 automotive atrocities from the past 20 years (Honest John, Fowler)
Chevrolet Corvette (Starkey)
Chrysler 300 – America's Most Powerful Car 2nd Edition (Ackerson)
Chrysler PT Cruiser (Ackerson)
Citroën DS (Bobbitt)
Classic British Car Electrical Systems (Astley)
Cobra – The Real Thing! (Legate)
Competition Car Aerodynamics 3rd Edition (McBeath)
Competition Car Composites A Practical Handbook (Revised 2nd Edition) (McBeath)
Concept Cars, How to illustrate and design – New 2nd Edition (Dewey)
Cortina – Ford's Bestseller (Robson)
Cosworth – The Search for Power (6th edition) (Robson)
Coventry Climax Racing Engines (Hammill)
Daily Mirror 1970 World Cup Rally 40, The (Robson)
Daimler SP250 New Edition (Long)
Datsun Fairlady Roadster to 280ZX – The Z-Car Story (Long)
Dino – The V6 Ferrari (Long)
Dodge Challenger & Plymouth Barracuda (Grist)
Dodge Charger – Enduring Thunder (Ackerson)
Dodge Dynamite! (Grist)
Dorset from the Sea – The Jurassic Coast from Lyme Regis to Old Harry Rocks photographed from its best viewpoint (also Souvenir Edition) (Belasco)
Draw & Paint Cars – How to (Gardiner)
Drive on the Wild Side, A – 20 Extreme Driving Adventures From Around the World (Weaver)
Ducati 750 Bible, The (Falloon)
Ducati 750 SS 'round-case' 1974, The Book of the (Falloon)
Ducati 860, 900 and Mille Bible, The (Falloon)
Ducati Monster Bible (New Updated & Revised Edition), The (Falloon)
Ducati Story, The – 6th Edition (Falloon)
Ducati 916 (updated edition) (Falloon)
Dune Buggy, Building A – The Essential Manual (Shakespeare)
Dune Buggy Files (Hale)
Dune Buggy Handbook (Hale)
East German Motor Vehicles in Pictures (Suhr/Weinreich)
Essential Guide to Driving in Europe, The (Parish)
Fast Ladies – Female Racing Drivers 1888 to 1970 (Bouzanquet)
Fate of the Sleeping Beauties, The (op de Weegh/Hottendorff/op de Weegh)
Ferrari 288 GTO, The Book of the (Sackey)
Ferrari 333 SP (O'Neil)
Fiat & Abarth 124 Spider & Coupé (Tipler)
Fiat & Abarth 500 & 600 – 2nd Edition (Bobbitt)
Fiats, Great Small (Ward)
Fine Art of the Motorcycle Engine, The (Peirce)
Ford Cleveland 335-Series V8 engine 1970 to 1982 – The Essential Source Book (Hammill)
Ford F100/F150 Pick-up 1948-1996 (Ackerson)
Ford F150 Pick-up 1997-2005 (Ackerson)
Ford Focus WRC (Robson)
Ford GT – Then, and Now (Streather)
Ford GT40 (Legate)
Ford Midsize Muscle – Fairlane, Torino & Ranchero (Cranswick)
Ford Model Y (Roberts)
Ford Mustang II & Pinto 1970 to 80 (Cranswick)
Ford Small Block V8 Racing Engines 1962-1970 – The Essential Source Book (Hammill)
Ford Thunderbird From 1954, The Book of the (Long)
Formula 1 - The Knowledge 2nd Edition (Hayhoe)
Formula One – The Real Score? (Harvey)
Formula 5000 Motor Racing, Back then ... and back now (Lawson)
Forza Minardi! (Vigar)
France: the essential guide for car enthusiasts – 200 things for the car enthusiast to see and do (Parish)
Franklin's Indians (Sucher/Pickering/Diamond/Havelin)
From Crystal Palace to Red Square – A Hapless Biker's Road to Russia (Turner)
Funky Mopeds (Skelton)
The Good, the Mad and the Ugly ... not to mention Jeremy Clarkson (Dron)
Grand Prix Ferrari – The Years of Enzo Ferrari's Power, 1948-1980 (Pritchard)
Grand Prix Ford – DFV-powered Formula 1 Cars (Robson)
GT – The World's Best GT Cars 1953-73 (Dawson)
Hillclimbing & Sprinting – The Essential Manual (Short & Wilkinson)
Honda NSX (Long)
Immortal Austin Seven (Morgan)
India - The Shimmering Dream (Reisch/Falls (translator))
Inside the Rolls-Royce & Bentley Styling Department – 1971 to 2001 (Hull)
Intermeccanica – The Story of the Prancing Bull (McCredie & Reisner)
Italian Cafe Racers (Cloesen)
Italian Custom Motorcycles (Cloesen)
Jaguar - All the Cars (4th Edition) (Thorley)
Jaguar from the shop floor (Martin)
Jaguar E-type Factory and Private Competition Cars (Griffiths)
Jaguar, The Rise of (Price)
Jaguar XJ 220 – The Inside Story (Moreton)
Jaguar XJ-S, The Book of the (Long)
Japanese Custom Motorcycles – The Nippon Chop – Chopper, Cruiser, Bobber, Trikes and Quads (Cloesen)
Jeep CJ (Ackerson)
Jeep Wrangler (Ackerson)
The Jowett Jupiter – The car that leaped to fame (Nankivell)
Karmann-Ghia Coupé & Convertible (Bobbitt)
Kawasaki Triples Bible, The (Walker)
Kawasaki W, H1 & Z – The Big Air-cooled Machines (Long)
Kawasaki Z1 Story, The (Sheehan)
Kris Meeke – Intercontinental Rally Challenge Champion (McBride)
Lamborghini Miura Bible, The (Sackey)
Lamborghini Murciélago, The book of the (Pathmanathan)
Lamborghini Urraco, The Book of the (Landsem)
Lambretta Bible, The (Davies)
Lancia 037 (Collins)
Lancia Delta HF Integrale (Blaettel & Wagner)
Lancia Delta Integrale (Collins)
Land Rover Design - 70 years of success (Hull)
Land Rover Emergency Vehicles (Taylor)
Land Rover Series III Reborn (Porter)
Land Rover, The Half-ton Military (Cook)
Land Rovers in British Military Service – coil sprung models 1970 to 2007 (Taylor)
Laverda Twins & Triples Bible 1968-1986 (Falloon)
Lea-Francis Story, The (Price)
Le Mans Panoramic (Ireland)
Lexus Story, The (Long)
Little book of microcars, the (Quellin)
Little book of smart, the – New Edition (Jackson)
Little book of trikes, the (Quellin)
Lola – The Illustrated History (1957-1977) (Starkey)
Lola – All the Sports Racing & Single-seater Racing Cars 1978-1997 (Starkey)
Lola T70 – The Racing History & Individual Chassis Record – 4th Edition (Starkey)
Lotus 18 Colin Chapman's U-turn (Whitelock)
Lotus 49 (Oliver)
Making a Morgan (Hensing)
Marketingmobiles, The Wonderful Wacky World of (Hale)
Maserati 250F In Focus (Pritchard)
Mazda MX-5/Miata 1.6 Enthusiast's Workshop Manual (Grainger & Shoemark)
Mazda MX-5/Miata 1.8 Enthusiast's Workshop Manual (Grainger & Shoemark)
Mazda MX-5 Miata, The book of the – The 'Mk1' NA-series 1988 to 1997 (Long)
Mazda MX-5 Miata, The book of the – The 'Mk2' NB-series 1997 to 2004 (Long)
Mazda MX-5 Miata Roadster (Long)
Mazda Rotary-engined Cars (Cranswick)
Maximum Mini (Booij)
Meet the English (Bowie)
Mercedes-Benz SL – R230 series 2001 to 2011 (Long)
Mercedes-Benz SL – W113-series 1963-1971 (Long)
Mercedes-Benz SL & SLC – 107-series 1971-1989 (Long)
Mercedes-Benz SLK – R170 series 1996-2004 (Long)
Mercedes-Benz SLK – R171 series 2004-2011 (Long)
Mercedes-Benz W123-series – All models 1976 to 1986 (Long)
Mercedes G-Wagen (Long)
MG, Made in Abingdon (Frampton)
MGA (Price Williams)
MGB & MGB GT– Expert Guide (Auto-doc Series) (Williams)
MGB Electrical Systems Updated & Revised Edition (Astley)
MGB – The Illustrated History, Updated Fourth Edition (Wood & Burrell)
Micro Caravans (Jenkinson)
Micro Trucks (Mort)
Microcars at Large! (Quellin)
Mike the Bike – Again (Macauley)
Mini Cooper – The Real Thing! (Tipler)
Mini Minor to Asia Minor (West)
Mitsubishi Lancer Evo, The Road Car & WRC Story (Long)
Montlhéry, The Story of the Paris Autodrome (Boddy)
MOPAR Muscle – Barracuda, Dart & Valiant 1960-1980 (Cranswick)
Morgan Maverick (Lawrence)
Morgan 3 Wheeler – back to the future!, The (Dron)
Morris Minor, 70 Years on the Road (Newell)
Moto Guzzi Sport & Le Mans Bible, The (Falloon)
Moto Guzzi Story, The – 3rd Edition (Falloon)
Motor Movies – The Posters! (Veysey)
Motor Racing – Reflections of a Lost Era (Carter)
Motor Racing – The Pursuit of Victory 1930-1962 (Carter)
Motor Racing – The Pursuit of Victory 1963-1972 (Wyatt/Sears)
Motor Racing Heroes – The Stories of 100 Greats (Newman)
Motorcycle Apprentice (Cakebread)
Motorcycle GP Racing in the 1960s (Pereira)
Motorcycle Racing with the Continental Circus 1920-1970 (Pereira)
Motorcycle Road & Racing Chassis Designs (Noakes)
Motorcycles and Motorcycling in the USSR from 1939 (Turbett)
Motorcycling in the '50s (Clew)
Motorhomes, The Illustrated History (Jenkinson)
Motorsport In colour, 1950s (Wainwright)
MV Agusta Fours, The book of the classic (Falloon)
N.A.R.T. – A concise history of the North American Racing Team 1957 to 1983 (O'Neil)
Nissan 300ZX & 350Z – The Z-Car Story (Long)
Nissan GT-R Supercar: Born to race (Gorodji)
Nissan – The GTP & Group C Racecars 1984-1993 (Starkey)
Northeast American Sports Car Races 1950-1959 (O'Neil)
Norton Commando Bible – All models 1968 to 1978 (Henshaw)
Nothing Runs – Misadventures in the Classic, Collectable & Exotic Car Biz (Slutsky)
Off-Road Giants! (Volume 1) – Heroes of 1960s Motorcycle Sport (Westlake)
Off-Road Giants! (Volume 2) – Heroes of 1960s Motorcycle Sport (Westlake)
Off-Road Giants! (Volume 3) – Heroes of 1960s Motorcycle Sport (Westlake)
Patina Volkswagens (Walker)
Pass the Theory and Practical Driving Tests (Gibson & Hoole)
Peking to Paris 2007 (Young)
Pontiac Firebird – New 3rd Edition (Cranswick)
Porsche 356 (2nd Edition) (Long)
Porsche 908 (Födisch, Neßhöver, Roßbach, Schwarz & Roßbach)
Porsche 911 Carrera – The Last of the Evolution (Corlett)
Porsche 911R, RS & RSR, 4th Edition (Starkey)
Porsche 911, The Book of the (Long)
Porsche 911 – The Definitive History 2004-2012 (Long)
Porsche – The Racing 914s (Smith)
Porsche 911SC 'Super Carrera' – The Essential Companion (Streather)
Porsche 914 & 914-6: The Definitive History of the Road & Competition Cars (Long)
Porsche 924 (Long)
The Porsche 924 Carreras – evolution to excellence (Smith)
Porsche 928 (Long)
Porsche 930 to 935: The Turbo Porsches (Starkey)
Porsche 944 (Long)
Porsche 964, 993 & 996 Data Plate Code Breaker (Streather)
Porsche 993 'King Of Porsche' – The Essential Companion (Streather)
Porsche 996 'Supreme Porsche' – The Essential Companion (Streather)
Porsche 997 2004-2012 – Porsche Excellence (Streather)
Porsche Boxster – The 986 series 1996-2004 (Long)
Porsche Boxster & Cayman – The 987 series (2004-2013) (Long)
Porsche Racing Cars – 1953 to 1975 (Long)
Porsche Racing Cars – 1976 to 2005 (Long)
Porsche – The Rally Story (Meredith)
Porsche: Three Generations of Genius (Meredith)
Powered by Porsche (Smith)
Preston Tucker & Others (Linde)
RAC Rally Action! (Gardiner)
Racing Colours – Motor Racing Compositions 1908-2009 (Newman)
Racing Line – British motorcycle racing in the golden age of the big single (Guntrip)
Rallye Sport Fords: The Inside Story (Moreton)
The Red Baron's Ultimate Ducati Desmo Manual (Cabrera Choclán)
Renewable Energy Home Handbook, The (Porter)
Roads with a View – England's greatest views and how to find them by road (Corfield)
Rolls-Royce Silver Shadow/Bentley T Series Corniche & Camargue – Revised & Enlarged Edition (Bobbitt)
Rolls-Royce Silver Spirit, Silver Spur & Bentley Mulsanne 2nd Edition (Bobbitt)
Rootes Cars of the 50s, 60s & 70s – Hillman, Humber, Singer, Sunbeam & Talbot, A Pictorial History (Rowe)
Rover Cars 1945 to 2005, A Pictorial History
Rover P4 (Bobbitt)
Runways & Racers (O'Neil)
Russian Motor Vehicles – Soviet Limousines 1930-2003 (Kelly)
Russian Motor Vehicles – The Czarist Period 1784 to 1917 (Kelly)
RX-7 – Mazda's Rotary Engine Sportscar (Updated & Revised New Edition) (Long)
Sauber-Mercedes – The Group C Racecars 1985-1991 (Starkey)
Schlumpf – The intrigue behind the most beautiful car collection in the world (Op de Weegh & Op de Weegh)
Scooters & Microcars, The A-Z of Popular (Dan)
Scooter Lifestyle (Grainger)
Scooter Mania! – Recollections of the Isle of Man International Scooter Rally (Jackson)
Singer Story: Cars, Commercial Vehicles, Bicycles & Motorcycle (Atkinson)
Sleeping Beauties USA – abandoned classic cars & trucks (Marek)
SM – Citroën's Maserati-engined Supercar (Long & Claverol)
Speedway – Auto racing's ghost tracks (Collins & Ireland)
Sprite Caravans, The Story of (Jenkinson)
Standard Motor Company, The Book of the (Robson)
Steve Hole's Kit Car Cornucopia – Cars, Companies, Stories, Facts & Figures: the UK's kit car scene since 1949 (Hole)
Subaru Impreza: The Road Car And WRC Story (Long)
Supercar, How to Build your own (Thompson)
Suzuki Motorcycles - The Classic Two-stroke Era (Long)
Tales from the Toolbox (Oliver)
Tatra – The Legacy of Hans Ledwinka, Updated & Enlarged Collector's Edition of 1500 copies (Margolius & Henry)
Taxi! The Story of the 'London' Taxicab (Bobbitt)
This Day in Automotive History (Corey)
To Boldly Go – twenty six vehicle designs that dared to be different (Hull)
Toleman Story, The (Hilton)
Toyota Celica & Supra, The Book of Toyota's Sports Coupés (Long)
Toyota MR2 Coupés & Spyders (Long)
Triumph & Standard Cars 1945 to 1984 (Warrington)
Triumph Bonneville Bible (59-83) (Henshaw)
Triumph Bonneville!, Save the – The inside story of the Meriden Workers' Co-op (Rosamond)
Triumph Cars – The Complete Story (new 3rd edition) (Robson)
Triumph Motorcycles & the Meriden Factory (Hancox)
Triumph Speed Twin & Thunderbird Bible (Woolridge)
Triumph Tiger Cub Bible (Estall)
Triumph Trophy Bible (Woolridge)
Triumph TR6 (Kimberley)
TT Talking – The TT's most exciting era – As seen by Manx Radio TT's lead commentator 2004-2012 (Lambert)
Two Summers – The Mercedes-Benz W196R Racing Car (Ackerson)
TWR Story, The – Group A (Hughes & Scott)
Unraced (Collins)
Velocette Motorcycles – MSS to Thruxton – Third Edition (Burris)
Vespa – The Story of a Cult Classic in Pictures (Uhlig)
Vincent Motorcycles: The Untold Story since 1946 (Guyony & Parker)
Volkswagen Bus Book, The (Bobbitt)
Volkswagen Bus or Van to Camper, How to Convert (Porter)
Volkswagens of the World (Glen)
VW Beetle Cabriolet – The full story of the convertible Beetle (Bobbitt)
VW Beetle – The Car of the 20th Century (Copping)
VW Bus – 40 Years of Splitties, Bays & Wedges (Copping)
VW Bus Book, The (Bobbitt)
VW Golf: Five Generations of Fun (Copping & Cservenka)
VW – The Air-cooled Era (Copping)
VW T5 Camper Conversion Manual (Porter)
VW Campers (Copping)
Volkswagen Type 3, The book of the – Concept, Design, International Production Models & Development (Glen)
Volvo Estate, The (Hollebone)
You & Your Jaguar XK8/XKR – Buying, Enjoying, Maintaining, Modifying – New Edition (Thorley)
Which Oil? – Choosing the right oils & greases for your antique, vintage, veteran, classic or collector car (Michell)
Wolseley Cars 1948 to 1975 (Rowe)
Works MGs, The (Allison & Browning)
Works Minis, The Last (Purves & Brenchley)
Works Rally Mechanic (Moylan)

www.veloce.co.uk

First published in 1994 by Veloce Publishing Limited, Veloce Publishing Limited, Veloce House, Parkway Farm Business Park, Middle Farm Way, Poundbury, Dorchester, Dorset, DT1 3AR, England. Fax 01305 250479/e-mail info@veloce.co.uk/web www.veloce.co.uk or www.velocebooks.com. Reprinted April 2016, October 2016 and April 2019.
ISBN: 978-1-787115-24-8. UPC: 6-36847-01524-4

British Library Cataloguing in Publication Data – A catalogue record for this book is available from the British Library.
Typesetting, design and page make-up all by Veloce Publishing Ltd on Apple Mac. Printed and Bound by CPI Group (UK)Ltd, Croydon, CR0 4YY.

- Revised Paperback Edition -

ROVER

P4

Malcolm Bobbitt

VELOCE PUBLISHING
THE PUBLISHER OF FINE AUTOMOTIVE BOOKS

ACKNOWLEDGEMENTS

One of the most pleasurable facets of researching a particular motor car or marque is meeting the dedicated enthusiasts who brave all to keep their cars on the road, sometimes against great odds, and who never lose the enjoyment of driving them. The Rover P4 enthusiasts are no different and I am very appreciative of the help they have freely given to assist me in writing this book.

My sincere appreciation extends to Stan Johnstone, who has not only suffered my innumerable questions, checked the manuscript for technical accuracy and offered valuable suggestions and advice, but also allowed me access to both his own and the Rover P4 Drivers Guild's photographic archives.

I am grateful also to Matt White, editor of the Rover P4 Drivers Guild magazine, *Overdrive*, for the loan of photographs from his private collection and also the use of reference material collected from the magazine.

Bill Henderson has provided a vast amount of information concerning the prototype 2.6-litre Cyclops car, as well as the Tickford drophead coupé, and I am particularly grateful for Bill's hospitality and access to his collection of vehicles.

Thanks are due to Anders Clausager, Trevor Lord and Karim Ram at the British Motor Industry Heritage Trust for allowing me to search through the Trust's archives and photographic library. My gratitude also to James Taylor, Richard Stenning and Daniel Young for their advice and information concerning the P4. I am grateful also to Les White, a Rover enthusiast of many years, for lending me documents and information.

Friends have been very supportive in looking out for anything connected with Rover and the P4 in particular and, in this respect, thanks to Andrew Minney, who not only sought out some interesting snippets of literature, but also read through my manuscript.

The efforts of the library staff at the National Motor Museum are much appreciated, especially those of Annice Collet, Jonathan Day and Linda Springate, who have unfailingly assisted in my searches for information.

My thanks to Rod and Judith at Veloce who have given much in the way of support and helpful advice and who suggested this book in the first instance.

Last, but not least, my appreciation to my wife, Jean who, as always, has provided unending support and encouragement.

Malcolm Bobbitt.

CONTENTS

INTRODUCTION

As a youngster taking a serious interest in anything motorised during the mid-1950s, the instant recognition of every car was considered virtually mandatory. There was a degree of one-upmanship in being able to identify a vehicle, both from its characteristic shape and its bonnet-mounted mascot. To have to peer at the badge in order to realise the car's pedigree was to admit failure!

The Rover P4 was easy to spot, such was its broad outline and majestic stance; its proud and stately frontal design indicating superiority over the rest. It exuded a calm presence, reserved well-being and, above all, an enviable degree of sophistication and comfort. The latter attribute was all-important, appealing, as it did, to the discerning motorist who considered the car's opulent high quality walnut and leather as desirable as its undisputed engineering excellence.

Ownership of the Rover was a statement about one's social position: Rovers attracted the professional classes – doctors, solicitors, bank managers and the like. The P4 commanded respect; its owner did not have just a car but a Rover!

Its esteem and desirability was altogether in the same class as that of Daimler and Jaguar, and touching on even Bentley and Rolls-Royce. The P4 never lost its traditional touches and retains the image of the essential classic British motor car of the postwar era.

Now, in middle life, I enjoy watching the new generation of classic car enthusiasts deliberating over the cars built in an earlier age. Remarkably, the P4 captures for them the steadfast image of an age when only the best was good enough. The excellence of the car's engineering can be experienced through the steering wheel, the smell of the finest leather and the smoothness of the polished African walnut. The P4 is a car that wants to be loved, cherished and lavished with care and attention. In return, it will comfort and cosset and go on forever.

Then, of course, there is the P4's background, nurtured from the ashes of a war-torn motor industry. Gordon Bashford, following in the careful wake of Spencer and Maurice Wilks, created a car proud enough to carry the Rover emblem into the fifties and sixties. He ensured its longevity by designing a sturdy car with all the character of the British Bulldog – a belt-and-braces job, though Bashford would never admit to the car being over-engineered.

Ironically, the P4, the staunch British establishment car, had some of its roots not in the motor producing towns of the West Midlands, but South Bend, Indiana, deep in the USA. Spencer Wilks had uncharacteristically fallen for the American dream machine of the forties, designed by the progressive

Almost without doubt the most famous Rover of all time, JET 1, set new standards in motoring achievement. Not only did this P4 pioneer the gas-turbine engine in the motor car, it also established a world record by topping 151mph (244km/h) on the Jabbeke highway in Belgium in June 1952. Here, JET 1 in its original Cyclops styling, rests outside the Rover Company's offices at Solihull after successfully completing initial trials on a nearby airfield. (Courtesy National Motor Museum)

and controversial Raymond Loewy for the Studebaker Corporation. Such was Wilks' determination to follow in the American idiom that he had two Studebaker Champions delivered to the Rover works, where they were used as models to replace the ageing, prewar designs that heralded the return of car production in the immediate postwar austerity period.

A Studebaker body married to a Rover chassis and dubbed the 'Roverbaker', gave rise eventually, via a number of prototypes, to arguably one of the most notable cars of the immediate postwar period. The Rover 75, with its extraordinary frontal styling and distinctive Cyclops foglamp,

arrived at the 1949 London Motor Show, exhibiting luxury and refinement in a car unashamedly destined for the middle and upper classes.

The Rover P4 also had a hidden side to its character in the shape of gas-turbine engined models: who would have thought that safe, comfortable 'Auntie' Rover would be capable of breaking all records by thundering along a Belgian autoroute at something in excess of 151mph in the summer of 1952?

The Rover P4 is, therefore, more than what it seems and is, without doubt, one of the best admired of all postwar British cars. This is its story.

Note to the Fourth Edition

Although the first edition of this book appeared more twenty years ago, it has been a pleasure to revisit the Rover P4. The British motor industry has changed much since the last of the traditional Rovers rolled off the production lines, and since this book first appeared the Rover name, like so many other famous British marques, has fallen into oblivion. And yet this Rover, *One of Britain's Fine Cars*, continues to survive in healthy numbers thanks to its sound design, attention to detail and excellent build quality. That alone would not be sufficient for the P4 to withstand the vagaries of time, use and road and traffic conditions,

One of Britain's Fine Cars

and therefore the cars' enthusiastic custodians have to be applauded in keeping their Rovers in good fettle and saving those examples which might have otherwise been destroyed.

It is my good fortune to write the foregoing as the fourth edition of this book appears, and to affirm that this is the story of one Britain's best loved cars.

Malcolm Bobbitt

This emotive image taken from a Rover publicity brochure typifies the P4, in this instance a Rover 90, as a high quality family car suitable for continental touring. (Author's collection)

P4

STARLEY, WILKS AND THE P4

Below: Hands and feet were required to propel this tricycle of 1884 which used Starley's Patent Automatic Double-driving gear. (Courtesy Rover P4 Drivers Guild)

Sewing machines, cycles and cars
James Starley started it all in the middle of the 19th century: from a career in marine engineering he took a side-step into the business of sewing machines, where he excelled in the development and manufacture of new models, each better than the one before. A move from London to Coventry saw Starley set up a company with Josiah Turner, whom he had met

THE "ROVER.

THE POPULAR MACHINE FOR 1884.

Specially constructed for gentlemen requiring a light machine with vertical or bicycle position, very easy, comfortable, perfectly safe, and the best hill-climber yet made. OPEN FRONT, fitted with Starley's Patent Automatic Double-driving Gear, Ball Bearings to all Wheels, Adjustable Handles and Seat, safe yet effective Band Brake, Plated Parts, Hubs, Handle Brackets, Seat, and Steering Rod, &c.

Independent motivation arrived in 1886 with the Rover Safety Cycle. (Author's collection)

in London, to produce and sell a sewing machine which Starley had designed and patented. With Starley's design and engineering prowess and Turner's business acumen, the duo founded the Coventry Sewing Machine Company in 1861.

Just as many British car makers grew out of cycle manufacturing, so also Rover developed. The link between sewing machines and cycles was Josiah Turner's nephew who had an interest in Michaux cycles, which were made in Paris where he was studying. Soon, Starley and Turner's sewing

FOR LADIES & GENTLEMEN "THE ROVER"

THE "ROVER" HAS SET THE FASHION TO THE WORLD
— THE CYCLIST

FOR PARTICULARS & PRICE LIST APPLY

J.K. STARLEY & CO. LTD.

METEOR WORKS, COVENTRY.

machines were being sold in France and, by way of agreement, the Coventry Sewing machine Company was building Michaux cycles, albeit under the new name of Coventry Machinists Company.

The new company was formed in 1869 but, within a year, Starley and Turner's partnership was over; Starley wanted to build a cycle of his own design but Turner was not interested.

Another famous name in motor history – Hillman – now enters the story. William Hillman, who was employed by the partnership, agreed to join forces with Starley to build Ariel cycles. However, he, too, eventually went his own way to build bicycles and James Starley was joined by his nephew, John Kemp Starley.

After four years of partnership the two Starleys decided by mutual agreement to part company: John Starley set up business with William Sutton to produce cycles, with James Starley backing the venture, and moved into premises at West Orchard in Coventry which was also known as the Meteor Works.

Business boomed for John Starley and it was not long before expansion was necessary and further premises were acquired nearby in Queen Victoria Road. During this period of intense activity Starley niggled away at improving the concept of the bicycle, away from the penny-farthing design and peddling the front wheel, to driving the rear wheel in the now

accustomed fashion. Tricycles were also developed as they offered greater stability and it is with these machines the Rover name was first associated – simply because they were ideal for 'roving' around.

The Rover name was first used in 1884 but a significant development occurred in the early 1890s in the shape of an electrically-powered tricycle with rather feeble batteries stored in a wicker basket above the rear axle. Whilst never marketed and intended purely as an experiment, the whole question of adding mechanical power fascinated John Starley and his ideas would be put to good use at a later date.

The Rover Cycle Company was formed in 1896 with a capital of £200,000, £50,000 of which was in the form of debentures. Initial trading was excellent with some 11,000 cycles quickly leaving the factory gates and providing a reasonable profit for the company. The question of mechanically-powered transport surfaced again when Starley set about importing some Peugeot motor cycles from France for evaluation purposes and soon began to develop a machine of his own. Tragedy struck in October 1901 when John Starley died at the age of 46: his work was incomplete and it was a further year before the first Rover motor cycle was sold.

Starley's death meant a restructuring of the Rover Cycle Company. Harry Smith took over as general manager and Frank Ward

was appointed company secretary. John Starley's son, Jack, took the position of assistant works manager at the company's New Meteor factory in Queen Victoria Road.

Coventry, during the final days of the 19th century and the bright new epoch of the early 1900s, was fast becoming the centre of motor car development. Already Daimler had set up a factory headed by Harry Lawson, who had tried, without success, to recruit John Starley. Riley and Humber were also forging ahead. Rover, under Harry Smith's guidance, decided it, too, should be looking at car manufacturing and Edmund Lewis was secured from Daimler to lead them in the right direction.

As it happened, Edmund Lewis's 8hp Rover was a milestone in automobile development: whereas chassis development had followed the style of the horse-drawn carriage style, Lewis opted for a vehicle with a steel backbone frame and so out-dated all other designs. There was more from Lewis: he devised the '6', a cheaper version of the 8hp which served Rover well and sold for a mere £105.

One of the first Rovers to win international acclaim was driven by Dr Jefferson in 1906, the year the company name was changed to The Rover Company Limited: this was an 8hp car which endured the positively traumatic journey between London and Constantinople. The 6s and 8s survived with their single cylinder

Where it all began ... Rover's first car, the 1904 8hp pictured outside the registered offices of the Rover Cycle Co. Ltd. (Author's collection, courtesy Les White)

engines until 1911 when Owen Clegg, having taken over from Lewis who had moved to Armstrong-Siddeley, introduced the 12.

Owen Clegg had been poached from Wolseley where he had worked his way up to the position of works manager. Clegg joined Rover in 1910 and it took him just a year to introduce the new car. Priced at 300 guineas, the 12hp was an elegant machine with its 4-seat phaeton body and was well worthy of the 'Silent Knight' designation bestowed upon it. For £15 less, the 12hp could be bought as a 2-seater.

There is no doubt the 12hp was an excellent car. Rover placed so much importance upon it that it remained as the company's sole product, along with a larger engined version known as the 18hp, until the outbreak of the 1914 war. The

18 was never as popular as the 12 and the production figures speak for themselves as only 150 were built during 1912-13.

War, boom years, the Depression

The Rover Company was forced to stop making private cars in 1915 and, like so many other manufacturers, turned their resources to production of armaments before taking on the building of 16hp Sunbeams, some of which were built as ambulances, and Maudslay lorries for the war-effort. Along with the Sunbeams and Maudslays, Rover returned to motorcycle production with some 3000 machines leaving the factory gates, many of which were destined for use in war-torn Russia.

Rover's chief designers seemed to enjoy relatively short terms of

office: Owen Clegg stayed only 18 months before being spirited away by Darracq, where he was to build 12 and 16hp cars in a similar vein to the Rover. Mark Wild took over from Owen Clegg as both chief designer and works manager but appears to have progressed little in the way of producing new models before the First World War; it must be assumed the Rover Company, and Wild, were quite happy with the Clegg-inspired machines.

After the war there was a move towards change: Rover had acquired a munitions factory in Tyseley, a suburb of Birmingham, with the aim of returning to light car production. The enthusiasm with which Rover entered this particular enterprise was all due to a young engineer by the name of Jack Sangster who, having designed a little 8hp air-

Early days on the road: a Rover 12hp in idyllic Edwardian setting. (Courtesy BMIHT/Rover Group)

Overleaf: 1924 saw the 12hp models re-rated at 14hp; the Weymann saloon could be purchased for £550 whilst the range started at a mere £470. (Author's collection)

cooled, flat-twin runabout, was keen to sell his car to the highest bidder. Rover, appreciating the car's potential, seized the opportunity and struck a deal with Sangster.

Production of Sangster's 8hp began in 1920. The Tyseley factory, where Jack Sangster was installed as assistant works manager, built the rolling chassis of his cars before they were transported to the Meteor works at Coventry for the bodies to be attached. The 998cc 8hp initially went on sale for £300 after receiving almost rave reviews in *The Autocar*; during a few years of impressive production figures the price dropped to £180 before reaching a low of £160.

The reason for this discounting was in part the introduction of Herbert Austin's ubiquitous Austin Seven, which was to have such an impact upon the British motor industry. In those immediate post-war years there appeared a number of inexpensive cars which were aimed at the mass market – apart from the Austin there were such machines as Citroën's small but ever-popular 5CV, which was hardly any match in price at £260. On the horizon, William Morris was set to take on the popularity of Ford and eventually secured 41% of British car production in 1925.

Jack Sangster, while achieving

impressive results for Rover, left the company in 1922, preferring a position with Ariel as assistant managing director. His 8hp lived on until 1924 when a new engine, a 1074cc water-cooled four, replaced the air-cooled twin and the 'new car' emerged as the Rover 9.

A year later another new car was launched by Rover, the 14/45 which was joined by a sister model, the 16/50, a year later. Both cars – designed by Peter Poppe who had been brought in by Rover to secure the company's future – were a disaster: underpowered and heavy, they were costly to build and unattractive to potential customers. Only something like 2000 were built over a four year period which exacerbated Rover's financial predicament. In desperation Poppe produced another machine, this time with a 2-litre, 6-cylinder engine. This was not enough to change Rover's fortunes and it looked as if the company would fold, like many other concerns that failed in the depression of the twenties.

Spencer Wilks arrives

With the prospect of failure and loss of substantial investments, Rover shareholders took the initiative and formed an action committee to head a deputation, led by W D Sudbury and Herman Jennings, to

Rover's chairman, Colonel Wyley, who had been appointed in 1909. The outcome of the meeting was that Wyley stepped down as chairman and tendered his resignation immediately.

In this difficult situation Sudbury and Jennings were elected to the board of directors, with Sudbury being further elected as Rover's new chairman. Influencing Sudbury was Sir Alfred Mays-Smith, a fellow director, and it was by his suggestion that Sudbury approached Colonel Frank Searle to join the Rover board.

Searle's appointment was the beginning of major changes to Rover's directorship: acting as joint managing director alongside John Kemp Starley junior, the last of the Starley association with Rover, Searle it was who was instrumental in deposing of Starley, who went off to Australia with a compensation payment of £4500. Searle opened the way for the position of general manager to be created and suggested the board consider Spencer Wilks. A relatively short career was destined for Searle at Rover as he, too, was deposed in 1932.

Spencer Bernau Wilks was 38 years of age when he was appointed general manager of Rover in 1929 and with his arrival so Hillman re-enters the story. Not only had Spencer Wilks started working for Hillman in 1919, he rose to the position of joint-managing director alongside John Black, later of

ROVER

14 h.p. Cars

THE famous "12 h.p. Rover" has been re-rated at 14 h.p. in order to avoid confusion: as heretofore, the Treasury rating is 13·9 h.p., the bore and stroke of the 4-cylinder engine being 75 mm. × 130 mm. Actually, however, the engine develops more than 40 b.h.p.

A four-speed gearbox has been standardized, with ratios of 4·375, 7·15, 11·4 and 18·5. The open models can be supplied with three-speed gearbox if desired.

The range of enclosed models meets every requirement of the growing number of motorists who prefer to travel in comfortable seclusion from the elements. The 4/5 seater Weymann type saloon, which is both low in weight and noise-proof, is extraordinary value at £550.

The coupé is eminently suitable to the professional man, whilst the Light Saloon and Saloon are unequalled examples of "quality" coachwork at the extremely reasonable prices quoted.

The equipment of the 14 h.p. Rover is complete in all the details which make motoring a pleasure. The full specification is attractively set forth in our latest four-colour catalogue: may we send you a copy? It is free on request.

NOVEMBER 1923

OPEN MODELS.

2/3-SEATER (4-SPEED)	.. ..	£485
Ditto (3-SPEED)	.. ..	£470
4/5-SEATER (4-SPEED)	.. ..	£495
Ditto (3-SPEED)	.. ..	£480

SALOON (WEYMANN TYPE)

With 4-SPEED GEAR-BOX	.. ..	£550
LIMOUSINE COUPE (4-SPEED)	..	£585
LIGHT SALOON, Coachbuilt (do.)	..	£595

SALOON, Coachbuilt (4-SPEED) .. £695

The above model has B20 m.m.× 120 m.m. Tyres.

Left: Pre-war scene? Early Rovers, including P2s and P3s, gather at Crich for a Rover Sports Register meeting in post-war days. (Photo: Keith Austin, courtesy Rover P4 Drivers Guild)

Below: The Rover 10 earned a reputation for being both nippy and reliable. In 1927 the 2-seat touring model cost £220 while another £5 bought the 4-seat model. (Author's collection)

Maudslay and Standard Triumph notoriety. Black was distantly related to Wilks by marriage to one of Hillman's daughters.

Hillman's involvement was further extended as Spencer Wilks had married into the Hillman family, his wife being another of Hillman's six daughters. Following the death of William Hillman in 1926, his company was bought by the Rootes brothers; Wilks was less than happy with his position in the Rootes empire and it was with some relief on the part of both Wilks and Rover that Spencer accepted the offer to take the helm at the ailing Rover company.

It wasn't only Spencer Wilks who arrived at Rover from Hillman: quite a crowd changed allegiance, amongst them was Maurice Wilks, Spencer's younger brother by thirteen years, and Jess Worster and Geoffrey Savage – both of whom were to apply their skills on Rover's behalf in later years.

At this point it is pertinent to provide some background to the Wilks family and its significance to Rover. Spencer Wilks was born in Rickmansworth, Hertfordshire, in 1891 and attended Charterhouse school. His education stood him in good stead for training as a barrister, which he undertook for five years after leaving Charterhouse and before joining the army as a captain in the 1914-18 war. It was after the war that he joined forces with William Hillman. Spencer stayed with Rover after leaving Hillman until his retirement in 1962.

Maurice Wilks is probably best known for introducing the Land Rover concept after the Second World War. His career in the motor industry began with General Motors before he transferred his talents to Hillman. After joining his elder brother at Rover he eventually took over as managing director.

Both Spencer and Maurice Wilks were involved in the development of Frank Whittle's jet engine, while Spencer's nephew, Spen King, was largely responsible for the development of Rover's turbine cars. Keeping it in the family, Peter Wilks, who was a of nephew Maurice Wilks, played a prominent part in the development of the Marauder, a sporting variant of the P4 which will be discussed later. Maurice's brother-in-law, William Martin-Hunt, also played a salient role in Rover's affairs, as he, too, eventually aspired to the position of managing director.

On joining Rover, Spencer Wilks was faced with a formidable situation: the company had an overdraft approaching a quarter of a million pounds with losses amounting to between £2000 and £3000 a week or, putting it a little more succinctly, approximately £130,000 a year. The two main creditors were Joseph Lucas and Pressed Steel and both concerns demanded to see a new strategy from the company's top line management – a policy with some positive forward planning and firm measures to stabilize the company's affairs.

It was very clear to Wilks that his ideas for the future of Rover were quite different to those of Colonel Frank Searle. Whereas Searle was convinced the future lay with a market for less expensive cars which were turned out in large quantities with small regard to quality, Wilks favoured a more cautious approach. Rather than take a back seat in standards of quality, Wilks implicitly believed quality should become the company's hallmark.

Searle had already made a start on planning the ultimate utility car and decided it should have an enormous impact on its intended low-price market where four wheels were preferred to a motorcycle combination. He christened his brainchild the Scarab, the Egyptian name for beetle. Wilks' enthusiasm for the project, however, was somewhat less than Searle's.

The tiny, 2-door, 4-seater open tourer, with the minuscule air-cooled 840cc V-twin in its tail, was advertised in both *The Motor* and *Autocar* at just £89. The engine was something of a technological curiosity; its cast-iron cylinders were set at an angle of 60 degrees, the crankcase was built from aluminium, while the crankshaft and big-ends ran in roller bearings. All-round independent suspension, inboard rear brakes and an engine and gearbox built as a single unit were all part of the machine's intriguing specification.

It is said that Ferdinand Porsche showed a distinct interest in the car and had even travelled to Britain to try it out for himself. There were extensive plans for the Scarab: a production figure of 30,000 cars has been mentioned but ultimately only 12 prototypes were actually built. Some £15,000 had already been spent on the project by the end of 1931: enough was enough and the tiny Scarab was buried forever, leaving the cycle-car brigade to press on with such unusual designs. Had the project succeeded, however, it would have provided the British motorist with a simple machine at well under £100.

Wilks, obviously relieved at the demise of the Scarab affair, looked to the immediate future to strengthen Rover's position. Poppe's unwieldy engine had to go and it was to another Hillman ex-patriot that Spencer Wilks turned for help. Major Thomas, understanding Wilks' predicament, produced a neat and well-balanced 6-cylinder unit of a little over 1400cc which, although eventually up-rated to 1577cc, formed the basis of the company's 'Pilot' models for some time to come.

The early thirties were, without any doubt, very trying times for Rover and it is almost a miracle that the company survived at all. In 1931, after losses amounting to almost £80,000, the company's bankers finally moved in and nominated an independent financial adviser to be appointed to the board of directors.

This is where Howe Graham – an accountant with a reputation of immense insight and providence – enters the story. Graham and Wilks shared something of an accord: on Graham's influence Wilks was appointed to the board of directors. There followed a period of change and new direction at Rover, resulting in a streamlining of costs and production. Within a relatively short space of time savings of £100,000 had been realised.

Spencer Wilks turned his attention to the company's production operation. There was no room for sentiment: the premises at the Meteor works were unceremoniously shut down and a new factory to the north of Coventry, at Helen Street, which had been bought in 1929, formed the basis of car construction. Known as the 'New Meteor Works', Helen Street was the company's main finishing plant: Tyseley continued in operation but for the manufacture of engines and transmission systems only.

The Rover Light Six made history by beating the famous Blue Train by 20 minutes, averaging 38mph over the 750 mile run from the French Riviera to Calais. The feat was achieved by Dudley Noble, Harold Pemberton and a Rover test engineer named Bennett in late January 1930, thus predating a similar triumph by Bentley Chairman Woolf Barnato and his golfing friend Dale Bourne, over 13-14th March the same year, aboard Barnato's Bentley 6½ Litre. (Author's collection)

Quality, not quantity

An early casualty of Wilks' and Howe's management shake-up was Colonel Frank Searle. Whether he was dismissed or tendered his resignation is now irrelevant, but at last Spencer Wilks felt he had the all-important control over Rover's future and prosperity.

In retrospect it was more than sheer luck and good fortune that had allowed Rover to survive as long as it had. Weaknesses, wrong decisions and wrong-headed policies had meant the company lumbered along like a machine out of control. However, it is important to understand the general state of the motor industry in the late 1920s and early '30s. Companies were being forced out of business and in America – the land of plenty – all was doom and gloom. Ford, once the great success story, had idle factories and a rioting workforce. At least Rover was alive, even if only barely conscious.

Rover's hopes of competing directly with the like of Austin were sheer folly; in recognising his company's best tactical position Spencer Wilks proceeded with a policy of quality against quantity.

Perhaps not to Wilks' entire amusement, but nevertheless a milestone in Rover's achievement, was Dudley Noble's epic 750 mile sprint across France in a Light 6, a car that Wilks wished to see killed off. The dash from St Raphael to

ROVER beats the BLUE TRAIN

Get the best from your car by using Wakefield CASTROL as recommended by over 230 leading Motor Manufacturers.

The CASTROL Grade for your needs is shown on the Wakefield Index Chart at any Garage—but when asking for it, emphasize the word CASTROL, and so make sure that you do not receive an inferior oil.

Wakefield CASTROL will mix with other oils—but naturally is best uncontaminated.

FOR twenty hours on end, the little ROVER Light Six raced the lordly Blue Train from the Riviera. Despite darkness and fog, the ROVER beat the Train by 20 minutes over the 750 miles from St. Raphael to Calais, averaging 38 miles per hour.

The ROVER engine ran like a clock (but considerably faster !) from start to finish, lubricated with Wakefield CASTROL "AA", as used and *exclusively recommended* by the Rover Company Limited.

Using WAKEFIELD CASTROL "AA"

C. C. WAKEFIELD & CO. LTD. (All-British Firm) Wakefield House, Cheapside, LONDON, E.C.2.

MENTION of "The Light Car and Cyclecar" when corresponding with advertisers assists the cause of economical motoring.

R39

Calais, racing the famous Blue Train express, was a favourite event and one that always ensured good publicity. Dudley Noble's car performed exceptionally well and arrived at Calais 20 minutes ahead of the express. Rover and Dudley Noble celebrated what was then a heroic accomplishment by storming their way to headlines across the nation's newspapers.

As Wilks' measures and Graham's financial expertise began to take effect, so losses turned to gains and profit margins increased. In 1933 Rover's net profit reached

a little over £7500 but a year later stood at a thundering £94,439, with an increase of an additional £60,000 in 1935.

The turn-around in model line-up also progressed at a steady rate: the 10 Special arrived with a pressed-steel body identical to that of the Hillman Minx – a fact that neither Rover nor Hillman ever admitted publicly. Then came the 'Pilots' and, in 1934, the 4-cylinder P1s in 10 and 12hp ratings, together with a 14hp version powered by the Thomas 6-cylinder engine.

For 1935 Rover's model range changed little except for some streamlining extravaganza on the Speed Fourteen. It was the fashion to sport elongated wings and curved tails: Standard produced the chic Flying 12, Riley the 1.5-litre and Citroën the sporty British-built Light Fifteen complete with front wheel drive and integral chassis. Independent front suspension was excitingly talked of for the Speed Fourteen but, in the event, failed to materialise.

Heading the range for 1936 was the 10hp Saloon at £248, while another £30 bought the 12hp. For the more adventurous-minded a further £20 secured what was then considered the trendy 12hp Sports Saloon and still with some change from £300. It was 1937 before any major changes were announced which heralded the appearance of the P2 Rover. The company was driving out of recession; net profits were riding at almost £153,000 for

1935 and edged towards £165,000 for '36 and then smashed through £200,000 for 1937.

One of Britain's fine cars

There is no doubt that Wilks was aiming Rover's products at a particular market. The P2 was well built and equally well appointed to the highest of standards; with its classic styling and the Wilks pedigree it was this car that was the mainstay of Rover's future until the Second World War and beyond.

The adoption of the corporate phrase 'One Of Britain's Fine Cars' promoted the Rover company from the general market to one of serving a particular clientele. Stately advertisements carried the Rover image to the professional classes: evocative drawings appeared in such esteemed journals as *Punch* and depicted a handsome Rover 16 leaving the Houses of Parliament carrying dignitaries seated in style and comfort while the regulatory policeman saluted his peers. *The Autocar* was equally stirring in its praise: "The Rover 16 ... a really beautiful job ... gives one

the impression of being a £1000 car scaled down, so quiet is its performance and so splendid its interior finish."

The P2s were not entirely Spencer Wilks' brainchild: we must not forget Maurice, Spencer's younger brother, who was by then in charge of engineering and who devised much of the model along with Robert Boyle. Although the Thomas-designed engine lived on, Maurice Wilks was keen to look at some new ideas which consisted of some V6 and V8 options. From this development work, none of which actually saw production, came the idea for a product of the next decade: the sloping head, inlet over exhaust in-line engine.

The *Daily Telegraph* on 13th June 1938 likened the Rover – certainly elegant and with a hint of stately dash – to the "Rolls-Royce of light cars". No doubt Spencer Wilks joyously greeted the paper's views!

Whilst mass production was commonplace in Britain, Europe and America, this method was not for Rover. Production had almost

doubled from 4960 cars built in 1933 to 8335 built in 1936, but by 1938 output had only grown to 10,516 units, which represented only 3.1% of Britain's total car output. With profits of £169,000 Wilks was hardly concerned and although, by 1939, Rover's share of the market had only crept up to 3.2%, company profit was up to almost £206,000.

During the mid-1930s Rover extended the Helen Street factory and in 1937 the company raised a further £260,000 capital. Success seemed assured and for 1939 an all-new 6-cylinder 14hp car was announced which spearheaded a model range comprising the 1389cc 4-cylinder 10hp and a 1496cc 12hp, whilst two other 6-cylinder models consisted of the 2147cc 16hp and Speed 20hp with its 2.5-litre engine.

1940 models were announced but so was the Second World War. The effects of a nation fighting again were to be far-reaching for both Britain and Rover as a company; even after the outbreak of war Rover was still making a few cars but only until May 1940.

Shadow factories and the war effort

As early as the spring of 1936 the air ministry, worried at events in Europe, put into operation a scheme of 'shadow factories' to prepare for war. Rover, along with Austin, Standard, Daimler and Rootes, was approached in this respect,

which concerned the production of aircraft components in new factory sites built and paid for by the government.

Agreements had been reached by 1936: Rover, together with Daimler, and Standard with Austin, were to build aero engine components; assembly of complete engines was to be undertaken by Bristol and Austin and airframes built by Rootes and Austin. 'Shadowing' the aero industry, Rover's aircraft engine plant was situated at Acocks Green near Birmingham which was quite close to the Tyseley works.

Acocks Green was up and running by the end of 1937 and Rover was supplying engine parts to Bristol. Some changes took place after the outbreak of war and to ensure continuity of supply Rover and Austin, who were both based in Birmingham, and Standard and Daimler, who were Coventry based, began to produce complete engines between them.

The war effort quickly spread to Rover's other factories with Cheetah aero engines being built at Tyseley, airframes for the Albermarle were constructed at Lancaster and Bristol as well as Helen Street.

Enter Solihull

As the grimness of war continued the British Government asked for more commitment from Rover by way of a second but much larger shadow factory. The plan was for Rover, in association with Rootes,

to build complete Hercules radial engines. The location of Rover's second shadow factory was on a greenfield site to the north of Solihull known as Lode Lane.

The British Government, having approached the Rover company in April 1939 concerning the second shadow factory, instigated building work at Lode Lane within two months and, by September 1940, production of aircraft engines was underway. Initially, the site at Solihull had extended to 65 acres but the Rover directors chose to purchase an additional 200 acres; a decision proved, in time, to be one of considerable foresight.

Rover's shadow factories eventually amounted to several sites throughout the Midlands and north of England. By far the most bizarre of these was a highly secret underground plant at Drakelow, near Kidderminster, comprising some 50 acres which was used as a machining shop for Centaurus, Hercules and Pegasus engines.

The war over, Rover was left with the Helen Street factory in ruins. The decision was taken to sell off the premises and a ready buyer was found in the form of machine tool maker Alfred Herbert. Spencer Wilks had decided he wanted to move his company's main business to Lode Lane and, by 1944, plans were afoot to lay the factory out for car production, signalling an end to the connection between the Rover company and Coventry as a manufacturing base.

Rover's attempt at producing an out-and-out economy vehicle resulted in the M1 prototype developed between 1945 and 1946. The front-end styling has a suggestion of the P4 shape combined with that of the P2, but using a full-width design. Proposed as a 2+2, the overall design of the diminutive M1 is very similar to Fiat's 500 Topolino, especially in its 500C guise. The M1 was finally abandoned even though Harry Loker and Gordon Bashford had put many hours into the project. (Courtesy BMIHT/Rover Group)

A further and very important aspect concerning Solihull as the hub of Rover's activities was the experimental work carried out during war time on Frank Whittle's gas turbine engines: an intense exercise which was to have far-reaching effects for the company as we shall discover later.

The transition between Coventry and Solihull was not immediate; the Meteor works, too, were very badly damaged and, although conversion to motor production was underway at Lode Lane, it was essential the company was in a position to deliver as many cars as possible, albeit pre-war models. A satellite factory in Coventry's Clay Lane and Stoke Road was quickly set up and in 1945 a pilot production of 4-cylinder cars was leaving the premises. Steel shortage being so accute, the delivery of new cars from Clay Lane was nothing more than a nominal number. Production at Clay Lane and Stoke Road was never intended to be anything other than a temporary measure and by 1948 the operation had ceased.

Rover's range of post-war cars was announced in *The Motor* and *Autocar* during the early part of October 1945. This, however, did not preclude the company from reviving its advertising from the summer of 1944, even though there were no cars to sell. Four models were launched which were, in essence, identical to the pre-war cars: the 1389cc '10' and 1469cc '12', both of which had 4-cylinder engines, and the 1901cc '14' as well as a 2147cc '16' which had 6-cylinder motors.

Rover did not plan the post-war models until after VE (Victory in Europe) Day. Naturally, at first, there was no alternative but to resume production of pre-war cars, but what of the future? There were two considerations: firstly, with post-war austerity Rover might have anticipated building a small economical car for a money-starved nation or, secondly, the company's total commitment to quality and finesse should have prevailed – after all, was not the Rover 'One of Britain's Fine Cars'?

The M1 project

Although the ill-fated Scarab affair may have reminded the Wilks brothers of the 'not so good old Rover days' the decision was taken to press ahead with another concept of the ultimate economy vehicle in light of the growing trend towards smaller and more frugal family cars.

Designated M1, Rover's mini was under development in 1945 and by 1946 a prototype machine was being evaluated. The two people mostly responsible for the M1's design were Harry Loker and Gordon Bashford and it is interesting to see how the car finally took shape. The original concepts of the car were by far too avant garde by Rover standards and it is said that Maurice Wilks ordered a much more conventional style. Early body shapes – which included an open tourer and a coupé – featured full-width frontal treatment with integrated headlamps, slab sides and an absence of running boards. The basis of these outlines, however, was to re-emerge later in the general shape of the P4, which was but four years away. Perhaps too progressive for the Rover clientele, the futuristic shape of the early M1 reverted to more conservative lines with separate wings but with headlamps recessed into the full-width nose.

There was something about the M1 prototype that was oddly familiar: the frontal treatment, design of both front and rear wings, body shape and overall dimensions were remarkably reminiscent of Fiat's baby car, the 500C Topolino.

The M1's similarity to the Topolino was more than skin deep: the wheelbase was virtually identical, as was the interior layout to the extent of both cars sharing sliding windows. The Rover's engine, although of a different design, was also positioned ahead of the front axle in Fiat style.

The engine of the M1 was of some interest in itself. Although only

The P3 followed traditional Wilks styling while Rover engineers struggled to find a new formula for the fifties. Underneath the bonnet the IoE engine paved the way for the P4. (Author's collection)

New era: post-war design and the P3 stopgap

Developments in the early style of the abandoned M1 prototypes were still being nurtured by the Rover design team, although forsaken for the eventual road-going experimental car. For the immediate future, however, there would have to be some compromise with tradition.

The Wilks brothers plans were affected by other influences: America had a distinct influence over automobile design in Britain due, in the most part, to its later involvement in the war. By the early '40s running boards and separate front wings had been pushed into relegation and were

699cc in capacity, the design was a scaled-down version of Rover's inlet over exhaust unit destined for the P3 cars and, of course, the subject of this book, the P4.

Talking to James Taylor, whose authority on Rover matters is well appreciated, he recalls seeing evidence that a Fiat Topolino was purchased by Rover and subsequently taken apart for examination of the finer details of the Italian manufacturer's masterpiece in miniature. Other small European cars were also evaluated, including the rather novel DKW.

The mini Rover, however, was not to be. In retrospect, the abandonment of the project might be judged a lost opportunity as the little 2-seater with its 2 occasional seats at the back might have pre-dated such cars as Austin's A30 and A35. The reasons for the car's still-birth was not out of concern with breaking the Wilks tradition of quality, and certainly not with regard to how Rover's customers might react to a utility car within the model range, but due to circumstance.

The demand for economies in fuel consumption did not happen to the extent the Wilks brothers had anticipated, not until the Suez crisis

anyway. The need for rationalisation and concentration of one-model policies, produced in part by the virtual non-availability of steel for such a project, together with changes in the taxation laws, were relative, as was Maurice Wilks' plans for the Land Rover. The bottom line of the whole affair is that the project became lost within a complicated chain of events and was eventually laid to rest and quickly forgotten in the spring of 1947.

Few P3 dropheads have survived in this condition. GAC 120 is a tribute to Rover engineering and its caring owner.
(Photo: Stan Johnstone)

ONE OF BRITAIN'S FINE CARS — NOW MADE FINER

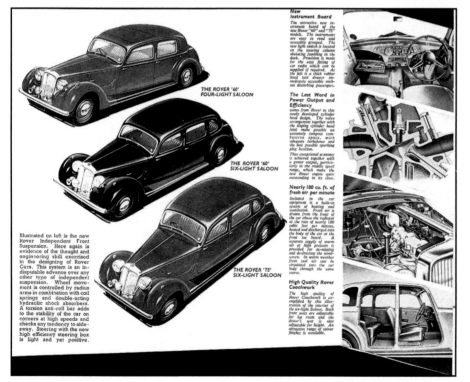

THE ROVER '60' FOUR-LIGHT SALOON

THE ROVER '60' SIX-LIGHT SALOON

THE ROVER '75' SIX-LIGHT SALOON

Illustrated on left is the new Rover Independent Front Suspension. Here again is evidence of the thought and engineering skill exercised in the designing of Rover Cars. This system is an indisputable advance over any other type of independent suspension. Wheel movement is controlled by radius arms in combination with coil springs and double-acting hydraulic shock absorbers. A torsion anti-roll bar adds to the stability of the car on corners at high speeds and checks any tendency to side-sway. Steering with the new high efficiency steering box is light and yet positive.

New Instrument Board
The attractive new instrument board of the new Rover "60" and "75" models. The instruments are easy to read and accessibly grouped. The new light switch is located on the steering column obviating fumbling in the dark. Provision is made for the easy fitting of car radio which can be supplied if required. At the left is a thick rubber lined tool drawer immediately accessible without disturbing passengers.

The Last Word in Power Output and Efficiency
comes from Rover in this newly developed cylinder head design. The valve arrangement together with the sloping cylinder head joint make possible an extremely compact combustion space, with adequate turbulence and the best possible sparking plug location.
This exceptional economy is achieved together with a power output, particularly in the middle speed range, which make the new Rover engine quite outstanding in its class.

Nearly 100 cu. ft. of fresh air per minute
Included in the car equipment is a built-in system of heating and ventilation. Fresh air is drawn from the front of the car above the radiator at the rate of nearly 100 cubic feet per minute, heated and discharged into the body of the car at the front toe board. A separate supply of warm air at high pressure is provided for de-misting and de-frosting the windscreen. In warm weather fresh cool air can be circulated into the car body through the same source.

High Quality Rover Coachwork
The high quality of Rover Coachwork is exemplified by this illustration of the interior of the six-light Saloon. Both front seats are adjustable for leg room and the driver's seat is also adjustable for height. An attractive range of colour finishes is available.

replaced by full-width bodies, integrated headlamps and curved windscreens. There was also a fascination for bakelite, from which

the fascias were often formed.

The American influence was soon marked in Britain by the appearance in 1948 of the Austin

This brochure illustration of the P3 gave the car an aggressive appearance. Clearly, the car's styling originates from pre-war days. (Author's collection)

Below: The P3 was the essential link between the pre-war cars and the post-war era. Although essentially a pre-war derivative, the 60 and 75 P3s were the test-beds for the Rover P4. (Author's collection)

A90 Atlantic and its pretty sister saloon version a year later. Hillman, too, was quick to adopt the American attitudes with its phase III Minx which was inspired by Raymond Loewy's designs. Continuing the Rootes' corporate image, Humber followed in similar vein to that of the Minx but with its big-car appeal. Morris showed a lead with an American theme in 1948 with the substantial Oxford and, of course, the lovable and ubiquitous Minor. Understandably, Vauxhall, the British arm of the General Motors empire, displayed aggressive new designs for '48 and the Wyvern and Velox sold in not unreasonable numbers.

In the transition from pre- to post-war styling Rover engineers were confronted with some difficulty. Not that there was any lack of innovation, on the contrary – remember those initial ideas for the M-type project? – there was plenty, but they had to fit in comfortably with what Rover customers might expect from a highly respected and traditional motor company.

The new shapes emanating from across the Atlantic, as well those emerging from European manufacturers, were all noted and applied, if somewhat cautiously, to influence the style of the Solihull product. Integrated headlamps and full-width radiator grilles were all tried out on the P2 design with not especially pretty results.

Rover was caught between two stools: they had the right chassis

Vintage Rovers offer unique ownership potential – when restored. (Author's collection)

and a new engine but nothing to clothe it with. Taking a cautionary route a stopgap measure was decided upon: use the newly developed chassis and engine but return to the P2 theme, albeit with a few cosmetic changes. The result was the P3 in two designations, the 60 and 75.

The P3 was successfully launched in 1948 at the Brussels show and followed Britain's government directive of a one-model policy. With the arrival of the new car all four variants of the P2 disappeared completely, replaced by a choice of four cylinders and six cylinders, 1.6- and 2.1-litres respectively.

The main feature of the P3 was its engine and chassis which set new parameters for the future. For the power unit a design of inlet over exhaust (IoE) had been resurrected from pre-war development and it is claimed that bench testing amounted to the equivalent of some 600,000 road miles. In principle, of course, there was nothing new about IoE; Sir Harry Ricardo of engine design fame had advocated such a concept twenty years earlier.

The choice of engine stemmed from an outline for a V6 which never materialised; Maurice Wilks had been enthusiastic over plans laid down by Jack Swain, who eventually

graduated to head of Rover's engine development department.

The inlet over exhaust engine can be traced back in automotive history to before the Great War, after which it was abandoned and later revived in the mid-1930s. Rover's IoE unit, a 4-cylinder version, convinced both Jack Swain and Maurice Wilks that a similar concept should be used for the proposed post-war car. In essence, the IoE is something of a hybrid, a combination of both side and overhead valves. Trials with the IoE engine had proved it to be highly efficient; it was possible to obtain high compression ratios using low octane fuels, especially useful after the war when there was only low-grade petrol available. With this obvious advantage in flexibility, performance could be virtually guaranteed, and even when using 72-octane fuel the engine would respond instantly to heavy accelerator pressure.

The Studebaker affair

In introducing the P3 Rover gave itself a breathing space in which to consolidate its position from frenzied wartime activities to peacetime production and reassess market position. It also gave the Wilks brothers time to launch one of the motor industry's greatest phenomena, the Land Rover.

It was no secret that the P4 development was not going exactly to plan. There were difficulties in getting the body styling together and finding an easy route to using the P3 chassis. Indeed, some of the designs that were being considered to form the basis of the P4 were quite dreadful and certainly would not have appealed to the discerning motorist that Rover was targeting.

Spencer and Maurice Wilks had given themselves time to analyse what was happening elsewhere in the motor industry and, like so many of their contemporaries, they looked to America for inspiration. The 'is it coming or going' look had been created in America – rounded edges, curved screens, equal length bonnets and trunks – had arrived. Maurice Wilks liked what he saw. In particular it was the Studebaker that set his thoughts racing into action and, after studying the car's profile and aesthetics, he decided there was room for such a car, modified to suit the particular British taste, of course.

It could be said that both Rover and Studebaker shared some empathy: both companies had enjoyed a long association with powered transport, Studebaker being associated with the car for far longer than any other American manufacturer. Dabbling with electric vehicles was a common factor between the two companies and each had developed its first petrol-engined car in the same year, 1904.

American styling heavily influenced the prototype designs for the P4. Early thoughts for the car, seen here as scale models in clay, were based upon the Studebaker Champion which resulted in the fledgling P4 being known as the 'Roverbaker'. (Courtesy BMIHT/Rover Group)

Left: Three Roverbaker designs were modelled, 500, 501 and 502. Here, 500, as in the previous photograph, is seen with the huge bumper extension along the sides of the car. Note the massive snout which was a feature of the American car. (Courtesy BMIHT/Rover Group)

Right: Prototype 500 featured split windscreens and faired-in headlamps. (Courtesy BMIHT/Rover Group)

Studebaker had not been frightened of displaying new ideas and, as an independent manufacturer, sold more cars than its rivals in 1941. The company was not shy in experimenting with alternative types of engines and produced for testing purposes flat-six units which were both water and air-cooled.

For the first few months of 1946 Studebaker continued selling its face-lifted models which were first introduced in 1942. However, during the month of May that year an all-new and controversial range of cars was announced for 1947. Behind the startling and futuristic design was Raymond Loewy, not a motor engineer but an industrial designer, famous for his streamlining of American travel, for he had already applied his skills to trans-American railways and buses. He became responsible for Studebaker's corporate styling in 1939 and his post-war 'wrap-around' design with its choice of 2.8- or 3.7-litre engines had found almost a quarter of a million customers by 1949.

Unlike other American car makers, Studebaker did not design cars in-house, therefore, Loewy was considered something of an outsider. His views were, in the most part, quite different from other auto designers and his ideas were not always readily accepted by the car giants in the USA. Perhaps that is why the post-war Studebakers were so charismatic.

Loewy firmly believed that the American car industry had a lot to learn from its European counterparts, especially in the areas of fuel consumption, suspension techniques and stability. In fact, Loewy proposed to the Studebaker board that he ask Ferdinand Porsche to design a whole new chassis and

Prototype 501 has a sleeker tail arrangement than 500; the bonnet styling is also more pronounced and the side protectors have disappeared. (Courtesy BMIHT / Rover Group)

The side profile of 501 shows that the split windscreen is still favoured but the bonnet now has a chrome strip. Note the doors are hinged on the central pillar. (Courtesy BMIHT / Rover Group)

power train. Following a visit to Stuttgart Porsche responded with his proposals for a rear-engined car: the Studebaker hierarchy recoiled in near panic deciding to stay with more the conservative principles they knew and understood.

Would Rover's selective customers approve of anything so radical as a Studebaker lookalike? There was only one way to find out and Wilks set about getting his hands on a Studebaker to pull apart.

Not one but two Studebakers arrived at the Rover works and were, most likely to the privileged few involved with the project, the source of much interest and amusement.

The slab-sided and full-width bodied effect with moulded contours suggested only a hint of a previous classic style, which was something quite new to Britain's car designers; the extravagant frontal treatment of the American car was a daunting prospect to conservative eyes and whether it befitted a Rover is a matter of conjecture. The chassis dimensions of the Studebaker Champion and that of Gordon Bashford's P3 were almost identical and it was therefore a relatively easy task to transplant the Studebaker body on to the Rover chassis.

Known at Solihull as the 'Roverbaker', this odd machine lived on in service for several years before being dismantled and the Champion body reunited with its original chassis. The car was acquired by a member of the Rover staff after the

research department had finished with it and it survived for a further period of time as a Studebaker. Although it had been subjected to some alterations in its career, the car was a cherished and familiar sight at the factory.

Full-width body styling was not entirely new to Rover before the P4 – a special-bodied P3 completed by Graber of Zurich in 1948 resulted in an extremely handsome 2-door tourer.

Delays in the development stages of the P4 were, ironically, a help instead of hindrance. Certainly the company was seen to be trading in old ideals with the pre-war design of the P3, but to many a Rover customer, however, that was no bad thing. In the rush to imitate American styling Rover was able to let the dust settle before choosing a design to see them into the '50s. Standard, for example, had introduced the Vanguard with its prominent nose and fast-back shape which followed the style of the

Plymouth and it was not until 1952 that a more contemporary design was achieved with the advent of the phase 1A and II models. Rover, therefore, was seen as wise to wait and, in effect, stole a march on its competitors.

It is important to stress that there was no intention of 'copying' the Studebaker Champion or of allowing the Studebaker design to totally influence Rover thinking. The styling department at Rover – if it can be called that – was a two-person affair with Harry Loker taking direction from Maurice Wilks. Harry Loker, of course, had been responsible for the shaping of the P3 and, before it, the P2.

The P4 emerges

Three scale model P4s were constructed and numbered 500, 501 and 502. From these early designs the shape of the definitive car can be seen to emerge, although some areas of the styling were not exactly pleasing.

The front end had ugly bulbous features with a predominant bonnet line, giving the impression of a whale. At this stage the headlamps were positioned immediately above the bumper but either side of the air-intake. The inclusion of a split windscreen was a leftover from earlier ideas and had appeared on the ill-fated M1.

An interesting feature of the 500 and 501 designs is the configuration of the doors. Originally both front and rear doors were hinged on the central pillar, the front following the 'suicide' front-opening style, a relic of the P3, while the rear doors mirrored the modern idiom. Later, the design was turned about with both doors being reverse-hinged and so closing together upon the centre pillar. This design withstood the passage of time and persisted throughout the car's life-span. Plain windows were fitted to the scale models; quarter-lights, at this stage, were not a feature.

The basic styling between all 500 series designs was essentially similar; the sides of 500 were completely flush and slab-shaped, the only relief being a continuation of the bumpers along the entire length of the car. The outline of 501 was enhanced by the scalloped bottom edges of the doors, which even gave a hint of running boards, and contoured wheelarches pronounced the car's rear styling. The effect was even more enhanced with 502 which had a bright embellishment along the scalloped edge. However, without doubt 501 was the more attractive design.

Headlamps on all cars were protected behind perspex covers, but as for the bonnet two different themes were displayed. The three prototypes were fitted with a distinctive wedge-shaped nose all the more accentuated on the 501 by the addition of a chrome strip along the centre on the bonnet line, no doubt a throw-back to the centre-hinged bonnet of the P3.

Whereas the P3 had been available as a four or six-light saloon, there was no such option with the P4. Styling allowed for only a four-light design and, in common with contemporary cars, wide rear pillars were the fashion.

For the first time in designing a new Rover models were initially built in clay before being expertly shaped, sanded, sculptured and filed into the desired shape. Suffice to say that Maurice Wilks wrestled with decisions between what he considered the outrageousness of American styling over the more cautious and sophisticated dignity of the British Rover; time was taken to appreciate the P4's eventual overall design, especially in losing such time-honoured features as running boards and exposed chromed headlamps, not to mention the upright and distinctly proud radiator grille.

What, then, of the prototype's interior features? American influence resulted in the P4's bench seat and, horrifyingly, a column gearchange and a horn ring built into the steering wheel. Even the dashboard had tones of the New World: the fascia supported rectangular instruments.

Having an affect upon the interior styling was the P4's chassis, modified in slight detail to the P3's from which it was derived. A problem with earlier P-type chassis had been their inability to provide anything other than limited wheel movement. Now Gordon Bashford's careful

Almost there! The final prototype complete with Cyclops foglamp. The frontal styling has been smoothed out considerably since the 500 series design models. Note the Viking badge and that the car is left-hand-drive. (Courtesy BMIHT/Rover Group)

design changes incorporated a full chassis instead of a "three-quarter" type and semi-elliptic springs. Other revisions included telescopic dampers, which gave virtually a 50% increase in wheel movement, and an increase generally in stability. Understeer was a problem though, which was caused by moving the engine position forwards to provide more passenger accommodation. This was the price to pay for not increasing the wheelbase. On the plus side the P4 had a lower centre of gravity achieved by installing a joint in the propeller shaft with a flexible bearing which therefore lowered the floor.

Arrival of the Viking

By the definitive prototype the profile of the P4 had been considerably softened: the sharpened snout was smoothed into a friendly and less aggressive style, headlamps were positioned into the integral wings and flanked a deeply louvred air-intake, a feature of which was a centrally-mounted fog lamp left over from P3 days on the insistence of Maurice Wilks. Why Wilks should have approved of such a peculiar feature remains something of a mystery, unless it was his way of retaining a remnant of classic style. It was this single fog lamp so predominantly featured that quickly earned the car its 'Cyclops' nickname.

By this stage development was almost complete; above the air-intake the Viking mascot stood guard. At this point it should be noted there was probably every intention of dispensing with the model numbering system which was traditional with Rover cars, for above the radiator louvres, instead of the name 'Rover' there appeared 'Viking'.

In retrospect the development of the Land Rover had greater affect on the P4 project than was perhaps initially appreciated. In February 1949, Rover announced that in order to extend production of the Land Rover, the company was to issue 535,144 eight-shilling (40p) shares; based on a ratio of 1:3 the shares were priced at a figure of not below £1 each. In January 1950, Rover announced its export figures for 1949: these amounted to an impressive £4million, which included the relevant sales of Land Rover, whereas for 1946 the figure had been a mild £650,000.

Originally it had been decided to use sheet steel for the production of the P4 bodies but, due to the accute shortage of steel immediately after the war, the decision was taken to use the same material as did the Land Rover. Using Birmabright 2, which was produced by Birmetals and consisted of an alloy of aluminium with a content of 25% manganese, the weight of the metal was a third of the steel. As such this was good news; however, the cost was three times as much as steel! In the event there was no argument; the steel was not available but the Birmabright was.

With production of the Land Rover in full swing at Solihull there was some difficulty in planning for construction of the P4 bodies. A contract was placed with Pressed Steel at Cowley to the south-west of Oxford and tooling-up cost a quarter of a million pounds. There is probably some irony in the fact that the good reputation Rover acquired for the P4's durability was a direct

'Viking' poses for the camera. This is not a production car but a final prototype version used for evaluation purposes. The radio aerial seen on the off-side wing was moved to the roof when the car went into production. (Courtesy BMIHT/Rover Group)

result of the initial shortages of steel: had it been available the story might have been different ...

Maurice and Spencer Wilks were influential in Rolls-Royce's decision to contract Pressed Steel to build bodies for the post-war Bentley Mk VI and, later, the R-R Silver Dawn. When Roy Robotham was seeking a coachbuilder that was able to prepare Rolls-Royce and Bentley bodies to the desired quality, the Wilks brothers were unequivocal in their praise for Pressed Steel.

To conclude the package Rover decided initially to offer just one engine option for the P4, so complying with the government's one-model policy. The 4-cylinder engine from the P3 60 could have been used but would have resulted in chronic underpowering. It was not allowed to fade into obscurity however, destined, as it was, for use in the Land Rover, a role to which it was especially suited.

Rightly, the 6-cylinder engine was used, but not without some modification: twin SU carburettors were installed and cylinder bores chromium-plated. A revised aluminium cylinder head with an integral manifold was devised and this alone saved almost 14 kilograms in weight. Combining all the modifications not only raised power output to 75bhp, it also improved fuel consumption, even with the poorly graded fuel available in the post-war period.

With the all-new Rover some of the jealously-guarded values of

the P2 and P3 had been retained which included the Rover freewheel. Essentially, the freewheel device operated on engine overrun; once engine speed had been increased to the desired limit and the accelerator pedal relaxed, so the freewheel would engage and allow the car to coast. An obvious disadvantage was the lack of engine braking but in its day it proved popular, especially as it effectively reduced petrol consumption. As the engine speed reduced to a predetermined level, so the freewheel would disengage; if the driver so required it was possible to repeat the whole process over and over again. A safety factor built into the system ensured that by pressing the accelerator pedal at any time direct drive could instantly be engaged and, furthermore, the device could be permanently

deactivated by a control knob on the car's fascia.

Mechanically, the freewheel acted through a second clutch within the transmission system which was positioned between the gearbox and propeller shaft. Engagement of the freewheel occurred when the speed of the propeller shaft was less than that of the gearbox layshaft. A further aspect of the freewheel allowed gearchanging to be carried out while the device was in operation, without having to use the clutch pedal. Today, of course, such a device would not be permitted.

If post-war Rover was seen to be dragging its heels when designing the P3, when other manufacturers were falling headlong for full-width bodies, integral wings and three-box styling, the P4 set the seal

Two generations: Mike Cauldrey's Twenty has been joined by Tony Rowland's original 15-bar Cyclops P4. (Photo: Stan Johnstone)

on the future with a vengeance. Rover defied its critics with the P4's new look and to get some idea of the shock of the new, consider some of its rivals, which still had upright radiators, separate wings and exposed leadlamps. In 1949 Daimler was still producing the DB18 Consort and Triumph was finding ready customers with the razor-edged Renown; Lanchester plodded along with the LD10 but most significant was Citroën with its *Onze Legeres* and *Normales* – Light and Big Fifteens in Britain – virtually unchanged, apart from a little cosmetic treatment, since 1934. As far as Citroën was concerned it would be another six years before the stunning DS would make its shattering debut.

The launch pad for the P4 was the 1949 London Motor Show held at Earls Court which opened during the first week of October.

Being on home territory the P4, or rather the 75, as it was destined to become, attracted an inquisitive audience as crowds flocked to see Rover's new masterpiece. From the motoring journalists' point of view the emergence of the P4 was the final act in a drama which they were privileged to have been part of, for on various occasions they were invited to not only witness demonstrations of the prototype cars, but to ride in them as well!

There was certainly some surprise from certain quarters that the P3 had survived less than two years and even more astonishment at the P4's courageous styling. Perhaps, also surprising, especially considering the appearance of a totally new model, was the price tag of the P4 – £1106 – exactly the same as the P3 it replaced.

What else was fresh at the show? The new Daimler Conquest saloon was offered for export only, while both the Nash and Frazer Nash (no relationship here, of course) appeared with enclosed front wheels, a fad that died as quickly as it arrived; locking petrol caps suddenly became important due to the scarcity of petrol and the penalties imposed for being caught with the wrong colour fuel in the tank. More and more cars were being rust-proofed during manufacture, the roto-dip process providing the technology; 5-speed gearboxes had arrived with the Lancia Aprilia, the Lago Record had a guaranteed 125mph while, from Britain, the Jaguar XK120 claimed a maximum speed of over 130mph.

Priced the same as the P3, the P4 offered a lot of car for the money. It was just £20 more than the Citroën Six, £118 less than the Riley 2.5-litre saloon and almost £1000 less than

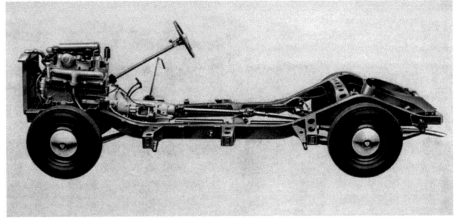

The chassis shop at Solihull. This picture actually shows Land Rover assembly, but compare this picture with those on pages 51 and 54. (Courtesy BMIHT/Rover Group)

the Daimler 2.5-litre Special Sports Coupé. Triumph's Renown, still with running boards and classic styling, was fetching £991, only £115 less than the new P4 Rover 75.

The Autocar, in describing the P4 in its motor show issue of 1949, summed-up the car quite eloquently: "It is a superb car, beautifully suspended, accurate and light in steering, steady and stable on corners, deceptively lively because of its quietness, and possessed of one the best steering column gearchanges so far experienced. Altogether a car of superlative charm."

Rover's display at the London Motor Show understandably created considerable attention. Five new 75s, like prima donnas, revealed their splendour, fit for a queen. As a car on a turntable pirouetted to show off its finest features, four others in static display showed their classic style to a curious audience, some of which were ecstatic while others mourned the passing of an era.

Along with the sparkling new cars with their abundance of chrome, Rover displayed a P4 chassis in cutaway section which exposed all its mechanical parts. The company had what amounted to a virtual obsession with cutaway models, no doubt out of some pride for their technical prowess. Modifications to the chassis from that of the P3 version were quite evident; the frame swept over the rear axle and the engine sat further

forward, so allowing increased cabin space. There were other features, of course; the generous width of the cabin was a result of the new body style and the front passenger space was remarkably clear due to the column gearchange and positioning of the handbrake on the right hand side of the driver's leg.

In fact, none of the quiet luxury and discreet appointment of the Rover had been lost: dignity still prevailed, soft hide adorned the seats and deep-pile carpets covered the floor; walnut embellished the fascia and door cappings while, throughout the car, an air of excellence prevailed. Lower and wider than the P3, extra

Coming out of the drying ovens, a row of P4 75s heads for the next stage on the production line. (Courtesy BMIHT / Rover Group)

This brochure illustration of a Cyclops P4 is a brilliant publicity period piece. The model depicted has received the first modifications of the range, having the new 8-bar grille and reduced chrome embellishments. (Author's collection)

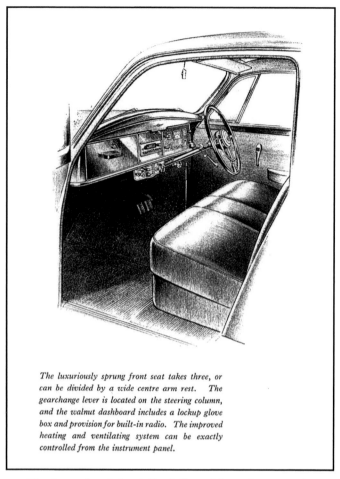

The luxuriously sprung front seat takes three, or can be divided by a wide centre arm rest. The gearchange lever is located on the steering column, and the walnut dashboard includes a lockup glove box and provision for built-in radio. The improved heating and ventilating system can be exactly controlled from the instrument panel.

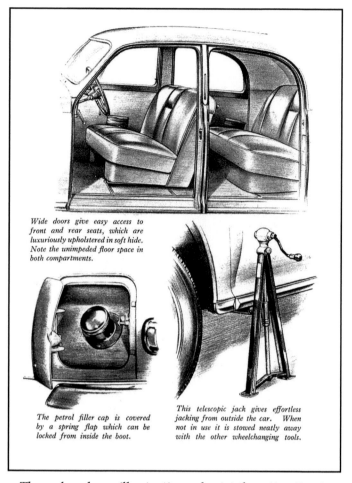

Wide doors give easy access to front and rear seats, which are luxuriously upholstered in soft hide. Note the unimpeded floor space in both compartments.

The petrol filler cap is covered by a spring flap which can be locked from inside the boot.

This telescopic jack gives effortless jacking from outside the car. When not in use it is stowed neatly away with the other wheelchanging tools.

The benefit of the P4's full-width styling can be seen in this delectable brochure drawing. Note the rectangular instruments, column gearchange and early handbrake lever. (Author's collection)

These brochure illustrations depict the attention to detail of the P4. The front bench seat enabled the car to be a full six-seater. (Author's collection)

passenger comfort was provided by way of more leg, elbow and head room. The boot, too, was 6 inches (150mm) wider and twice the depth of the P3; even so, its shape and capacity was the cause of prolonged controversy.

On display was the first P4 75 produced. Carrying chassis number 0430-0001 the car was built on September 26th 1949 and finished in Connaught green with grey trim. The car was eventually supplied to a Mr Stephenson who took delivery of the vehicle on December 30th 1950. The second, third and fourth cars built were all supplied to Rover staff or were used within company departments.

Car number 0008, again finished in dark green, was supplied to Spencer Wilks on 24th October 1949; Maurice Wilks took delivery of car number 0011 in black, while Peter Wilks at the company's service school received number 16. The dispatch records at the Heritage Motor Centre show that 4 cars, numbers 13, 14, 23 and 24, all from the early production run, were supplied to the Rover experimental department.

History reveals that during the early days of P4 production the experimental department was particularly busy in two highly significant areas which concerned gas-turbine cars and the prototype 2.6-litre model, both of which will

be discussed in some detail later. Car number 0053, finished in Connaught green, was also supplied to the experimental department and it can only be a matter of conjecture as to what purpose the car served.

The P4's export drive got underway with car number 0012 which was dispatched to Belgium, but it was not long before an order of 50 cars was on its way to Uruguay. During the first year of production 5220 cars were built and of these 3027 were destined to go overseas. The first production car to be registered was JNX 123, but it was JNX 124 that was emblazoned across the front cover of Rover's brochure in 1951.

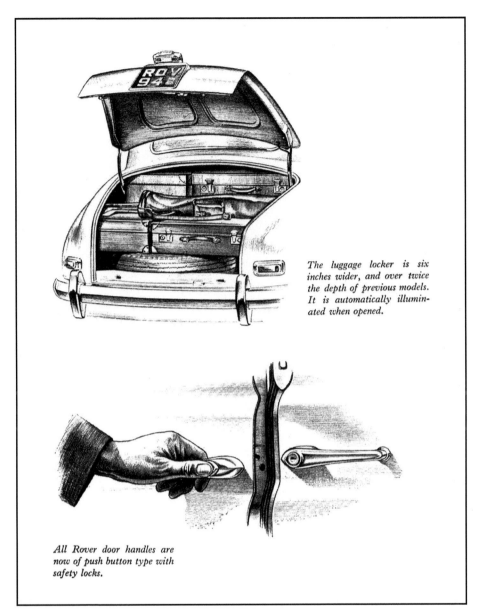

The luggage locker is six inches wider, and over twice the depth of previous models. It is automatically illuminated when opened.

All Rover door handles are now of push button type with safety locks.

Early P4s had the spare wheel laying flat on the boot floor which made the already meagre boot space even more restricted. Rover advertising would have you believe otherwise! (Author's collection)

To launch the 75, Rover produced an all-new colour brochure which depicted the fineness of the car; superb artist drawings exemplified the quality of the car's interior, its plushness as well as the latest features such as push-button door handles and the automatically illuminated boot. Comfort, too, was all-important and was provided for in the form of an interior heater and de-mister.

Colour co-ordination arrived with the 75. Five body colours were specified: two shades of green – Connaught, which was dark, and Lakeside, a lighter shade; pastel blue, ivory and the regulatory black. Grey upholstery was specified with Connaught green and black, a matching blue for the pastel blue exterior and red or green for the ivory and black cars. A further point concerning body colours is that Connaught green is normally presumed to be very similar to British Racing Green; Rover, however, decided it would be a very dark shade of green which was often mistaken for black. Interestingly, Rover experimented with different varieties of paint, the most notable being a pearlized finish applied to JET 1, the record breaking gas-turbine car, which, in essence, was an early metallic type.

So what did the motoring press think of the P4? *The Autocar* saw it as a result of the spirit of progress; *The Motor*, reviewing the car before its launch claimed '... the new Rover 75 ranks as one of the outstanding cars of 1950.'

The new Rover 75 had arrived in style, a new and modern motor car for a new decade, and predetermined a long and auspicious career. Although greeted with some misgiving by those fond of the old Rover image, the P4 – the symbol by which this latest and fourth phase in Rover development was known – quickly forged its own distinct niche in the British market. Its solid and dependable stance, built-in luxury and quiet good taste with reliable engineering soon attracted the discerning motorist and professional classes who preferred a car of distinguished sophistication.

With the export drive underway the Rover 75 was hailed with

The new Rover '75'

*One of the original publicity cars with the 15-bar grille. This
early P4 makes a fine contribution to the London scene.*
(Courtesy BMIHT/Rover Group)

*Above: The majesty of the P4:
few cars were built with such fine
attention and appointment.*
(Author's collection)

enthusiasm from abroad, where the
British car with its unique attention
to detail, quality and essentially
superior finish was regarded with
some enviable curiosity. There was
no doubt the new Rover was on its
way to becoming one of the most
desirable cars of the period.

II

DEVELOPMENT AND CHRONOLOGY

6-cylinder 75, 90, 95 and 100; 105 and 110.
Popularizing the P4, 60 and 80 4-cylinder cars.

Lucky were the relatively few customers who were able to take delivery of the early batches of the P4 75s which, in any case, were being produced at a lower production rate than the P3 had been. The demand for the new Rover, and, indeed, for any new British car at the time, was immense. To the committed Rover owner and enthusiast not successful in obtaining a new 75 there was a choice: accept a second-hand P2 or P3 (at least it was a Rover) and wait jealously in the hope that a car might turn up or join the ever-increasing queue to wait patiently while the covenant scheme imposed by the British Motor Trade Association lumbered on its difficult way.

The covenant scheme was devised owing to the massive demand for new cars, a demand that manufacturers just could not meet. With the majority of production going abroad – it was 'export or bust'–it could be several years before a car became available and the scheme was intended to put an end to profiteering and avoid a black market. The covenant scheme endured until 1953, the irony of it was that it often went against the very people it was intended to help: by the time a car was available the price had increased by such an amount as to be unaffordable.

As a digression, purchase tax on cars had a considerable effect upon price. Initially introduced towards the end of 1940, its effect, of course, was not completely apparent until postwar production of cars resumed.

Levied at 33.33% for cars priced under £1000 and at 66.66% for those costing over £1000, there was, quite naturally, a tendency to price more expensive motor cars at £999. There were anomalies in the system, of course, and one of these was the Land Rover which was classed as a truck! Double purchase tax was applied to all cars from April 1951; little help to an already distressed motor industry but this figure was scaled down to 50% in 1953.

What then would the lucky owner find on taking delivery of a new Rover 75? The large, three-spoked steering wheel was needed to haul the car around corners while the column gearchange and rectangular instruments were the result of American styling. The plain leather seats were of some contrast to the P3's and many other cars of the period but, nevertheless, of enormous comfort especially with armrests built into both the front and rear backrests.

Visibility from the driving position was vastly different to the P3's where a view along the tapering bonnet line to the separate front wings and chrome headlamps was what you got. The P4 offered a much broader vista across the

American influence is carefully combined with British traditionalism in this, the first of the Rover P4 advertisements timed to coincide with the 1949 London Motor Show. (Author's collection)

Right: Early Cyclops P4s were fitted with rectangular instruments. This arrangement, influenced more by American design than anything else, was not over-popular. Note the leather upholstery, African walnut dash and the free-wheel control just visible to the right of the steering wheel. (Author's collection)

Auntie explained

The 'Auntie' Rover was an exercise in dignified comfort and esteem and it is appropriate at this stage to explain how P4 Rovers earned the nickname.

It was all the fault of Denis Jenkinson, that celebrated journalist attached to *Motor Sport* magazine, who is attributed to christening a Rover he was travelling in as an 'Auntie' car. What, in fact, happened was that Ted Eves of *The Autocar*, together with Denis Jenkinson and Jesse Alexander of *Sports Car Illustrated* had taken a P4 to Morocco to cover the 1958 Grand Prix, which was being held at Casablanca. On the return journey a diversion was made to Turin to call in at the Motor Show, all in all a gruelling test for any car. It seems that the car, a Rover 90 which had been supplied to the motoring press as a demonstration machine, had completed the journey in exemplary fashion; it had not missed a beat, used a drop of oil or water and, what is more, had been the provider of the safest and most comfortable transport without any hesitation whatsoever.

Denis Jenkinson, being totally impressed with the Rover, which was registered UUE 991, remarked that the car had tackled the tortuous journey just as if going to Auntie's for tea. The term of endearment stuck and forever after the P4 has carried its 'Auntie' nickname.

full-width body. Facilitating far greater width and comfort inside the cabin compared to previous models, the absence of running boards was a notable feature of the car's external styling; open the doors, however, and there were the running boards in the style of a sill extending the length of the cabin. The P4 felt like a modern car in spite of its ancestry and P3 fundamentals; such luxuries as the standard fitment heater and layout of the interior saw to that.

Below: The 'Auntie' nickname for the P4 was meant as an endearment rather than criticism after journalist Ted Eves completed a marathon tour in the newly announced 90. In this picture the 90 has been sold and it would be interesting to know whether the car has survived ...
(Courtesy BMIHT/Rover Group)

Below: The Cyclops cars were soon modified with an 8-bar grille to improve cooling. Less chrome adorned the front in an effort to reduce the rather garish effect this gave on early cars.
(Courtesy BMIHT/Rover Group)

This story dispels the myth that Rover P4s were called 'Auntie' cars because they were the type of cars elderly aunts chose to drive during the 1950s; in retrospect the P4 is probably just the car elderly aunts would have chosen not to drive. The fact that it was the very car they may have preferred being driven around in is a different matter!

Early problems

In launching a completely new model a few teething problems are inevitable. The first to show itself concerned the cooling system which appeared to be a little too ready to overheat. The trouble was eventually traced to the design of the radiator grille and a message was sent out to Rover dealers to carry out modifications.

As designed, the front grille had fifteen slats which, because they were so close together, prevented adequate cool air passing over the radiator. During the colder months and on short runs there was little difficulty; long journeys and hot weather took their toll and the cars were soon enveloped in clouds of steam. After numerous and frantic complaints Rover service engineers devised a new front grille with only eight slats. These were fitted to new cars but the problem, nevertheless, remained with existing cars. Some dealers, in an effort to resolve the problems themselves, were removing the thermostat; this was not ideal and Rover engineers were forced to issue a service bulletin instructing their agents to overcome the situation effectively.

The remedy was to remove the radiator grille and foglamp assembly and cut out alternate louvres, starting at the bottom and using tin shears and a cold chisel. After filing off the remaining sharp edges and repainting the grille in a matt black finish, the job was complete and any further trouble avoided.

A further problem was discovered in the chassis: linking the rear axle to the frame to provide greater stability while cornering, a Panhard rod was installed to lift the roll centre. The rod mounting was found to have a weakness and this had to be rectified on early production cars. All this was somewhat in vain as later Rover decided that the tie rod served no useful purpose whatsoever and discontinued fitting it. The company decided to advise their agents to remove it from existing cars and it is highly unlikely any cars still retain this redundant mechanism.

Creature comforts

A feature of the P4 was the fascia and driving position which changed relatively little over the years. Whereas the fashion on a lot of cars was for pendant pedals, the organ-stop controls remained on the P4s until the end. What was seen by some enthusiasts as an ommission was the lack of a sunroof, opening windscreen and even a rear-window blind. Such items added to the cost of new cars so Rover, along with the majority of other British car manufacturers, quietly and conveniently ignored them.

As for the fascia and dashboard this was an essay in finery itself, brought up to date from the prewar design of the P2 and P3. Walnut surrounded the instrument panel which was visible through the steering wheel. In front of the passenger a lockable glovebox provided useful stowage; in the centre of the fascia a neat radio could be fitted as an option. To add even further to the car's fine appointment the windscreen and door cappings were also finished in the same walnut trim. A further item of Rover thoroughness and thoughtfulness was the set of essential tools stowed neatly and safely out of sight under the driver's seat. From 1952 the tool tray was relocated under the fascia rail, a position it retained until the very end of P4 production.

The instruments had the particular Rover touch: sophistication was evident by the presence of a rheostat for dashboard illumination and the fuel gauge doubled as an engine oil level indicator. Even a low-fuel warning light was fitted as a driving aide. For all its tell-tale quality, though, the instrument layout in its rather uninspiring formality lacked a certain panache and was not in keeping with the car's rounded lines.

To aid ventilation to the car's interior two air-intakes were fitted alongside the sidelights and directly under the headlamps. In addition, and what was then a novel feature, were the front window quarterlights which could be swivelled to force cold air into the car when at speed. There were compensations for the unimaginative instrument layout in the form of little touches of luxury within the cabin; twin reading lamps were installed above the rear seats and the glove box was illuminated, as was the boot.

It would be arrogant to suggest the Rover P4 was all perfection, even accounting for its pedigree and fineness; allowing for the car's foibles, however, the 75 justly lived up to its reputation of being 'One Of Britain's Fine Cars'. The centrally-placed Cyclops lamp was not popular and the frontal treatment of the car, controversial

November 16, 1949.   The **Motor**

Where to see the new

ROVER

AT THE SCOTTISH MOTOR SHOW,
Kelvin Hall, Glasgow

You will want to see the entirely new Rover Seventy-Five. With its versatile companion the Land-Rover, it will be displayed at the Scottish Show by the following distributors and dealers :—

Jas. Gibbon (Motors) Ltd. Stands 42 & 79	Rossleigh Ltd (Cars) ... ... Stand 26
Taggarts (Motherwell) Ltd. ... Stand 58	James Forrest (Cars) ... ... Stand 5
Jas. Tweedie Ltd. ... ... Stand 15	Rossleigh Ltd. (Commercial) ... Stand 64

Wm. Hamilton (Motors) Ltd. ... Stand 8

THE ROVER COMPANY LIMITED SOLIHULL BIRMINGHAM & DEVONSHIRE HOUSE LONDON

GVS-113

from the beginning, came in for some added criticism due to its over-use of chrome which, claimed some, was far too Americanised. The column-change gears were not overly well-received, either, and the traditionally-minded were not so keen on the instrument layout; round dials were considered correct and the rectangular type rather flippant in the American style.

Turning to the P4's performance and mechanical details, the cars produced between 1949 and 1964 derived their model designation from the engine bhp ratings, hence the first series, the Rover 75, developed 75bhp maximum

The ROVER *Seventy-Five*

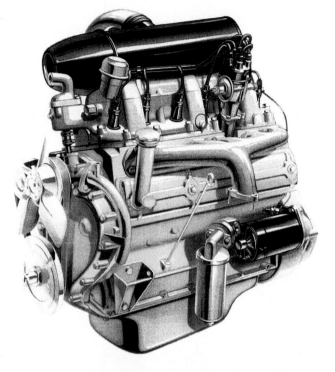

The central model in the Rover range of three fine cars, the Seventy-Five is attractive from any point of view. Inside and out it reflects the thoughtful care given to its design and the superb workmanship that has gone into its construction.

In every way the Seventy-Five maintains the Rover tradition of quality that is held in such high regard by motorists all over the world. It is a brilliant performer on the road, running with a smoothness and silence that must be experienced to be fully believed. Four, five or six people may relax in the restful comfort of its interior furnishings, enjoy the soothing action of beautifully balanced suspension and have confidence in the unfaltering operation of mechanical components that have been built for reliability and long service.

Rover engineers are proud of this car, so are Rover owners !

The engine of the Rover Seventy-Five is outstanding for its smooth, silent power and for the hard-wearing qualities of every individual component. Copper-lead main and big-end bearings, for instance, standard in all Rover units, have four times the life of types used in a great many engines. It is an extremely robust, six-cylinder unit with a capacity of 2,230 c.c., developing 80 brake horse-power at 4,500 r.p.m. Its horse-power by R.A.C. rating is 19.85.

The F-Head engine. (Courtesy BMIHT / Rover Group)

Stopping power: early P4 75s were fitted with Girling's Hydro-Mechanical system before total reliance was put on fully hydraulic systems. (Author's collection)

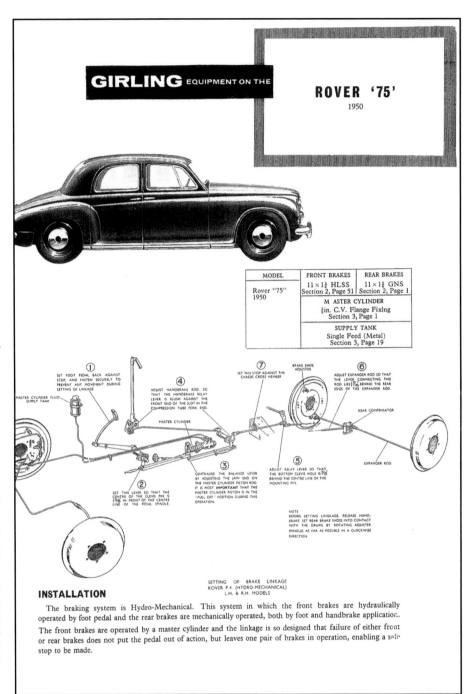

INSTALLATION

The braking system is Hydro-Mechanical. This system in which the front brakes are hydraulically operated by foot pedal and the rear brakes are mechanically operated, both by foot and handbrake application.

The front brakes are operated by a master cylinder and the linkage is so designed that failure of either front or rear brakes does not put the pedal out of action, but leaves one pair of brakes in operation, enabling a safe stop to be made.

power at 4200 rpm. The early 75s could manage a top speed of 82mph (132km/h) which, in retrospect, was a fair achievement for 1949-50, especially with the car's weight being in excess of 28cwt (1450 kilos). In comparison to the P3 75, the P4 had the advantage of a further 7mph (11.2km/h) margin of overall speed although acceleration through the gears was not quite so spirited. The old P3 found the urge to sprint along through its gears with several seconds to spare although it ran out of energy somewhat sooner.

In part, the P4's performance was due to its twin SU carburettors which fed the internal inlet manifold within the newly-designed cylinder head forged from aluminium instead of cast iron. Apart from increasing engine efficiency and, therefore, overall performance compared to that of the P3, a weight-saving of the power unit by some 30lbs (13 kilos) was also achieved. For its weight and size, the P4 boasted an average fuel consumption of 24mpg (12 ltrs/100km) which, in all respects, was decidedly abstemious.

A few words on the F-head Rover engine are necessary at this

Left: Gordon Bashford at the wheel of a prototype P4 chassis. Many considered the P4 over-engineered; Gordon Bashford preferred to say the car was 'properly engineered'. (Courtesy Rover P4 Drivers Guild)

point as there aren't many engines that can boast such longevity of life and production history without undergoing major mechanical design changes. Rover's inlet over exhaust design can only be matched in such comparison of long life by, say, Volkswagen's air-cooled flat-four for the pervasive Beetle and

its derivatives, as well as Citroën's well-loved 2CV flat-twin.

A similar design concept was also used by Rolls-Royce and Bentley in their post-war six-cylinder models, and the question has to be asked why was it eventually replaced? The answer, quite simply, lies in the quest for performance

and ever-increasing speed. Rover's product was, quite naturally, built for durability and reliability, its low-revving, heavy weight and relative low specific output saw to that. A further advantage of the F-head design was the engine's happiness with low-grade fuels and its capacity for enduring mileages of at least 'once round the clock' without even the hint of any difficulty.

In terms of longevity it must be appreciated the engine was still available into the 1990s as an option on the series III Land Rover. So durable was the F-head engine that it was claimed by the manufacturer it could run on 20% diesel without trouble and, as further evidence, a 7.5 compression ratio engine could run – on reduced power, naturally, – on blends of 83% octane petrol and even 62% octane paraffin.

Stopping power

Having got the P4 into motion and up to a respectable speed, let us consider its stopping potential. In essence the car inherited the Girling hydro-mechanical system from its predecessor with hydraulically operated brakes serving the front wheels and a mechanical system operating the rear wheels. In addition, a separate parking brake was provided which worked on the rear wheels.

Considered now something of a hybrid belt-and-braces system, both the front and rear brakes were operated by the foot pedal in the normal fashion. As a safeguard,

and due to the system's linkage arrangement, at least one source of braking power remained operative in the case of failure. As the plunger in the master cylinder pressurized the brake fluid to the front wheel cylinders and activated the brake shoes, so a mechanically-operated rod spurred the rear brakes into action. Rover was reluctant to rely completely upon a fully hydraulic braking system: should a failure have occurred within the front brake assembly, the lower travel of the foot pedal would, in theory, have ensured that the mechanical rear brakes were operated independently, so stopping the car. This caution was typical of Rover. A similar system was used by Rolls-Royce during the 1950s.

On such a prestigious car this cautious measure is not quite so overdone as it first appears. Girling hydro-mechanical systems were widely used and could be found on such cars as the AC 2-litre, Bentley, Daimler and Lagonda 2.5-litre models and the Riley 2.5-litre saloon. Fully hydraulic brakes were also gaining support, although they were by no means new; such systems had been around since the mid-1930s and were a feature of Citroën's Traction Avant model whose origins dated back to 1934.

When applied, the Rover's brakes were not so antiquated as might be suggested. While never fierce they stopped the car completely adequately, even in dire emergency, with relatively little pedal pressure being exerted.

One comment that is constantly hurled at the P4 – and it is hardly a criticism – is that the car was over-engineered. Gordon Bashford, who had so much to do with the car both in its development and planning stages and, indeed, during its life-span, was very much critical of the use of the 'over-engineered' expression. Without doubt Gordon Bashford was of biased opinion; he had every right to be and insisted the car was not so much over-engineered as the result of prudent thought and design, an argument that can hardly be faulted.

Gordon Bashford insisted the quality of engineering and build be simply the best that could be provided with the available technology: in those days computer-aided design was not even a dream. Engineering was mathematics, slide rule and the drawing board. Testing mechanical forces was done by hand and experience and the results evaluated on the test track to see if the ideas could stand the test of reality and endurance.

True, Gordon Bashford was careful to allow for failure margins and it was a matter of conjecture as to whether a stronger component or a belt-and-braces approach to essential areas of construction could be considered over-engineering. The ideas adopted for the P4 helped make the car the success it undoubtedly was and a machine of legendary durability.

At this point it is worth considering the impact Gordon

Typical fifties brochure detail of the driving position of the P4. Obviously Rover had the export market in mind with this left-hand-drive illustration.
(Courtesy BMIHT/Rover Group)

Bashford had upon both the Rover car and the company and the esteem with which each regarded the other. Bashford joined Rover at the age of 14 in 1930 after a friend had put in a good word for him to the head of the drawing office. As an apprentice in the Rover drawing office department he was expected, amongst other things, to be tea-boy, a task he must have executed with his usual tenacity and excellence for he was singled out to go to Chesford Grange to work on the designs of Sir Frank Whittle's jet engines during the Second World War.

Working as an apprentice during the 1930s on the Wilks brothers Rovers stood Gordon in good stead for applying the formula associated with the Rover tradition. After the war Maurice Wilks persuaded him to take charge of the future planning of Rover cars which meant that, as well as working some five years ahead of his colleagues in the production department, he had responsibility for the overall concept of all the models that were to emerge from Solihull.

Initially Gordon Bashford set out to prepare the ill-fated little M-type but it was the P4, P5, Land Rover and P6 Rover 2000 he was most associated with and, in this respect, he followed Spencer and Maurice Wilks in their quest for luxury, refinement and a quality approach to engineering that was second to none. Later, he was involved with the SDI and the Range Rover, the latter not only being a

development of the Land Rover but somewhat akin to the experimental Road Rover which will be discussed later.

Apart from the development of production cars, Gordon Bashford was also recognised for having an involvement in the development of research vehicles for Rover, namely an energy conservation model which had the potential of 100mph (160km/h) and 100mpg (2.8 ltr/100km). Up to the time of his retirement in 1981 he worked in conjunction with the Rover development centre at Gaydon – now the home of the British Motor Industry Heritage Trust – and the research department that was also based there. Even in retirement Gordon Bashford kept busy within the motor industry and helped with the design of cars for the disabled.

On his death in September 1991 *The Times* wrote of Gordon in its obituary: "... he leaves a considerable reputation: it is estimated 70 per cent of more than 1.6 million Land Rovers which have been built are still in regular use."

Of the original 3563 Rover 75s built in 1950, its first production year, some 28 cars are known to have survived. At 0.79% of the original cars, this figure is not as low as first it seems.

First changes to the P4
Lessons were learnt from the early batches of P4s that were delivered from Solihull and,

following a succession of criticisms and recurring faults, certain modifications were made to the 75 during its first year of production. The Cyclops foglamp, 15 bar radiator grille and chromed headlamp and ventilator facings gave the car a somewhat garish appearance which needed to be tidied up. This was achieved by replacing the headlamp bezels with painted types in the body colour and the facings on the rectangular ventilation intakes were removed.

As for the Cyclops lamp, this remained, but at this point the question must be asked whether this feature really was a Rover novelty or, as is more likely, a design copied from another American car. A similar creation was to be found on the ostentatiously designed Tucker and it may have been an attempt by the Wilks brothers to satisfy their love-affair in those immediate postwar days with the American automobile. American Fords, on some early Fifties models, featured a large roundel within the grille, and, while a lamp was not fitted within it, the styling association nevertheless remained.

The most significant design change was the modification of the radiator grille, undertaken not as an attempt to soften the frontal appearance of the car but in an effort to prevent over-heating. As has been described earlier it was found necessary to remove every other bar in order to provide extra cooling air and Rover engineers

43

The 2.6-litre prototype car: this sole surviving example out of 30 built has been painstakingly restored by Bill Henderson. KAC 471 was originally sent to Rolls-Royce at Crewe for evaluation, the car assigned to Roger Cra'ster, the firm's Export Manager. It was instructed that the vehicle be returned to Rover after a specific period but it was in fact lost within the Crewe system and later sold, only to be rescued by the present owner. (Author's collection)

produced a factory-made alternative as an effective solution.

A further point of customer criticism concerned the fascia with its American-inspired rectangular instruments and a year later, in 1951, additional changes were announced. As well as cosmetic modifications in which Rover conceded to public opinion and fitted round dials – which were so much more traditional – there were other changes of a mechanical nature.

Rover decided it was time to put complete faith and trust in fully hydraulic brakes instead of insisting upon the Girling-designed hybrid hydro-mechanical system. With all-hydraulic brakes the opportunity was seized to uprate the overall efficiency of the brakes themselves and a larger master cylinder and wider shoes were fitted. In addition, the handbrake, an upright lever to the driver's right, was modified for reach and given the famous 'shepherd's crook' handle.

Early 75s were fitted with push-button interior door handles which were never really fully appreciated for their ease of use: for 1951 they were changed in favour of conventional levers. Also affecting the doors, catches were fitted to stop them opening too wide and causing damage and courtesy lights redesigned to enable them to operate whenever the doors were opened instead of being switched through the sidelights.

Much of the experience with the early production cars was called upon in an effort to eventually offer a wider model range with an option of engine sizes. In preparing for the future some further modifications were found to be necessary, as well as detail changes dependent upon supply and demand of components. Steel radiators found their way into some cars and resulted in a number of owners soon complaining of poor running and over-heating which was hardly surprising. Larger cooling fans were fitted, carburettors modified and the fuel pump repositioned to provide greater efficiency. A further minor modification concerned the dashboard in as much as the clock was relocated to the passengers' benefit – before it had been visible only to the driver.

During the period of these changes the export of P4s to the USA began, albeit in relatively small numbers. These cars had certain modifications not seen on home market vehicles: the Cyclops lamp was removed although its housing remained and was made to look part of the car's frontal design; semaphore signals as found on the British cars were substituted with flashing indicators, a modification later available in Britain. Some cars were fitted with wire wheels, which had a peculiar effect to say the least, but the most striking feature was the fitting of white-wall tyres, a craze that had swept across the USA and found some following in Britain, thankfully, though, not on Rovers.

The 2.6-litre Cyclops Rover
In preparation for an additional model to the P4 range, or at least an alternative engine option, Rover specially commissioned a batch of 30 cars with a new 2.6-litre engine. For evaluation purposes the 30 special examples were, in effect, standard Cyclops 75s but with their engines modified with siamese bores to achieve a capacity of 2638cc. The first clue as to the existence of these cars is in the Rover dispatch records which show a set of chassis numbers 053 00001-053 00030; this numbering system was in contrast to the standard 75 model cars which had chassis numbers commencing with the 043 prefix.

It appears the existence of these experimental cars was, for a number of years, not readily appreciated and may have been confused with the eventual Rover 90 model which was also fitted with a 2.6-litre engine but of different design. Although of 2638cc capacity the design of the 90's engine was quite different and not simply an over-bored unit direct from the 75.

This was not the first time a larger engine had been fitted to the Cyclops model; in its experimental and prototype stage a 2.4-litre engine, which was basically the 2103cc unit bored out, was used by Spen King as a company car around 1949. In an interview with Spen King, in which he looked back over his career with Rover and, eventually, British Leyland, he admits to the 2.4-litre prototype Cyclops as being a jolly fast car for its time.

The whole reason for producing the special batch of 30 2.6-litre cars was to gain first-hand knowledge and experience of a larger engine over prolonged use and to gauge its characteristics. A number of specially chosen individuals were selected to provide a reliable source of information, and so delivery of the vehicles began. Further inspection of the company records reveals that nine of the cars were supplied to officials and directors of the Rover company which included the future chairman, William Martin-Hunt, and, quite naturally, Spencer Wilks. Wilks, in fact, received two cars, probably one in connection with business use and the other for private evaluation. Six cars were delivered to special customers, all reputedly in the Midlands area, while three cars were made available to specialist Rover agents Henlys of London, Midland Autocar company of Leamington and Ewens of Bournemouth. Apart from three cars which were supplied to Rover's experimental department, export division and the London service department based at Seagrave Road, the remaining cars found their way to specialist automotive companies who had connections with the Rover company: these were Leyland Motors, which was closely involved with the turbine project, Dunlop, Ricardo, Girling, Lucas and Sturgess and Sons of Leicester.

By way of digression, Dunlop had only recently returned to favour with Rover. When Spencer Wilks was hired to save the ailing company he toured the firm's creditors begging them to give more time; Avon and Lucas supported Wilks but Dunlop did not and it was some time before Rover did further business with that company.

The feedback from the specially selected test sources showed that the 2.6-litre engine lacked the ruggedness desired; the engines were subject to some abnormal piston wear which led the Rover engineers to decide upon a redesigned power unit for the 90 of 1954. In general, the problems had been encountered when the cars were driven hard and to the extreme of their limits. In common with the typical Rover belt-and-braces policy, this was deemed far from good enough.

In all other respects, apart from the engine, the 2.6-litre Cyclops cars were virtually identical to the 75s of the same period, even gear boxes and rear axles were the same. The thirty specials were all produced in 1950 between mid-April and mid-June with the majority of cars being delivered to their destinations during the middle of the summer.

Part of the deal in supplying the thirty specials was that after two years the cars had to be returned to Rover, where they would then be rebuilt with a perfectly standard engine, thereby disguising the fact that the specials had ever existed.

An interesting point concerning the specials was that five cars were finished in two-tone paintwork at a time when only single colours were available for the standard 75s. Spencer Wilks' two cars, chassis numbers 053 0001 and 20, were included, black with blue and black and beige respectively. The remaining three cars were finished in two-tone grey, two-tone blue and silver-grey. The five non-standard colour cars all remained in Rover ownership as they had been supplied to company directors and officials. The existence of the five specially finished cars does point to the fact that the company favoured this development which was later to become a feature of the P4s.

Side-by-side are two of the rarest P4s. The Tickford drophead coupé and the 2.6-litre prototype both belong to Bill Henderson and each have been subject to major restoration. (Photo: Bill Henderson)

For a long time precious little was known of this particular episode in Rover history and it was generally considered that none of the cars had survived in original form. As so often happens, the passage of time reveals fascinating quirks of circumstance, the like of which led to the discovery of a lone remaining 2.6-litre Cyclops model.

It appears that the car had originally been presented to Rolls-Royce and became personal transport for the Company's Export Manager, Roger Cra'ster. It escaped being returned to Rover after the initial two years, and the car was used regularly until 1969, by which stage it had covered some 75,000 miles. Over the following twenty four years the car seems to have been forgotten, although it changed ownership several times. KAC 471, the seemingly sole surviving

Rover was not normally associated with the motor show world of glamourous models publicising new cars – but exceptions were made! The occasion was probably the 1952 Geneva show; note the car is left-hand-drive.
(Courtesy BMIHT/Rover Group)

2.6-litre Cyclops, is now in the safe hands of Rover enthusiast Bill Henderson who also owns a unique 75 drophead coupé. It was touch and go whether the car could be saved, such was its condition: the front wings and boot floor had completely rotted away.

Part of the reason that little is known of the existence of the 2.6-litre specials is due to the fact that all but one did not survive. What happened to these particular cars remains a mystery and tracing them through their registration numbers has drawn a blank.

The design that replaced the Cyclops model. Mike Chenin's 1952 Rover 75 looks very smart with its whitewall tyres and diplomatic plates. (Courtesy Matt White)

This is unfortunate as it means an important stage of the P4's development remains unclear.

By sheer coincidence Roger Cra'ster was reunited with the Rover during the late 1990s. Roger, having met the author, mentioned that he was looking to use a Rover P4 to attend a family wedding. The author, unaware at this time that it was Roger who had used the car on behalf of Rolls-Royce, put him in touch with Bill Henderson, who agreed to officiate. Imagine, therefore, Roger's pleasure on seeing 'his' car again, and Bill's satisfaction knowing more of the vehicle's history.

Exit Cyclops; enter a new image
The first two years of the new 75 production had given Rover time to consolidate performance and standing with both the home and export markets, as well as being able to judge the overall success of the model. Useful time had been spent in evaluating feedback from Rover agents and customers alike with some modifications already implemented. The most obvious and significant however appeared in 1952.

From the outset the use of the Cyclops foglamp and the rather bland radiator grille had been controversial. These aspects of the car's frontal styling were less than appreciated and quite disliked by many of the company's customers. Rover engineers finally gave way to public opinion and criticism and, for the revised cars announced in March 1952 to coincide with the Geneva Motor Show, a completely new front-end headed a whole list of modifications. Instead of the horizontal slats with the Cyclops lamp in the middle, the radiator grille was neatly encased in a semi-rectangular chrome frame with thin vertical bars. A dividing bar in the middle which opened out at the top incorporated the Rover emblem with a '75' motif. Altogether this was far more elegant and remained almost the same – apart from minor modification – throughout the remainder of the car's production.

A careful examination of the revised 75 model showed the grille to be but one of a whole series of changes. At the front of the car the two small rectangular air intakes for cabin ventilation disappeared: these had been a problem from

the outset as they were set so low they picked up fumes and road dust which found their way into the interior of the car, much to the passenger's discomfort. In place of the grilles a centrally-positioned flap on the scuttle which could be opened and closed from within the cabin provided fresh air without the need for a lot of cumbersome ducting. At the same time the car's heating system was also improved with a more powerful heater unit capable of the equivalent of 3.5 kilowatt output.

Headlamp housings were also revised with the rectangular bezels being dropped in favour of the new Lucas PF700 headlights, which incorporated the double-dipping principle. This succeeded in giving the car's front a lighter appearance, which helped lose the oppressive boxy aspect of the original styling. Whereas on the previous model the front bumper had been separated from the lower scuttle, the gap was filled in with a valance which helped improve its appearance considerably.

Externally, the only other major modifications were to the rear window, which was made slightly

wider to give greater visibility; especially useful when reversing, and to the boot compartment. A common complaint from owners was the lack of useful boot space which, for a car of the Rover's size, was especially poor. The culprit was the spare wheel which, where it was positioned on the floor of the boot, took up valuable luggage space. Already drivers bemoaned the fact they had to watch their heads when packing and unpacking the back of the car and furthermore it was difficult to carry any bulky items. This was rectified in part by moving the spare wheel from the boot to its own separate compartment under the boot floor which could be accessed from a drop-down panel below the bumper. This modification was made possible by a slight change in the shape of the chassis crossmember and the re-designing of the petrol tank into a wedge shape. Getting to the spare wheel in an emergency was made all the easier by not having to remove all the luggage beforehand; however, the boot lid had to be in the open position in order to release the drop panel as the locking device operated both compartments.

Internally, there were modifications aimed at providing increased comfort: the seats were given extra springing while the back of the front bench seat was recessed to provide greater leg room for rear passengers. Instead of the single glove compartment in the fascia in front of the passenger seat, two separate hatches were fitted. A casualty of the new design was the tray containing the tool kit, which was repositioned underneath the fascia rail where it stayed for the remainder of the car's production. Minor revisions included the fitting of self-parking windscreen wipers, an organ-type accelerator pedal and re-designed circular horn push instead of the original D-shaped example. The new accelerator pedal was found to be vastly more comfortable on long runs and the horn ring was perceived as a safety feature.

Significant were changes to the chassis design which resulted in quieter running and increased comfort generally. 'Silentbloc' rubber bushes were used in the front suspension and these took the form of conical studs partly shrouded in steel which were fitted between the coil springs and wishbones. Elimination of any direct contact between the springs

and the body mountings helped enormously to reduce road noise and vibration. The modification resulted in an increase of one inch (250mm) to the height of the chassis at the rear which, apart from going almost unnoticed, provided a slight improvement in luggage capacity as well as increasing headroom for rear seat passengers.

On the mechanical side a higher output dynamo improved slow-running, while the latest Lucas higher voltage coil and distributor improved the car's specification. The fuel pump which was supplied by SU was moved to the boot where it provided improved performance and was not subjected to the atmosphere as on previous cars. A further modification took

The Cyclops styling of the P4 was not entirely without its critics: the smoother styling of the revised model enabled Rover to concentrate once more on its reputation for refinement. (Author's collection)

OCTOBER 31, 1952   The *Autocar*

 By Appointment to the late King George VI

 Manufacturers of Land-Rovers The Rover Company Ltd.

$\mathcal{T}$HERE'S considerably more to the immaculate Rover Seventy-Five than meets the first appraising glance. A wealth of skilfully co-ordinated refinements such as the Rover method of body silencing and controlled heating and ventilation help to make motoring in this outstanding new car a pleasureable and unprecedented experience.

THE ROVER COMPANY LIMITED, SOLIHULL, BIRMINGHAM   NSHIRE HOUSE, LONDON

the form of a metal-asbestos heat shield positioned between the front silencer and the floor of the car.

The detail changes for 1952 cars were put into effect some time before the Geneva Motor Show but were not available for home-market sales: British customers had to be content with the remaining Cyclops cars. Observers of Rover practice would, however, have noticed that some export markets were being supplied with the updated model for at least a couple of months or so before the changes were officially announced. Such was the importance levied on export sales.

Another feature of the car which had received its share of adverse publicity since conception was the column gearchange, not because it was unwieldy, inefficient or uncomfortable, or even cumbersome in use, but merely because it reflected American influence, an influence not always readily accepted in Britain. Rover felt no great desire to change this fad of immediate postwar gadgetry and retained column change for a little longer. In an effort to satisfy opinion and demand, however, it was left to a Midlands agent, Gethin's of Birmingham, to supply a floor change conversion. Its success is reflected by the fact that relatively few customers opted for the conversion, although there is some evidence that a number of police forces using the P4 were in favour of it. There are not any figures to suggest how many cars were so converted but it is clear that very few have survived.

The changes to the P4 were enough to give an added impetus to sales: from the 3211 cars produced for the British market for 1950/51 production dipped to 1927 cars in 1952. With the revisions production increased more than twofold with 4742 cars produced in 1953. Export sales showed 6942 vehicles produced as well as 126 CKD units for 1951; for 1952 and 1953 the figures evened out at 3841 and 3258 cars respectively.

Achieving increased sales had been an uphill effort but was good news to Maurice Wilks in his capacity as chief engineer at Solihull. His appointment to the board of directors was verified in May 1950 and he must have watched the company's

The Road Rover was but a glimpse of what might have been. In this photograph of a prototype model of a P4 estate car, the Land Rover influence is clearly evident. (Courtesy BMIHT/Rover Group)

Below: A further Road Rover prototype: SNX 36 appears to have overall smoother detail to PUE 41 in the preceding photograph. (Courtesy BMIHT/Rover Group)

market Fords and Chevrolets, and it could be out-run on the straight flat highway, but, on lesser roads, the Rover was capable of holding its own, the light and positive handling providing the necessary impetus in

financial and trading position with some considerable interest. For the year ending 2nd August 1952, the Rover company managed a net profit of £313,300 after tax; two years later this figure had increased to over half a million pounds – £553,617, to be precise.

The model range widens

Whilst the original Cyclops and revised 75 models were under production, the early to mid-1950s were a period of development and expansion. Earlier minor difficulties – which included discontinuation of the Panhard rod that dealers had been removing when necessary for some time under the guidance of Rover's service department – had been isolated and ironed out.

The good reputation of the P4 was spreading rapidly and was given a tremendous boost by Bob Dearborn writing in America's *Road and Track* magazine. The emphatic article graced the Rover as being in the league of only the best and Dearborn wrote: "I honestly believe (barring the Rolls-Royce) that there is no finer car built in the world today."

This fervent statement, together with Dearborn's glowing regard for the P4, elevated the car to a higher level of customer; the advertising world soon caught on to what

was seen as a tremendous fillip for British engineering abroad, as well as a boost for Rover products, and a series of evocative sales advertisements in the style of *The Autocar* and *Motor* did nothing but good for the car's following.

As further evidence of the esteem in which Rover was held in America, the P4 75 was deemed to have a completely honest approach to its overall quality, its luxury interior and mechanical excellence. True, the 2-litre engine was on the small side when compared to the motors that powered the USA's home

towns and on country roads.

Above all, American motorists respected the Rover for its pride and statuesque beauty and delighted over the Rover's refined touches: the starting handle, wheel jack and tyre pump all neatly stowed away and clipped to the inside of the engine compartment. The ultimate, of course, was the tray of tools packed under the fascia and especially the tyre pressure gauge engraved with the Rover crest.

Bob Dearborn's comments relating to the 75 have already been noted but it was left to Oliver

P4s alongside Land Rovers on the Solihull assembly line.
(Courtesy BMIHT/Rover Group)

Billingsley to sum-up his thoughts on the P4 after taking a 75 for a week-long run up and down the steep hills and rough streets of San Francisco, courtesy of Kjell Qvale of the British Motor Car Company: "I found myself with a genuine respect for the comfortable ride and quick-thru-traffic pace. Brakes were easy to fade but this has since been remedied by greater lining area. The many quality features of the Rover soon instil pride in the operator and it was with reluctance that I returned the 'junior Rolls' to Qvale."

In Britain there was a general relaxation of postwar austerity measures and there began to appear a glimmer of hope for the future. After adhering closely to the government-inspired one-model policy, apart from the production of the Land Rover, on which the Rover company were proud to display the insignia of royal approval, Solihull began to feel obliged to widen the P4's model range and desirability. Two areas were giving company engineers food for thought: the feedback from the 2.6-litre engine exercise and the Land Rover.

One particularly significant aspect of research and design was for an estate car derivative of the P4 which happened to take on the form of a utility vehicle – something of a hybrid between the Land Rover and the 75. Known as the Road Rover the vehicle first received detailed boardroom discussion in 1952 but history has revealed it really was the forerunner of the much later Range Rover. Although the Road Rover never materialised as such, it does have some importance in Rover genealogy, especially as its launch was originally intended for the mid-1950s. Other matters took precedence and eventually its plans were relegated to the filing cabinet in 1958, where it joined other

ROVER
1954

The 60 was Rover's attempt at popularising the P4. The light steering and 4-cylinder engine made the car responsive but fuel consumption was often no better than the 6-cylinder cars.
(Author's collection)

aborted projects. This and other P4 derivatives will be discussed in greater detail in a later chapter.

Whilst planning behind closed doors progressed it was Rover's current cars that were busy ensuring the public relations image was not lacking. The gas turbine cars were the subject of increasing public awareness and interest and had caused a steady stream of experimental turbines to appear on both sides of the Atlantic. The reputation of the P4 had spread worldwide and a major operation was mounted when an official from the British Embassy in Khatmandou ordered a brand new 75. The car had to be manhandled across fifteen miles of mountain tracks from the Indian frontier by an army of local volunteers. Although the wheels had to be removed the car arrived quite safely after its ordeal without any further dismantling.

In September 1952 a Rover 75 and Land Rover were taken on a gruelling 20,000 mile exercise to the Middle East, across the Sahara and through central Africa before returning via Europe. A tribute to both vehicles and Rover reliability was that the trip was completed without any faults except for a puncture or two!

Despite the apparently steadfast position of the expanding Rover concern there were, however, some doubts about the future. During the early part of March 1954 there was a simultaneous announcement from the Rover and Standard companies to the effect that preliminary talks had taken place regarding a proposed merger between the two concerns. The basis of the plan was that both companies would have a shared financial commitment, although both would operate and produce vehicles as a separate entity. A major stumbling block to this union was Rover's and Standard's commercial vehicle interests, ie., Land Rover and Ferguson tractors. The talks were, however, relatively short-lived for at the end of July that year a further announcement indicated the plans had been dropped.

On the finishing line at Solihull: 60s and 75s receive their final check.
(Courtesy BMIHT/Rover Group)

A major move in expanding the P4 range was to make the car more easily accessible to a greater car-buying public. En route to achieving this goal were a number of still-born exercises resulting in various prototypes and experimental cars using alternative body designs which will be discussed later. In the first real step in model expansion, Rover launched two new models in time for the London Motor Show in the autumn of 1953. The experiments with the 2.6-litre engines as fitted to the 30 special test and evaluation Cyclops models had paid off and Rover was able to offer the brand-new 90 model with a modified version of the larger engine. The other new model, the 60, was less successful in its attempt to attract greater sales: in effect it was the same reliable P4 but with a less-refined mechanical specification and therefore lower cost; the price difference, though, was not enough to attract customers of other marques. Placed between the two new models the 75 remained, offering good value for money.

The 1954 model range – enter the 60

While offering an alternative engine at a lower price, the 60's failure to attract custom from what were considered lesser makes was due, in part, to the far too narrow price difference between the new 60 and the existing 75. For the 1954 season the difference in price for what was, after all, a de-tuned luxury car,

was just less than £107; a year earlier the 75 had been priced at £1487 but dropped to £1269 on introduction of the new cars. The question prospective Rover owners had to consider was whether it was worth finding the extra £107 for greater refinement?

At the heart of the 60 which, like the 75, derived its model designation from its bhp rating – 60bhp at 4000rpm – was the 2-litre 1997cc 4-cylinder inlet over exhaust engine. Although in principle the 60's power unit followed in the P3 and P4 tradition, it had a greater affiliation to the engine used in the Land Rover. Its components were more refined, however, and more suited to a prestige saloon car than a utility vehicle.

Performance-wise, the 60 was capable of a maximum speed of just 2mph (3.2km/h) below that of the Rover 75 but made considerably more fuss getting there, taking 4 seconds longer on the 0-50mph (0-80km/h) and 6 seconds longer on the 0-60mph (0-96 km/h) figures. The benefit of the 4-cylinder engine was evident mainly in its fuel consumption, which was approximately 27-32mpg (10.5-8.8 ltrs/100km), as opposed to the 6-cylinder's 18-26mpg (16-11 ltrs/100km).

In contrast to its performance the interior of the 60 remained generally the same as the 75 and its more powerful sister, the 90. Certain items were lacking which were reserved for the more expensive cars

such as the windscreen washer; little, however, was lost in the way of finesse and standard of finish.

Financially, the 60 was something of an expensive enterprise for Rover: more cars were sold in its first year (1997 in 1954) than any other, although in its last two years, 1958 and 1959, it outsold the faithful 75.

The 90 makes its debut

From the outset the 90 became Rover's bread and butter model in the P4 range, vastly outselling the 75 and accounting for far greater production than the 60 and 75 combined.

The 90's engine sported 2638cc with 90bhp at 4500rpm; the compression ratio was slightly reduced, as were the ratios on both the 60 and 75, to make allowances for the improved quality of fuel finding its way to British petrol pumps. Whereas the 60 had an accent on economy, the 90 was most definitely directed towards performance: there were faster cars and larger cars and some enjoyed greater economy, but to find another car with as many attributes as the 90 would have been difficult.

Studying the manufacturer's figures, the Rover 90 had a top speed advantage of some 4mph (6.4km/h) over the 60, however, in its test of the car in late March 1954, *The Autocar* managed a best maximum speed of 84mph (135.2km/h). Identifying the 90 from its two stablemates was easy: a fog lamp was part of

Easy does it! On the Solihull assembly line a P4 is gently lowered onto its chassis. (Courtesy BMIHT/Rover Group)

Below: Possibly the same car as in the adjoining photograph, now safely lowered onto its chassis. (Courtesy BMIHT/Rover Group)

the standard equipment and was offset to the left of centre of the radiator grille; in addition 'Rover 90' badges were fixed to either side of the bonnet and to the boot lid, while the 90 insignia was incorporated in the grille emblem.

The expansion of the model range made possible a number of revisions which affected all three cars, some changes being a little more significant than others. Externally, apart from the adoption of badges for the 90, the most obvious modification was the provision of sidelights on the top of the front wings. Not only did this comply with the trend amongst British cars – Rover had fitted wing-mounted side lamps since the late 1920s – it also gave the driver a clear indication that the lights were working as tell-tale repeater neons were an integral part of the lamp casing.

Most significant of the changes was the adoption of a floor-mounted gearshift in favour of the column change. Public opinion finally won and there were few who mourned the passing of the column gearchange, although there is nothing to suggest

Following the end of Cyclops styling, early P4s retained the distinctive box headlamps which can be seen on these 1955 cars on the Solihull production line. (Courtesy BMIHT/Rover Group)

the system worked anything but efficiently and adequately. Column gearchanges on British cars rapidly lost support although, on some cars, however, column change gears remained well into the Sixties and Seventies; Citroën's DS retained the system until that model's demise in 1975.

Not only was the gearchange new, the gearbox itself was the subject of some revision with synchromesh being provided on second, third and top, whereas earlier it had been restricted to the third and top ratios only. A feature of the P4 had always been its capacity to seat three-abreast on the front seat, the column change facilitating this particular asset. The central lever still allowed this due to its positioning, which was adjustable for height and angle. By placing a turret at the gearbox end of the lever it was possible to find a comfortable position to suit all drivers and was especially useful when used in conjunction with left hand drive when only simple adjustment was necessary.

During the 1954 season a number of minor modifications were made to particular models and, in some cases to all three versions of the P4. Larger screenwash bottles were fitted to the 75 and 90, the 60 was left out for the good reason that such a device on the cheaper model was not deemed essential. Following problems concerning the cooling fan, the four-blade unit normally reserved for export cars

was made standard equipment on home-market vehicles. Lighting, too, became an issue on 1954 cars and a Heath-Robinson affair was thought up for fitting of rear reflectors; a temporary design allowed the reflector to be suspended from the rear light cluster but this was considered unsatisfactory and far from what Rover owners would expect. The conversion was withdrawn. Flashing indicators were attracting widespread popularity in favour of the difficult-to-see semaphores and a kit enabled the rear brake lights to double-up as flashers. Several makes of car were fitted with this device including the ubiquitous Morris Minor. Again, Rover was not entirely happy about the conversion and advised its agents against fitting it.

Internally, chrome-plated door handles were fitted as standard and the spare wheel was given a support to prevent it working loose and falling out of the compartment. A short-lived modification concerned the handbrake which, for the 1954 season, was relocated to a floor position alongside the driver's seat and between the door. Whilst

there was a lot of opposition to the change – both the Rover company and the agents were besieged with complaints – its adoption was not universally met with disapproval. The majority won through and almost immediately Rover reverted to the original shepherd's crook design which remained throughout production.

David Bache and the 1955 facelift
One of the most notable events at Solihull in the early 1950s was the recruitment of David Bache, who was brought to Rover by Maurice Wilks from Austin at Longbridge in 1953. Five years previously the young Bache had been fresh out of university but still continuing his studies at Birmingham's college of art. There was no doubt whatsoever of there being flair and potential in Wilks' young discovery and it was his intention that David Bache should head-up a fully-fledged design department, the existence of which had never been previously seriously contemplated by the company.

Such a department was becoming necessary if the company

was to increase its range of cars without economies. As a result, the Rover P5 – with its rakish lines – eventually came about, appealing to those customers demanding a large and fast luxury car.

It should be explained that the original concept for a P5 model was a car smaller than the P4. History has shown that Maurice Wilks was less than sure what he wanted for Rover: he was envious of the success that Jaguar was enjoying with its big, fast and opulent cars as well as the more compact sports saloon models. He was also aware that it would have been wrong to venture into a smaller class of car, even if it retained the traditional Rover characteristics, as such a car would be an unknown quantity. For a smaller car to be marketed successfully, Rover would have to produce it in large numbers, and the capacity for this it did not have. In the event, Maurice Wilks erred as usual towards safety and proceeded with the P5 as we know it, the designs of which were drawn up by David Bache following instructions from the master.

David Bache also had a considerable impact on the modification of the P4 for the 1955 season: for some time it had been considered the car needed a facelift to tidy up its overall appearance, especially the rear styling which had always presented somewhat of a problem to Rover's engineers.

Firstly, there was the shape of the boot, then the problem of rearward visibility, even though the back window had already been enlarged. Thirdly, the issue of the lighting and flashing indicators refused to go away and would have to be dealt with effectively. Rightly, all these aspects received attention in one fell swoop.

In general terms the modifications introduced for the 1955 season were retained through the 1956 season, apart from minor detail changes. The model range for 1955 consisted of the three existing cars – 60, 75 and 90 – offering a choice of trim and power options with the 90 showing an out and out lead in popularity. Of the 13,436 cars produced in the 1955 model year, 8728 were Rover 90s while of the remaining 4708 cars less than half (1488) were 60s; the Rover 75 accounted for 3220 cars. Prices were pegged at 1954 values which made the purchase of a Rover an attractive proposition, especially the 90 with its £1297 price tag, only £28 more than the 75.

The size and shape of the boot of the P4 models really had been quite a difficult problem for Rover; certainly it was larger than had

been offered on the old P3 but had nowhere near the capacity of contemporary cars. The drawback as far as Rover was concerned was what exactly should be done about it without changing the car's appeal or identity; David Bache was left to sort it all out.

To increase boot capacity it was necessary to raise the line of the rear wings and hence the boot lid, which gave the whole car an even more solid appearance. It also brought the car right up-to-date; the sloping effect of the original styling harked back to the American influence of a decade before. It was, therefore, possible to replace the horizontal rear lights with vertical clusters incorporating flashing indicators, so making redundant the ponderous and time-worn semaphores. Now, of course, properly working semaphores are a delightful period piece, even if they are hardly noticed in congested traffic conditions!

Having made two changes it was right to finish the job completely by designing a wholly new wrap-around rear window. In essence the window was built in three segments, the wrap-arounds sealed to the large section by plastic and rubber joints. As far as the indicators were concerned the front of the car had to be sorted out, too: the wing-top 'torpedo' sidelights were retained and in place of the old sidelights, which had been previously been utilised as reflectors, flashers were fitted.

Mechanically, the three models underwent a series of changes which concerned the 75 and 90 in particular. As far as the 60 was concerned revisions were kept to relatively minor details such as the provision of a windscreen washer and areas of trim that put the car, in terms of luxury, on a par with its two stablemates. Both the 75 and 90 were fitted with new front brakes which were more powerful and to achieve this the effective width of the brake shoes was increased by three quarters of an inch (20mm) from $2\frac{1}{4}$ inches (57mm) to 3 inches (75mm) and the brake drums enlarged accordingly.

David Bache was responsible for styling modifications to the P4 from the mid-50s. Here, a P4 is pictured in the experimental department with revised front wing styling that never materialised. Of extreme interest is the scale model in the background of an estate-car variant of the Road Rover.
(Courtesy BMIHT/Rover Group)

The most significant changes for 1955 consisted of a new engine for the 75 and a choice of final drive ratios for the 90. In effect, Rover had streamlined its engine options: the new 75 engine was basically the short-stroke unit taken from the 90, which itself offered increased performance from a 3.9 to 1 final drive ratio. The 75's new engine boasted an increase of 5bhp and a capacity of 2230cc with performance to match but without increased fuel consumption. Carburation was also modified from two units to one.

Changes to the 75 engine were made possible by adopting the 90 cylinder block with a redesigned crankshaft. The connecting rods from the standard 90 engine were used but modified pistons produced a compression ratio of 6.95 to 1, compared to 6.73 to 1 on the 90.

The 90, with its optional 3.9 to 1 final drive ratio, could outperform the standard 4.3 to 1 final drive ratio car: top speed was a full 90mph (144.8km/h) and fuel consumption averaged 22.3mpg (12.6 ltrs/100km). Where it lost to the standard 90 was in acceleration

through the gears, but that was a small price to pay for an extra 6mph (9.6 km/h) on the maximum speed and almost 3mpg (8.4 ltrs/100km) less in fuel consumption.

There were other less obvious changes: twin silencers were replaced by a single unit without any loss of efficiency, while interior trim was upgraded with the provision of map pockets on the front door panels. Later in the year it was found necessary to replace the fuel and screen-wash pumps with more powerful examples; louder warning horns were fitted and, at the same

What should have been the ultimate P4, the 105R, with its Rover-designed 'Roverdrive' automatic gearbox.
(Courtesy BMIHT/Rover Group)

time, revised brake shoes were fitted to the rear wheel drums to prevent the common complaint of brake snatch while reversing.

As already discussed the same basic models were retained for the 1956 season. There were small detail changes, mostly relating to body and interior trim. However, the most important mechanical modification was the option, on the Rover 90 only, of an overdrive unit in place of the free wheel.

Internally, the 1956 models were fitted with new seats, using only the finest leather of course, that were pleated and provided greater comfort due to revised springing. Individual front seats were offered for the first time on a P4 and featured centre folding armrests for both driver and passenger comfort. An identifying feature of 1956 models were the amber lenses fitted to the front indicators, a lead Rover took over other marques although these did not become a legal requirement until the early 1960s.

The overdrive option on the 90 was a popular move on the part of Rover. Certainly the model's production figures reflected this with 66.5% of the season's production supplied with this option; the combined sales of the 60 and 75 accounted for less than 5000 units. There are no figures to substantiate the number of Rover 90s leaving Solihull with the overdrive option but sources confirm that the majority of cars were fitted with overdrive in

preference to the free-wheel. In any case, Rover was able to offer overdrive in place of the free-wheel unit as an addition to existing cars.

In selecting the overdrive unit Rover opted for the Laycock-de-Normanville product which ensured effortless cruising at speeds of 80mph (128km/h) over long periods. Overdrive could be engaged electrically from a small lever on the steering column once the car was in top gear and could be sustained even when de-accelerating. Its disengagement could be delayed until either the accelerator was pressed down or the gearlever shifted to a lower ratio. On changing down from overdrive to normal top, the device could be usefully employed as a form of pre-selector: once selected, normal top would not be engaged until the accelerator pedal was depressed, which was especially beneficial when tackling bends at which extra performance was required.

Laycock engineering lost little time in taking out full page advertisements in *The Motor* and *The Autocar* claiming a petrol saving of up to 19%, according to use that is, and a reduction of engine speed by 22% for the same road speed as well as reduced engine wear and driver fatigue. Laycock's overdrive was no stranger to the British motor industry and a further claim assured the uninitiated that the system was then currently fitted to no less than 28 British cars.

For those drivers opting for free-wheel as opposed to overdrive there was concern when using it in conjunction with the car's servo brakes and the possibility – although very minimal – of running out of stopping power. James Taylor, in writing of his experiences with P4s, portrays the formidable prospect

Neil Laundeberry's magnificent 75 is patently at home in this aristocratic setting.
(Photo: Matt White)

David Bache's revised styling allowed both front wings to be seen from the driving position.
(Author's collection)

The Bache design was carried through to the end of production with only very minor modifications.
(Courtesy BMIHT/Rover Group)

of a car stalling while in free-wheel and the driver exhausting the servo reservoir, rendering the car virtually unstoppable with potentially disastrous results.

A further step in gearbox development was the work connected with fully automatic gearboxes. Rover engineers were still looking over their shoulders at the American motor industry and liked what they saw. They were hoping, of course, to produce an automatic version of the P4 that would be favourably received by American drivers who were already getting used to two-pedal motoring.

Expanding the range again

For the 1957 and 1958 seasons Rover introduced two new top-of-the-range models, the 105R and 105S, which were designed to supplement the existing 60, 75 and 90 cars. For 1959 both new cars were replaced by the 105 which was itself dropped for 1960.

The mid-1950s was a period of expansion for the Rover company. Spencer Wilks, who was appointed chairman during 1957, was partly responsible for a huge investment in setting up a subsidiary company in Australia, Rover Australia Proprietary Limited. Seen as probably the most important market outside the United Kingdom, a massive £350,000 was deposited in a combine between Rover Australia and the Pressed Metal Corporation of Sydney to finance the manufacture of Rover cars and Land Rovers at a

new plant at Enfield in the Sydney suburbs.

Before the new cars are discussed it is pertinent to provide an overview of the Rover company in order to put the new range of cars into perspective. The 105R and 105S had fragmented production figures to a considerable extent: sales for 1957 show that less than 1000 (828, to be exact) 60s were built with the 75s faring little better with 1087 cars; the most popular model was still the 90, of which 3299 were produced. As for the 105R and S joint sales amounted to 3393 cars between them.

The increased model range was all part of Rover's plan to offer greater choice and flexibility to the discerning customer. Apart from an additional number of model designations from which to choose, there was a further facelift, particularly to the car's front which would remain virtually unchanged until its demise. The P5 – which David Bache was developing – was obviously having an affect upon the styling of the P4 and a common theme started to emerge.

Quality, of course, remained the overall objective and stringent attention to detail was apparent in all aspects of build. In the construction of the wooden window surrounds extreme care was taken, not only in producing the precise shape for a tight fit, but also in matching up the colours and grains of the African walnut used solely in the P4's construction. The same

applied to the dashboard panels and the fascia rail with its cut-out ready for the clock. Throughout the P4's production run it is estimated that approximately half a million window frames were made by hand, which is no mean achievement.

Close attention was paid to the colour schemes and matching interiors offered for the P4. It was thought that the rather conservative tones should reflect the aura of the car itself. For example, the duo-tone finish was limited to sage green over light green and dark grey over standard grey with green and grey upholstery respectively. For 1957, in order to complement the expanded model, other special colours became available and, to quote a contemporary brochure, it was possible to order "a choice of colours from a recommended range".

The P4 was given a further and more significant design change for the 1957 season and the revised cars appeared in time for the 1956 London Motor Show. The most obvious difference was a redesigned front wing line and amber indicators faired into its leading edge. The new wing also made it possible to reform the headlamp assembly and gently smooth off the whole area, which had previously maintained its rather stubby and blunt characteristics from the beginning of the car's production. Looking at the new model and comparing its frontal treatment to that of the P5 introduced at the 1958 Earls Court Motor Show, the similarity

and family resemblance was there for all to see.

With the front indicators repositioned, the front sidelights were also moved to a position immediately beneath them, which helped develop a cleaner and neater style that gave an even greater 'establishment' feel to the car. Rover engineers had anticipated criticism over the minor detail of losing the tell-tale warning reflectors built into the torpedo wing-top side lamps and therefore designed a small chrome motif to reflect the illumination from the new sidelights. At once the company was applauded for caring about the smallest detail.

The announcement of the 105R and 105S arrived a little time after the facelifted 60, 75 and 90 appeared and prompted *The Motor* to announce 'A Double Surprise For Rover'. There is no doubt Rover had been eased into allowing an expansion of its range of cars because of positive sales and and full order books. This euphoric state was to be shortlived, however, as the Suez crisis was looming and its effects were to plunge the motor industry back into postwar austerity and uncertainty. Rover suffered just as much as other manufacturers producing cars for the luxury end of the market; those that fared the best were the producers of small and economical cars capable of running on the smell of an oil rag. More of Rover's fortunes and misfortunes later however.

With re-designed coachwork and two new models, it was time for Rover to seek some economies, not in build quality but by some means of rationalisation. Overdrive at last became optional on the lead-in 60 and the established 75 which resulted in the free-wheel receiving the death sentence, although it was still available for a little longer. Even though upgraded, the 60 and 75 were not given servo brakes, which was still a feature of the 90. Before the 105R and S models the 90 had been Rover's P4 flagship; now this accolade was awarded to the latest offerings.

The two 105 models gained their model designations in exactly the same way as the other models

in the series, by their bhp ratings. The more powerful cars offered a choice in comfort with relaxed, fully automatic motoring in the form of the 105R or, the same comfort but sparkling performance made possible by manual transmission coupled with an automatic overdrive from the S. The 105R, the 'R' representing 'Roverdrive', was seen as an attempt to develop the only all-British designed and manufactured automatic transmission system, while the 105S – 'S', incidentally, standing for 'synchromesh' and not 'speed' or 'sports' as is often erroneously suggested- was proof of Rover's wish to be associated with a high quality sports saloon.

Both 105 models were luxuriously equipped with fully adjustable reclining front seats, cigar lighter, map-reading lamp, full-comfort trim and, as would be expected, a revised mechanical specification which included twin SU carburettors. It was the 105S which impressed motoring journalists of the time: Raymond Mays considered it the best value for money car in the world while *The Motor's* correspondent wound the car up to a fraction above 101mph (161.6km/h) on a test run. *The Autocar,* too, was impressed: "Rover comfort and quality are now allied without compromise to decidedly high performance." Bill Boddy echoed Raymond Mays' praises for the 105S but it was left to John Bolster to admit being left in a state of starry-eyed enthusiasm over the car.

Mechanical revisions to the range were in general kept to a minimum but it was found essential to replace the valve springs on all models and to uprate the windscreen wiper motor. A strange problem had been encountered on the cars fitted with overdrive in the form of serious oil leaks. When cars had been parked facing downhill on a steep slope, the oil in the gearbox had an annoying habit of depositing itself on the road! In curing the problem the gearbox oil capacity was reduced from 5.5 pints (3.125 litres) to 5 pints (2.84 litres) and there was no further aggravation. There were some difficulties with clutch plates on the 105S and overdrive 60 models and therefore redesigned components were fitted during the 1957 season. Engines, too, received attention with the 90,

105R and 105S models all receiving modified pistons.

The 105S enjoyed rave reviews but not the 105R with its Roverdrive transmission. On the plus side it offered the ultimate in relaxed motoring, too relaxed for some however, but at the expense of poor performance and increased fuel consumption. *The Motor* considered it "ideal for those drivers seldom in a hurry", which, of course, emphasised the fact that, despite its 105bhp, it was no sprightlier than the 60.

The Roverdrive automatic gearbox, in spite of press criticism, did represent a considerable step forward in technology and Rover engineering. Other contemporary British cars fitted with automatic transmission such as the Armstrong-Siddeley, Bentley and Rolls-Royce used in the main

modifications were quickly made to the radius arms in order to improve the car's steering. Extra support had also to be provided for the gearbox as it was prone to collapse upon the radius arm's ball housing.

The 1957 season was not Rover's best: sales of cars were hardly half those of the previous year and deliveries of the 60 accounted for just 828 cars. Still the best-seller was the 90 with 3299 cars supplied while the two 105 models saw 3393 cars between them. The Suez crisis had a dramatic affect upon the P4 and Rover management looked long and hard at the model range. Nothing could be done for 1958 except weather the storm and cut out unnecessary items and improve on essential areas. For 1959, however, dramatic decisions would have to be taken.

Old friends depart – new arrivals

The future – and, indeed, the whole existence of the P4 range – underwent detailed assessment as the car approached a decade of production. The reason was twofold: the Suez crisis had left the British motor industry in a state of turmoil and just when it was returning to some normality, the P5, with its finery and luxurious appointment, threatened to steal considerable sales of the faithful 'Auntie' Rover when unveiled at the 1958 Motor show. Apart from the Land Rover, the P4 had been the company's sole model and was the epitome of solid and logical engineering. It was also

General Motors' Hydramatic unit which was built under licence in the United Kingdom. The promise of the Roverdrive system was that it used a normal two-pedal operation less complicated than the American-based unit.

In volume production the Rover automatic gearbox promised a cheaper unit price and one with less components as it comprised only four major parts: torque-converter, vacuum-operated single dry plate clutch, two speeds and reverse synchromesh gearbox with an automatically operated Laycock overdrive providing the third ratio. A feature was the facility to manually override the system by pressing the switch button on the gear selector to engage 'emergency low' for extra-steep hill starts.

Early Roverdrive cars soon presented teething troubles and

On show at Earls Court the 100, considered by some to be the ultimate P4. On the dias is the P5 and behind the 100 on the pillar can be seen a photograph of the T4 gas-turbine car. (Courtesy BMIHT/Rover Group)

seen as being representative of the very best in British cars and second to none in terms of quality.

In producing five versions of the P4 and being committed to the larger 3-litre P5 with its three transmission options, it was clear there would have to be some model rationalisation, even if only to control output from Solihull.

For the 1959 season, therefore, we see the demise of the 105R and 105S after just two years and less than 9000 units between the two cars. Production figures such as these are hardly inspiring, yet, it did represent almost half of

Rover's total output of saloon cars for that period. In the place of the 105R and 105S Rover announced for the 1959 model year the 105 which was, in effect, the old 105S. As this meant the company had discarded its P4 automatic option, there was no alternative for the customer who wanted fully automatic transmission but to order the new P5, which was available with Borg-Warner's DG system. The 90 was also revamped and upgraded in respect of its braking system and clutch mechanism.

The 105 must be one of Rover's most shortlived models for at the

end of the 1959 season it, too, was discontinued after just 2030 units had been built – a little fewer than a quarter of the total number of P4s produced for that year.

By the time the 1960 range was announced, Rover's rationalisation programme had been fully augmented. All P4s had received trim alterations inspired by the new P5 which meant consolidation of a number of components such as bumpers overriders. Amongst the changes was a revised radiator grille, which appeared slightly recessed, and the outline of the car was enhanced, in the opinion of

The 80 had its enthusiastic followers, none more so than Derrick Partridge, whose superb 1961 car is shown here. (Photo: Matt White)

some observers, by the addition of a bright strip along the waistline of the body as well as a large chrome numberplate lamp which adorned the boot lid. A padded top to the dashboard was seen by some as a safety feature and a compromise by others who considered it a cheapening factor. Rover owners

Rover enthusiasts loved the 100 as it featured all the attributes of P4 development, including overdrive, but without the complications of the Weslake head engine found in the 110. (Author's collection, courtesy Les White)

Stan Johnstone's 100 pictured at Hagley Hall in 1987.
(Photo: Matt White)

were, and are, traditionalists and perhaps took exception that 'One Of Britain's Fine Cars' no longer appeared in company advertising. Gone for 1960 was the 105 and with it the 60. Also dropped was the long-running 75 and the family favourite 90. Replacing the four models were two new models, the 4-cylinder 80 and 6-cylinder 100. If Rover enthusiasts thought they had lost something to consolidation, they had also gained. The two new P4s did represent some compromise; the new 80 engine was similar to that developed for the series II Land Rover, while the 100 received a short stroke version of the 3-litre's power unit – which, in turn, had been developed from the 2.6-litre P4 unit.

The engine fitted to the 80 was singular in compromising Rover and Land Rover development in as much as its design was closely akin to that of the diesel engine fitted to the all-terrain vehicle. Most obvious was the fact that it no longer complied with Rover's inlet over exhaust design so long associated with the company's postwar cars. Compared to the 2-litre Rover 60 engine the 80 had a cubic capacity of 2286cc developing 77bhp at 4250rpm, which demonstrated a far greater urgency than the 60. *The Autocar* found the machine no slouch and obtained a maximum speed of 87mph (140km/h) while average fuel consumption hovered around the 20mpg (14.3L/100km) mark. Flexibility and quiet running

were the car's main features and handling was noticeably lighter than that of the 6-cylinder model; half a hundredweight (25.5kilos) less over the front wheels was the chief reason for this.

The new 6-cylinder engine fitted to the 100 was slightly down in capacity compared to the previous 'six' – 2625cc as opposed to 2638cc – and it had a single carburettor as opposed to two on the Rover 105. Fitting neatly between the 90 and 105, the 100 developed only 4bhp less than the 105 but 11bhp more than the 90. Performance of the 100 was more than adequate making it almost a 100mph (160km/h) car although when *The Motor* staff tested it

they could only achieve 93.3mph (149km/h) at best. Most important about the new engine was its 7-bearing crankshaft which boded well for smoothness, performance and longevity.

Impressive was the equipment lavished on both cars: servo-assisted brakes as standard with disc brakes fitted to the front wheels; this called for a minor modification of the wheels themselves and hence the rear axle to allow the same track front and rear. The free-wheel device was dropped entirely and in its place overdrive became standard, although it was still possible to place a special order for a car without it. In such cases, which were quite rare, the car was supplied with the

The smooth shape of the 95 embodies late P4s. (Author's collection)

3.9 to 1 axle ratio inherited from the old 90. Interior trim retained its former elegance and luxury: deep pile carpets, sumptuous leather and that wonderful feeling of well-being that the P4 managed to so successfully project.

There is no denying the 80 was prone to engine problems and that there had been several attempts to eliminate them. Noisy timing chains proved highly aggravating and, ultimately, the troubles were traced to the chain tensioner assembly which underwent modification; flat spots and poor running at slow speeds were rectified by modifying the carburettor and eventually a lighter clutch was provided which was later fitted to the 100.

From 1960 when 9670 P4s were produced, sales of the faithful Solihull 'Auntie' gradually diminished. 8361 cars left the factory in 1961 and fewer than 5000 in 1962. Certainly some sales were lost to the more grandiose P5 but, in a changing world of sleeker cars with all the hype of a new decade, the P4 was beginning to look its age.

In an attempt to revive sales the P4 range received a further, and final, facelift for the 1963 season which saw the demise of the 4-cylinder engine. Two new models were announced to replace the 80 and 100 and so entered the 95 and 110. Both had 6-cylinder engines and the cars were further evidence of product rationalisation. In essence the 95 took over the market of the 80 and,

95s and 110s receive finishing touches at Solihull. (Courtesy BMIHT/Rover Group)

Late model P4s on the production line. The car in the immediate foreground is destined for export: the split bench seat and pleated upholstery suggest this to be either a 95 or 110.
(Courtesy BMIHT/Rover Group)

before it, the 60. Although virtually identical to the defunct 100, it was stripped of its overdrive and was fitted with the 90's 3.9 to 1 axle; its engine was de-tuned to provide 102bhp but could still manage a respectful 94mph (150.4km/h), so keeping up with the 100 and 105R models.

The 110, therefore, was the ultimate P4 with 123bhp at 5000rpm and a maximum speed of over 105mph (168km/h). In many respects the new 110 was a completely different machine to the 95: the heart of the car was a significantly improved engine which shared the modified cylinder head of the P5 3-litre. It should be noted at this point that Rover engineers had shown concern over the 3-litre's engine for some time and had called upon Harry Weslake to apply his experience and engineering finesse in this direction. The result was successful and from that moment the redesigned cylinder head was referred to as the 'Weslake head'.

Further modifications bore the mark of parts rationalisation: the seats from the 3-litre found their way into the 110 and provided even

greater luxury; instruments and controls were interchanged and even the badge from the P5 grille adorned the P4. Surprisingly, the one component from the P5 not fitted to the P4 was the 3-litre engine. Whether it was actually planned that the P4 should eventually receive the larger engine is unknown, some observers suggest it was never an intention while others consider that had the all-new Rover 2000 been delayed in its introduction – or failed to attract massive interest – the 3-litre option might have been used.

The last major modification was to the car's construction. From the outset of production in 1949, alloy instead of steel had been used for doors, bootlid and bonnet but, from March 1963, all cars produced were built of steel throughout. The decision to revert fully to steel at this particularly late stage in the vehicle's production seems rather odd, although history shows it was all part of a cost-cutting exercise. This cynicism on the part of Rover was not universally approved of and Spen King in interview looks back at this development in the P4's history with some regret.

There is an intense, three-fold argument as to the use of alloy against steel: firstly, the provision of alloy as a material for the P4's body panels had been expensive but this, of course, was fully appreciated at the outset of planning and production; secondly, alloy was inclined to damage far more readily than steel and, thirdly, it did effectively allow more common usage, especially with the introduction of Rover's P6 model, the 2000. Whether Rover had plans to further modify the P4 range using an even greater number of common parts with the P5 and P6 is debatable, however, what is appreciated is that the all-steel cars were not only more prone to corrosion but were considerably heavier.

In retrospect, the P4 probably enjoyed a considerably longer production run than originally intended. Boardroom proposals would, no doubt, have seen the P5 as a direct replacement for the P4 but demand for Auntie was by far too great. Dropping the P4 when the P5 was launched would not only have been retrospective in terms of sales, it would have done Rover's reputation little good. It was, however, the intention to replace the P4 with the P6 and it was not originally planned the two models should overlap by a year.

From a driver's point of view the 110 was a magnificent machine, traditional in all respects and retaining all that Rover had ever

End of an era. The very last P4, a 95, rolls off the assembly line on 17th May 1964. (Courtesy BMIHT/Rover Group)

stood for. Its quality and performance – the latter perhaps a trifle archaic in terms of its contemporaries, especially in its cornering abilities – was a joy and reflected the Wilks brothers' concern and constant quest for quality and engineering excellence.

Quality and design, though, was not enough to ensure the car's appeal and demand, neither was its price: in 1963 the 95 could be purchased for £1373 while £1534 bought the 110. 1964 saw a dramatic reduction in price, the 95 was dropped to a little over £1236 and the 110 priced at just £8 above what the 95 had cost a year earlier.

Production figures show that following the 4493 cars built in 1962 demand increased slightly in 1963 with sales of the 95 reaching a point almost level with that of the 110 with 2387 and 2802 cars respectively. A further downturn in 1964 provided gloomy news and finally proved the P4 was no longer economical to build. These production figures were all the more disturbing for Rover P4 owners and enthusiasts who waited for the company's decision to halt production.

That decision was taken all too quickly. The last P4 built was a 95, which rolled off the production line on the 17th May 1964. It was an auspicious occasion in terms of Rover dignity and tradition; company stalwarts involved in the P4's sedate career were there to see faithful Auntie close a chapter in the company's history and bring to an end one of British motor industry's most illustrious cars.

In its last production year 3100 Rover P4s were built; with the car's demise so ended production of not only a brilliant and well-loved car full of the British tradition so keenly revered the world over, but also a whole era of car design.

In total, 130,342 Rover P4s were built. By far the best-selling model was the 75, the car that had started the great Solihull tradition with its infamous Cyclops fog lamp, possibly the one feature that is best and most associated with the entire P4 series. Possibly the most successful car as an overall package was the 90, the driving force behind the earlier models which spearheaded future development. Ironically, the one car that should have been the epitome of the series, the 105R with its luxurious appointment and specification – even to the extent of its stately automatic transmission and cautious turn of speed – was the one model left trailing in the popularity stakes.

If there has ever been one car that encompasses all that is the classic British motor car, it is the Rover P4. For this reason the car will live on, cared for and loved by a growing band of enthusiasts and admirers who appreciate everything it, and its engineering, stand for.

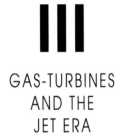

III

GAS-TURBINES AND THE JET ERA

Anybody with an interest in automobile history would certainly know of Rover's famous record-breaking and pioneering JET 1 gas-turbine car. This acknowledged leader in the development of gas-turbine cars is forefront in automotive history, with good cause, of course, and completely overshadows almost all other progress in this field. Such was the importance and charisma of this bullish, open 2-seater version of the seemingly staid, comfortable and well-mannered Rover P4, it pointed motor car design in a wholly new direction, albeit for a relatively short but nevertheless immensely innovative period.

Although Rover gas-turbine technology advanced at a gallop other developments plodded away behind the scenes. In America,

where Sir Frank Whittle's invention of the gas-turbine jet engine was received and applauded with seemingly greater enthusiasm than in the inventor's native Britain, it could only be expected that some major development in the way of turbine cars would get underway sooner than later. As early as 1951 General Motors was announcing plans for a road-going prototype car, but it was not until 1954 that the machine made its first appearance. Perhaps General Motors' ideas were too grand, too big and too beautiful, following in the American idiom of the time but, at 370bhp, the car was true to style.

In a somewhat less ostentatious manner Austin also became involved in gas-turbine cars, not surprising in view of the company's involvement with aero-engines during the

One of the most powerful keys in motoring history. (Photo: Matt White)

Jet-age Rover style. Rover's designers considered their gas-turbine car to be more akin to the aircraft age.
(Courtesy BMIHT/Rover Group)

Second World War. Austin, like Rover and a number of other motor manufacturers, had been prominent in the shadow factories scheme. Austin chose the huge and lumbering Sheerline model as a test-bed to front the gas-turbine development as it was able to accommodate the 125bhp engine.

Austin Healey was also involved in developing gas-turbine cars; MG was loathe to be left out in the cold and attention was focused in the same direction. For their proving ground Austin Healey and MG looked towards America, and where better than Utah and the famous Bonneville salt flats? Interest in gas-turbines as a source of motive power for the future was being taken seriously; so seriously that Ford of America was determined not to be seen lagging behind. This company, too, planned for the ultimate in technology and by 1955 its prototype was also ready.

Unlike Rover's development of gas-turbine cars which received universal acclaim, the competitor's progress advanced initially at a much relaxed rate and it is noticeable that their efforts received only an occasional line or two in *The Motor* and *The Autocar* which provided the barest of information.

Rover's involvement with the jet engine extends further back in history, far further than any other motor manufacturer, save Rolls-Royce, of course, who contained its development to the aero-engines

division. It is important, therefore, to take a step back into an era before the forties and fifties, to Sir Frank Whittle's invention of the jet engine and the tortuous path its development followed.

This is not the place to discuss Sir Frank Whittle's pioneering achievements with the Turbojet project and his invention that quickly revolutionized aircraft design and air travel. Suffice to say that out of Whittle's work emerged Power Jets Limited, which was incorporated as a company in March 1936 with Whittle himself as its honorary chief engineer together with an authorized capital of £10,000.

Whittle little doubted his progress would not be smooth and his trials and tribulations have been well documented. It was following the establishment of Power Jets that the Rover company became involved with gas-turbine engines. Whittle, together with Power Jets, stumbled from one financial crisis to the next and their relationship with supporting companies proved no more successful. From the establishment of Power Jets Whittle had been in frequent contact with the British Thomson Houston

Company – better known as BTH – to carry out experimental work on his engines; at the same time he was trying to elicit positive interest from the Air Ministry towards his Power Jets company. All this proved a constant uphill struggle but a breakthrough eventually materialized when Sir Henry Tizzard, chairman of the Aeronautical Society, believed Whittle's Turbojet worthy of financial support and considered it be given some priority.

Power Jet's relationship with BTH finally began to suffer after prolonged trials and experiments, failures and successes, and Whittle was anxious to be a little less reliant upon them. Rover's involvement with Whittle's developments occurred towards the end of January 1940 when Sir Frank Whittle met with Maurice Wilks and discussed the possibility of Rover carrying out work for Power Jets.

The meeting occurred, in the first place, as a direct result of a friendship between Barbara Wilks, Maurice Wilks' wife, and Nancy Tinling, the wife of J C B Tinling. Tinling, a fellow ex-RAF pilot, had been a constant friend and believer in Whittle's ideas and this link was

As well as engines for car production, the gas-turbine department at Rover saw potential in stationary engines. This is the IS 60 unit. (Courtesy BMIHT/Rover Group)

sufficient to get both Wilks and Whittle together.

Even as chief engineer of the Rover company Maurice Wilks did not have the total power to agree to Whittle's proposals; consent had to be granted by his brother, Spencer Wilks. Maurice anticipated his brother's response and suggested that Rover might be prepared to consider entering into a contract with Power Jets, even to the extent of providing some financial commitment towards the combined venture.

A further meeting was set up with the two Wilks brothers on behalf of Rover and a foursome from Power Jets, which included both Frank Whittle and J C B Tinling. The Rover works at Coventry was the chosen venue and the outcome of the meeting was the result of some hard bargaining on both sides: as far as the Wilks brothers were concerned they were required to put up a decidedly higher share of the capital than they had anticipated – £50,000 was the sum suggested in return for a shareholding in Power Jets.

Although somewhat apprehensive, Spencer Wilks did not dismiss the matter out of hand and agreed to consider the issue, returning to Whittle after he had been able to talk to the right people. The 'right people', in this case, was the Air Ministry through Major Bulman, Director of Engine Development. The action that followed was confused, worsened by a series of blunders which resulted in Whittle and Wilks parting company over the project. The Air Ministry, now at great odds with Frank Whittle, arranged a meeting between BTH and Rover; Power Jets had been left out of the discussions which had led to the arrangement whereby the two companies would each take a controlled share of engine production.

Whittle's Turbojet project was seen by the Air Ministry to be of extreme importance to the war effort. Time, of course, was of the essence and the ministry considered the Rover company best suited to further the Whittle invention which, understandably, was treated with the utmost secrecy.

The ill-feeling between Whittle and the Air Ministry was, however, no secrecy: the Ministry was keen to exploit Whittle's engine as a weapon of war and knew that Rover had the expertise and equipment to carry the development forward, the company's shadow-factory aero-engine work having proved that beyond all doubt. Whittle, on the other hand, cannot be blamed for feeling angry knowing his invention was being taken out of his hands. At the same time he felt he had been betrayed by the very people he was trying to help.

The Wilks brothers' initial association with Frank Whittle was seen as a blessing – a gift, even – by the Air Ministry, who worked behind the scenes to provide for Rover's further involvement. The operation to develop the Whittle Turbojet engine for aircraft use was code-named 'Supercharger' and led to an enormous amount of work and progress for the Rover company.

Leading Rover's developments in the design of the jet engine was Maurice Wilks, who took overall charge of the project and worked very closely with Robert Boyle. Between them they expanded Whittle's ideas and theories and were able to tweak the straight-through combustion jet to a high level of performance. When even more expertise was required to make the engine completely suitable for aircraft trials the Air Ministry brought in Rolls-Royce to take over Rover's work.

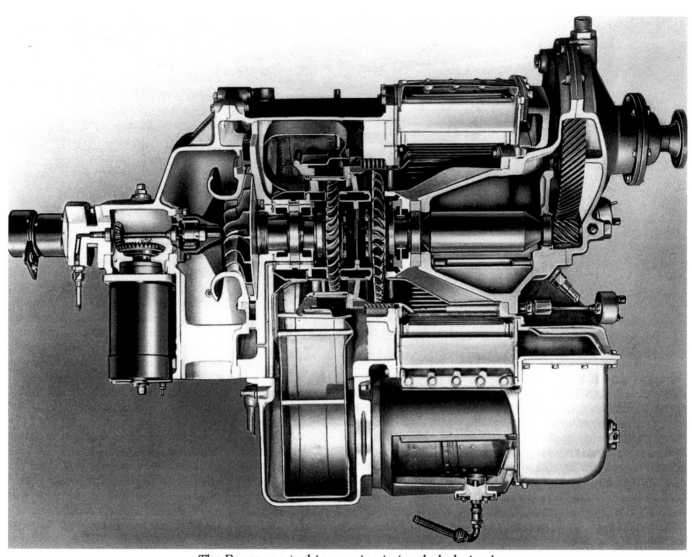

The Rover gas-turbine engine in 'exploded-view'.
(Courtesy The Science Museum/Science & Society Picture Library)

The move to transfer the project from Rover to Rolls-Royce stemmed from December 1942; Frank Whittle had been told that, in the Ministry of Aircraft production's view, both he and Power Jets were in danger of losing control of the jet engine undertaking. Rover was equally anxious about the situation and were perturbed at Whittle's attitude and petulant behaviour.

Maurice and Spencer Wilks were not too unhappy at relinquishing the jet development in favour of Rolls-Royce; Spencer Wilks openly admitted to Lord Hives, chairman and general manager of Rolls-Royce, that he had great difficulty getting on with Whittle and that, as a company, they would like to be shot of the whole business. In return for their share of gas-turbine work Rolls-Royce handed over to Rover their Meteor tank engine production and, at once, a close liaison was established between the two companies. Rolls-Royce quickly appreciated Rover's efforts in gas-turbine development and was able to mould the project with some haste into the "Welland" engine.

Gas-turbine – the potential power
The Whittle affair had left a deep impact upon the Wilks brothers; for all the harassment they had endured they could have been forgiven for wanting to be rid of gas-turbines forever. In fact, just the opposite was true for the two brothers realised the Rover company was quite adept at turning its hand to new and undeveloped technology. The brothers' appetite was whetted and Maurice was keen to look towards the future to peacetime and consider gas-turbines as a wholly realistic propulsion method for the motor vehicle.

If the elder brother was just as enthusiastic he was somewhat

reluctant to show his true feelings, as was his cautious manner. It was not long before the prudent Spencer Wilks was weighing up the whole situation though, evaluating the costs and benefits of such an enterprise. Certainly the Wilks brothers knew it would be possible to develop a gas-turbine engine for motor vehicle use but the cost was going to be far greater than Rover could afford to invest. Clearly there had to be a defined strategy.

At Rolls-Royce, meanwhile, delivery of the Welland engine was underway, ultimately powering the Meteor jet aircraft, the first batch of which was delivered to the RAF by the end of June 1944. A month later the Meteors were in active service. The close liaison with Rover still existed and allowed the Wilks brothers to interest Frank Bell in changing allegiance and accepting the offer of a post with them. Frank Bell's experience of gas-turbine engines at Rolls-Royce was perceived to be of exceptional value and, together with another Rolls-Royce engineer, Spen King, it was decided he would head-up Rover's new venture with considerable skill and adeptness.

Spen King was no stranger to the Wilks brothers as he was their nephew. To give him his full name, Charles Spencer King had started work at Rolls-Royce's Derby factory in 1945 and his move to Rover came at the time the company was still at Red Lane in Coventry. It was only a few weeks before Rover

left Coventry in favour of Solihull but, once there, Frank Bell and Spen King set up Rover's Project Department 'C' under the watchful eye and dedicated direction of Maurice Wilks.

Project Department 'C' was set up expressly to develop the gas-turbine engine as an alternative source of power for the motor vehicle to that of the piston engine. However, it is quite likely the venture would never have come to fruition had it not been for Spencer Wilks' friendship with Henry Spurrier of Leyland Motors. The cost of funding the whole idea of a gas-turbine engine was potentially enormous, but Henry Spurrier had agreed to take Wilks' idea seriously and invest in his proposals. The demand from Spurrier was that as long as Leyland Motors was involved with the gas-turbine project the company would be associated with any engines produced. In the event, Leyland's involvement turned out to be of a purely financial nature.

Once Spencer Wilks had given the green light, the establishment of Project Department 'C' evolved very quickly with the team in place and hard at work within three weeks. Working under Frank Bell's and Spen King's leadership, the Rover design team had its first engine running by 1947. Team effort had been superb with its members working round the clock to perfect every detail: at one point none of the team went home for three days!

There had been problems,

naturally, but in the main, it was a question of scaling down the engine design to approximately 150bhp, which was deemed suitable for a motor car. Materials, too, were a problem. Previous applications of gas-turbine engines had been used in connection with aero engines, which demanded special metals at huge prices; for a motor car engine such materials and costs could not be entertained. Having little experience in producing gas-turbines at such a small scale it was very much a case of 'suck-it-and-see' but, ultimately, dedication to a project usually saw it through to a successful end. If materials had been difficult to obtain for ordinary production cars in the immediate postwar era, just imagine what complications existed in obtaining them for gas-turbine use!

Rover's gas-turbine engine had completed extensive bench-testing by the very earliest days of 1947 and the design team had every reason to be pleased with its achievement. The future looked promising with the 100bhp engine, which had a designed speed of 55,000rpm and showed the direction their development should take.

It was obvious Rover was not alone in considering the use of the gas-turbine engine for road vehicle use: *The Autocar*, in its issue of June 20th 1947, featured an article by G Geoffrey Smith entitled *Gas Turbines for Cars*, while *Motor Transport* published a sister-article the following day, again by Smith,

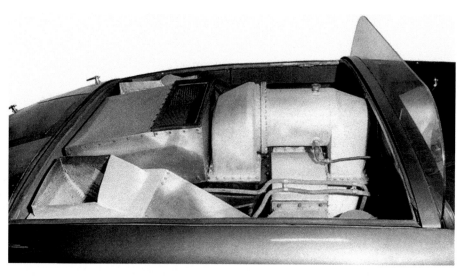

on the theme of *Gas Turbines for Coaches*. Whether Smith had any inside information is unknown but his article of June 20th 1947 showed a graphic illustration of a saloon car with a suggested layout for the rear-mounting of a gas-turbine engine. Why the drawing should display some similarity to the Studebaker and the eventual P4 is a matter of conjecture ...

Rover's gas-turbine operation was obviously a top-secret affair and there was no doubt other manufacturers were working on the premise that it was feasible for gas-turbine engines to be used in driving cars and utility vehicles. In 1948 *The Autocar* announced to the world that Rover was planning to install the 100bhp gas-turbine unit in the chassis of its 75 model, thus replacing the 2103cc petrol engine. This information had purposely been leaked to the press by Spencer Wilks in an attempt to divert publicity away from another design built and exhibited by Centrax Power Units of Acton, West London.

Centrax had exhibited a gas-turbine at the British Industries Fair with the claim that it could be used in a motor car. Spencer Wilks, obviously concerned at this development, took the unprecedented step of leaking Rover's own plans to the press. In the event the Centrax unit never

materialized as a useful tool, it had been exhibited in an unfinished state and never saw commercial production or installation in a motor vehicle.

The cat was out of the Rover bag, however, and from then on there appeared a steady stream of articles and features on the theory and development of gas-turbine engines for popular use. *The Autocar* reproduced further illustrations of theories and proposals for gas-turbine installations and the whole subject reached virtual fever pitch. With Rover's commitments clearly advised, the motoring world waited anxiously for news of its Turbocar.

As progress continued at Solihull Frank Bell and Spen King began to perfect their engine, which had the codename T5. The question arose as to what it should propel? With the parallel development of the P4 there really was little choice in the matter and Gordon Bashford was summoned to prepare a blueprint for an adaptation of the Cyclops 75.

In essence, the choice of the P4 Cyclops 75 was out of necessity: it would have been far too expensive to develop a specific design purely for a gas-turbined machine; it was also felt that the gas-turbine car would undoubtedly be met with some scepticism – suspicion, even – so association with a standard model would counteract these

reservations. A further particularly significant point was that the P4 was completely new in itself and an experimental gas-turbine car could only consolidate the P4's image.

The design Gordon Bashford produced for Project Department 'C' resembled a sleek 2/3 seat open tourer, essentially a Cyclops P4 with its top completely removed and bodywork smoothed out in a streamlined fashion, even to the extent of the rear doors being welded into place. Against a normal production P4 75 the turbine car looked decidedly aggressive with little or none of the softness of good old 'Auntie'. The car had a full-depth windscreen, later changed in favour of individual aero-screens; frontal treatment remained very much the same as the saloon and even sported the same 15-bar radiator grille and central foglamp. Along the flanks of the car, rear of the doors but ahead of the rear wings, three air intakes gave a distinct sporting appearance. However, before the car could undergo its trials there was a lot of work still to be done.

The original engine developed by Frank Bell and Spen King was considered underpowered and therefore a revised version, code-named T8, was prepared and ready for extensive testing by the end of 1949. The engine's first run under its own power away from test bench conditions was not in a motor vehicle at all but in a boat which belonged to Spen King. Its performance was far better than could have been

Not only for cars but also boats. The 2S/150 gas-turbine was designed as a marine engine. (Author's collection)

Rover's gas-turbine engine was originally tried out in Spen King's boat with good results. This is a further development! (Author's collection)

applications of over 40,000rpm. It was only the exhaustive efforts of Rover's engineers that eventually produced the right material. The machining – from a solid disc of nimonic nickel alloy – of the numerous aerofoil section blades of the turbine rotor had not been without extreme difficulties; the work on the turbine blades

Problems were experienced with early turbine fan blades, as this illustration shows. (Courtesy BMIHT/Rover Group)

expected and the way was at once clear to begin the final phases of testing. *The Autocar* recorded the event with its news item which described the engine installation in a 60 foot launch on the River Thames; the engine, which was rated at between 100 and 120bhp, was said soon to be increased to between 180 and 200bhp. The most outstanding feature of the test was the engine's vibration-free running and comparative quietness.

Getting the gas-turbine's development to this stage had not been easy: one particular point of frustration had been the search for a type of ball-bearings suitable for such an engine design. Quite simply, they just did not exist for

themselves represented some pioneering achievement and, while everything performed well under moderate testing, complete durability was something of an unknown quantity.

It should be explained that the Rover engine designed for road-going use needed to differ somewhat from the jet engine intended for aeronautical use. Whereas, in a jet engine, the mixture is burnt in a combustion chamber (similar to a blow-lamp) and expanding gases pass through a turbine before being expelled at tremendous speed creating thrust, some form of power controllability in relation to the driving of the road wheels had to be established for road-going use. The Rover unit employed two combustion chambers and air was fed by a centrifugal compressor, the impellor of which was completely encased. It was possible to use almost any fuel, petrol, paraffin or diesel which, once sprayed directly into the chambers, would burn continuously.

The heated air, once it had passed through the first turbine which drove the compressor, was fed to a second turbine which directed power to the drive mechanism. The Rover design team soon realised that in order to reduce fuel consumption it would be necessary to install a heat exchanger.

By nature, gas-turbines are extremely fast running; 55,000rpm had been the design speed of Rover's

first engine and the second unit built to achieve 230bhp at its full limit idled at a mere 7000rpm. In layman's terms, the engine required a separate starting unit but once underway the engine performed in a similar fashion to a vast torque converter, eliminating a need for either a conventional clutch or gearbox.

Initially, it had not been possible to bench-test a gas-turbine engine for much more than ten minutes at a time: as confidence in the machinery and its development grew so running time increased, but not by the amount Maurice Wilks and Frank Bell would have liked. The real breakthrough came when the Henry Wiggin company produced a nimonic blade material which dramatically increased blade life and running time from what was tens of minutes to hundreds of hours.

The secret of the nimonic blade material was its stress factor and ability to withstand immense temperature differences over relatively short periods. Tremendous heat could be generated in almost no time at all but the blade could cool almost as quickly.

A major hurdle in perfecting the gas-turbine engine was the question of fuel consumption. The effective remedy would be to fit a heat exchanger into the system but this in itself was presenting the design team with a major headache. As a result, testing continued for the time being without any heat

exchanging device, which meant that fuel consumption remained at an unacceptable level, often no more than 6 miles per gallon, less than three or four times that of a conventional petrol internal combustion engine. Once a suitable heat exchange unit had been developed, running costs would drop substantially but, even so, would remain slightly in excess of those on a conventional engine.

Work on the ultimate fuel and combustion system was helped by constant attention and guidance from the Lucas company, whose engineers often worked alongside Rover's design team.

Once the decision had been taken to try the gas-turbine engine under proper road-going trial conditions it took just six weeks to build the Gordon Bashford turbocar. The chassis, in effect, was the same as that for the standard Rover P4 75, although it received its own special allocation number. Code-referenced XT1, the suggestion was obviously that it pertained to Rover's very first experimental turbine car.

JET 1 makes its debut

Gordon Bashford's 2/3 seater P4 Special was never intended to represent Rover's ultimate gas-turbine car development for a planned production model. Its role was seen by Rover management as that of an essential tool, providing the basics of a mini laboratory on wheels.

Rover's designers chose to

Being wheeled out for action is JET 1, displaying its smooth profile. Note the bubble over the gasifier and the exhaust vents over the rear wings. (Courtesy BMIHT/Rover Group)

position the gas turbine engine aft of the cockpit but forwards of the rear axle. There was no technical motive for this engine location other than it afforded simplicity for the design team, the open body styling facilitating mechanical research.

There was, in fact, no reason why in a definitive model the engine position should be anything other than conventional, ie front mounted and driving the rear wheels or, for that matter, rear mounted over the back axle and driving the rear wheels. Perhaps front wheel drive was too adventurous at this stage –

certainly for the ever-cautious Wilks brothers, anyway.

The T8 engine was installed into Gordon Bashford's car on February 15th 1950. This was an auspicious occasion, for Maurice Wilks and Frank Bell had given their consent at last to the engine's full road-testing. Their decision acknowledged not only their approval of the prototype car but also the results of the engine's exhaustive test-bench programme. Watching the installation of the gas-turbine was G. Geoffrey Smith who had been following Rover's,

and its competitors', progress with considerable interest.

Although much of the running-gear was taken directly from the P4, the layout of the car was distinctly transformed. With the engine positioned behind the cockpit it had been necessary to move the fuel tank to a new position under the bonnet in place of the normal Rover inlet over exhaust engine. An important component was an oil-cooler, the same as that used on the Land Rover, which was installed behind the air-intake in place of the normal radiator. From

JET 1 at the Science Museum. (Courtesy The Science Museum/Science & Society Picture Library)

Right: Looking the worse for wear, JET 1 takes a well-earned rest after initial trials on an airfield adjacent to the Rover factory at Solihull. The speed JET 1 attained on this occasion is not known but it was impressive enough for Spencer Wilks to immediately arrange an RAC observation test followed by a press day at Silverstone. (Courtesy National Motor Museum)

the oil-cooler a feed was taken to the oil tank, positioned out of the way under the seats in the cockpit. Having the engine midships the transfer gearbox with its propeller shaft drive to the rear axle formed a relatively compact assembly.

Due to the size and weight of the engine the chassis of the turbocar had to be specially adapted, modifications in the form of bracing supports forming

JET 1's smooth design is evident here. Note the styling modifications compared with the picture on page 81. (Author's collection)

a platform which anchored the turbine in place being necessary to the rear section. Overall, the engine was considerably larger than the normal inlet over exhaust F-head unit; it appeared somewhat square in shape but a particular feature was that it required far less in the way of external components to the conventional engine. Prominent were the two exhaust stacks positioned on either side which drew the turbine efflux away. An important point is that the velocity of the exhaust amounted to approximately 100mph (160km/h) which was in direct comparison to that of the blast of a jet propulsion engine which could measure as much as 1200mph (1920km/h).

The engine having been installed, it was some two to three weeks before Jet 1 underwent trials under its own power. The date was Saturday March 4th 1950. The time between the engine installation and the first test run was spent getting the car together and presentable with all the running gear and equipment in complete readiness.

The trials were held on an airfield adjacent to the Solihull works: loaded into a plain lorry the turbocar made the short journey well concealed and away from prying eyes. The Wilks brothers were, of course, present at the trials, as were Frank Bell and Spen King. Both the Wilks brothers took turns at putting the car through its paces and even Spencer Wilks' wife was allowed to try the car out for herself. There is little information concerning the speed the car was allowed to reach but certainly its performance was impressive enough for Spencer Wilks to immediately arrange a press day, where performance trials were to be held under strict RAC observation and supervision.

Apart from the engine and transmission, the turbocar's mechanical specification was very much standard in relation to the production P4: the suspension, braking system and steering gear all resembling that of the Cyclops 75. What was different, though, was the cockpit, as the rectangular instruments were replaced by a whole array of switches and dials recording essential information and readings. Compared to a normal car the dashboard was more akin to an aircraft's instrument panel.

Rover's gas-turbined car received its registration number on 13th May 1950, almost two months

JET 1 with its modified frontal design as it was displayed at the London Science Museum. Note the well-worn leather seats, twin visors and the 'pearlised' paint finish, an early example of metallic paint.
(Courtesy Science Museum & Society Picture Library)

after the car's official premier in front of a specially invited audience, which included journalists, the RAC and notorieties of the motoring world. Having JET 1 on the turbocar was no accident; the number belonged to the Rotherham area and that particular series of index marks was not issued until almost two years later in March 1953.

It has been suggested that securing the special index mark was the doing of Spencer Wilks who negotiated the registration number through contacts both in the motor industry and elsewhere. Even so, the actual registration of the car must have presented a few problems: never before had a gas-turbined car been licenced and there was nothing on the registration documents to cater for a car running on paraffin. The fact that the car could run equally as well on either diesel or petrol only complicated matters. The saving

grace, however, was that petrol was a source of fuel and this was seized upon to smooth the way through the civil service bureaucracy. Ironically, the registration number of the car has, over the years, become as famous as the car itself.

On Wednesday and Thursday, March 8th and 9th 1950, JET 1 – although still unregistered at this time – was put on public display. Again, the car was loaded into a plain lorry and taken to the Motor Industry Research Association's (MIRA) proving ground at Lindley, near Nuneaton. The following day the car was sent off to Silverstone, one of the great homes of British motor racing.

On that Wednesday in March 1950 JET 1 performed admirably at Lindley; putting the car through its paces were the Wilks brothers, Spen King and Frank Bell. During the day the whole design team and

backroom boys turned out to see their car make history. It was a calm day, a light wind prevailed and the temperature of 54°F (12°C) and a dry surface made the test conditions almost ideal. With kerosene in the fuel tank, the push-button starter on the dashboard thrust the turbine into life, the time taken to get the engine to idling speed was some 13 seconds and after a few seconds more the car surged away from standstill.

Control of JET 1 was simple enough, with just accelerator and brake pedal. Five laps were taken at Lindley that day which accounted for 13.75 miles (22km) and the highest speed attained was officially 85mph (136km/h), although it is claimed the car actually reached between 89 and 90mph (142.4 and 144km/h) with 0-60mph (0-96km/h) in 14 seconds. By no means was the car taken up to top speed;

JET 1's dashboard looking very similar to an aircraft's control panel. (Photo: Matt White)

with just 35,000rpm recorded there was plenty of capacity for another occasion. That day, a world speed record for a gas-turbine car had been established.

In charge of the RAC observation was Maurice Hudlass, chief engineer of the organisation. For the test run he sat in the passenger seat alongside Spen King and no doubt was put in mind of G.Geoffrey Smith's sentiment about graceful power being released as JET 1 was let off the leash. As well as being timed around the proving ground circuit, speed tests over a 2000 yard (1.82 kilometres) straight were included. Alternative laps were taken with Maurice Hudlass at the wheel and it is very unfortunate that his personal comments were not recorded.

The starting technique of JET 1 was completely different to any other motor vehicle. Although the dash-mounted starter push-button brought the quite ordinary Lucas starter motor into use, its other purpose was to energize the two Lodge ignition plugs, one in each combustion chamber. Air was then forced through the combustion chambers via the compressor and mixed with kerosene which was sprayed through atomizers by means of a mechanical pump. 'Light-up' was achieved after a few seconds with the compressor working hard enough to sustain combustion, so allowing the turbine to settle at its optimum 7000rpm idling speed. The electric current was then cut off automatically and the mixture continued to burn without any further support ignition.

Depression of the accelerator increased the fuel and produced a much greater heat; the compressor-turbine rotated at higher speed resulting in increased airflow and, once sufficient energy was available to turn the power turbine, the car's brake could be released and the car was away.

In his impressions of driving JET 1, G Geoffrey Smith tells of "speeding around the perimeter of the Lindley proving ground in exhilarating fashion, the wind pressing hard on our faces". He recalls the car being completely stable and the steering perfect and "as the car gathered speed in a crescendo of sound, the speedometer needle showed 89-90mph (142.40-144km/h), whilst the compressor-turbine registered 36,000rpm".

Two significant features of the car were its complete lack of gear changing and surprising quietness. Certainly it was no noisier than a sports car at speed but without any of the mechanical cacophony

History in the making. The RAC's report on JET 1's trials, dated Wednesday March 8th 1950.
(Author's collection)

associated with a piston engine. Much of the noise, apart from road sound, was made by the exhaust which, not surprisingly, was more of a roar.

The day at Silverstone was nothing other than a wonderful publicity event: JET 1 was shown off to the world's press amid whole myriads of journalists and photographers. Every conceivable aspect of effective publicity for Rover was assured and for a long time afterwards Rover prospered upon the car's success. The JET 1 and the turbocar theme continued to be exploited throughout Rover's advertising and, understandably enough, the company capitalised accordingly.

A clamour of would-be orders for the Rover turbocar flooded into Solihull from all parts of the world: all, of course, to no avail. The car was not for sale and neither was production planned, certainly for the foreseeable future. In an interview with the motoring press the Wilks brothers had been emphatic it would be at least four to five years before a suitable gas-turbine car could be near ready for marketing.

What *was* assured, though, was JET 1's success in New York.

The car was shipped across the Atlantic in time for an exhibition especially designed to feature and sell British cars and, as such, not only represented all that was best in British engineering, but was the perfect ambassador for the British motor industry. The enormous interest in JET 1 was only to be expected, particularly as the American car industry was developing gas-turbine cars of its own.

A significant step forward had been taken by Boeing, who had produced a 175bhp unit which had been installed in a Kenworthy commercial vehicle. Rover further consolidated its position with a 200bhp gas-turbine which was displayed at Geneva at the same time: the future appeared positively encouraging.

The culmination of Rover's success was the presentation of the Dewar Trophy, awarded by the RAC to the Rover company in 1951. The trophy was awarded in recognition of the turbocar as being the outstanding engineering feat of 1950. The whole issue of the Rover gas-turbine car had been enough to stimulate the RAC to re-establish the Dewar Trophy after a gap of

22 years. Originally, the trophy had been presented for what was considered the most outstanding pioneering achievement in 1906 when it was awarded to Dennis Brothers Limited in recognition of that company's 4000 mile (6400km) run in its 20hp car. Before Rover, the trophy had previously been awarded to Miss Violet Cordery for her 30,000 mile odyssey on an Invicta chassis at Brooklands in 1929.

The Jabbeke Trials
Once returned from its American trip little more was seen or heard of JET 1 until 1952. Although Rover kept the gas-turbine theme alive and to the fore within its advertising, and the motoring press duly rekindled the subject of turbine cars every so often, JET 1 was conspicuous by its absence.

The reason for the car's non-appearance was due to the need for its evaluation and further research. Successful as the trials of March 1950 had been, they provided Solihull's Project Department 'C' with a whole new resource of information and directed the way towards further progress and development. Most of the major research unquestionably involved

Good for more than 150mph (240km/h). JET 1, with Spen King at the wheel, is pictured in more relaxed surroundings. (Courtesy BMIHT/Rover Group)

the refinement of the gas-turbine engine itself: whilst it had performed beyond all expectation it had as yet not been tested to its full limits or potential.

Rover engineering supremacy sought to squeeze every ounce of energy from the T8 gas-turbine engine and full potential power was calculated at being almost 230bhp at 40,000rpm. This was achieved purely because the continued work on the turbine blades resulted in a completely satisfactory level of durability. By the middle of 1952 Rover was ready to wheel out JET 1 once more into the public arena. Since the car had last been seen a few changes had taken place.

To separate the gas-turbine work completely from its everyday car manufacturing business, Rover had decided earlier in 1952 to establish a subsidiary company, Rover (Gas-Turbines) Limited. Under Frank Bell's direction renewed track testing had resulted in speeds in excess of 100mph (160km/h) and it was universally accepted that the new company was far in advance of any other concern interested in gas-turbines for motor vehicle use.

The most obvious change in the development programme was to JET 1 itself: the frontal styling now echoed the design changes applied to the P4 saloons and gone was the central foglamp and the 15-bar radiator grille. Instead, JET 1 appeared very smart and stylish with the new vertical bar grille and headlamp assembly. In fact, the changes went far deeper with an even greater streamlining effect: no more were the bumper and box-shaped headlamp fairings; gone, too, were horizontal air-intakes and sidelights, all in the cause of a more windcheating design.

There was also something of a mystery concerning Frank Bell. In almost sinister circumstances Rover's revered gas-turbine boffin had suddenly decided to leave Rover in favour of returning to his native New Zealand. This had happened at around the time of the setting-up of the subsidiary company and unveiling of the shapely new-look JET 1. Also at about the same time *The Autocar* featured an in-depth article on Rover's gas-turbine development which was written by Frank Bell. An editorial comment appeared to the effect that the author was "taking an extended holiday of some months, and his future plans were undefinite".

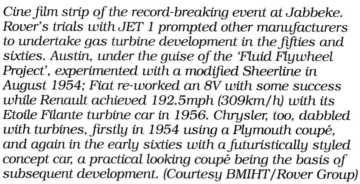

Cine film strip of the record-breaking event at Jabbeke. Rover's trials with JET 1 prompted other manufacturers to undertake gas turbine development in the fifties and sixties. Austin, under the guise of the 'Fluid Flywheel Project', experimented with a modified Sheerline in August 1954; Fiat re-worked an 8V with some success while Renault achieved 192.5mph (309km/h) with its Etoile Filante turbine car in 1956. Chrysler, too, dabbled with turbines, firstly in 1954 using a Plymouth coupé, and again in the early sixties with a futuristically styled concept car, a practical looking coupé being the basis of subsequent development. (Courtesy BMIHT/Rover Group)

The venue for Jet 1's return to public life was not in its native Britain but Belgium. Spen King had assumed control of the turbine project in respect of engineering and immediately started pushing it well into the media gaze. He decided to return to the record-breaking scene and arranged for what was intended to be spectacular trials on the newly-constructed Jabbeke motorway. The autoroute, its long straight stretches forming the main road between Ostend and Ghent, was ideal and added to the general charisma of the event. Fronting the experiments alongside Spen King was Peter Wilks, Maurice Wilks' nephew.

Peter Wilks and Spen King shared not only a firm friendship but also an enthusiasm for all things Rover (their association went far back to when they had built and raced a single-seat Rover Special based upon the P3), which extended to a common commitment to automobile engineering and the British motor industry. Peter Wilks had, in fact, left the Rover Company some years earlier to establish the Marauder Sports Car, which was based firmly upon Rover technology and is discussed at length in the next chapter. Despite his interest in the Marauder concern Peter Wilks still considered himself part of the Rover team and could not keep away from such events as the Jabbeke affair.

Rover had been given permission to use a stretch of the motorway to officially test the re-vamped JET 1. The west-bound carriageway was closed to traffic over two days, Wednesday and Thursday June 25th and 26th 1952, to enable the trials to be carried out. The whole affair was treated something like a military exercise by the Belgian police who patrolled the motorway area with Land Rovers full of officers. In charge of the scrutineering and test arrangements were the Belgian Royal Automobile Club and Britain's own RAC, with Maurice Hudlass again supervising the event.

The trials began shortly after 9.00 on the Wednesday morning. Spen King was at the wheel of JET 1 for the first run in which the car reached virtually 83mph (133km/h) over the standing kilometre. By the end of three runs JET 1 was getting into its stride and warming up nicely. The flying kilometre was then taken: JET 1 thundered down the Jabbeke highway – 90, 100, 120, 130mph (144, 160, 192, 208 km/h) and still faster, clocking a whisper under 142mph – 141.756mph (228.136km/h), to be precise.

After lunch on the Wednesday it was Peter Wilks who took the wheel of JET 1. With the turbine reaching a shrill scream he released the handbrake and let the car surge away from the start line, accelerating at a speed almost beyond belief. Over the flying mile JET 1 was just as lively as it had been during the morning's trials, although top speed was marginally lower at a fraction over 137mph (221km/h).

ROVER

For the trials JET 1 had been fitted with Dunlop racing tyres and as a safety measure the wheel hub caps were removed in case they should fly off. No longer were the drum brakes as fitted to the P4 considered capable of providing adequate braking and Girling disc brakes were fitted on Maurice Wilks' instructions. This was at the time disc brakes were in their infancy and considerably ahead of when they were fitted as standard to production P4s. At that time there was only one other car fitted with disc brakes and this happened to be the BRM V12 racing car.

Following the first speed attempts on the Jabbeke highway a problem was encountered with the car's oil pump: a leak in the intake pipe was eventually diagnosed and rectified before any further trials could be carried out.

On the Thursday JET 1 was prepared for another onslaught on the Jabbeke motorway: once the car's rear axle and lubricant had warmed up sufficiently the car was in sparkling form and ready to do fierce battle. Overnight Maurice Wilks, after consulting with Spen King and Peter Wilks, instructed his team of engineers to change the axle ratio, increasing it to 3.275:1 from 3.64:1, which would utilize the engine's last drop of power. As JET 1 warmed up the atmosphere was tense, everybody breathed excitement and great expectation.

Conditions that early Thursday morning were almost perfect; the air was still and cool as Spen King climbed into JET 1's cockpit. Even as it was manoeuvred in readiness for the first test run it was noted the car was appreciably faster and more responsive and already there was some betting from the spectators as to how fast the machine would actually go.

First the flying kilometre and then the flying mile: those watching saw the car thunder along the concrete road and disappear into the distance before it turned round and repeated the trial in the opposite direction. Then came the results; JET 1 had attained a speed of 150mph (240km/h) but it was on the west-east run over the flying kilometre that it broke all expectations of performance and clocked the distance in a mere 14.05 seconds with a speed of 152.691mph (245.73km/h).

Throughout the Jabbeke trials JET 1 had performed without a heat exchanger. Fuel consumption, whilst somewhat academic, did cause some concern, especially when returning 4mpg (1.4km per litre). It was evident that further intensive research would be necessary to enable the car to achieve real credibility.

As far as JET 1 was concerned it was the most successful and best-known car in Britain and it had attracted the attention of the government. Geoffrey Lloyd, minister of fuel and power at the time, decided to try the car out for himself and returned from his trial run very much smitten by his experience, extolling the virtues of gas-turbine engines. Obviously convinced this was the power and fuel of the future he overstated the entire issue by announcing a warning to the oil industry to the effect that gas-turbine cars "raised new problems for oil refiners". In the event, of course, he need not have worried.

In the time between JET 1 returning from Jabbeke and Geoffrey Lloyd taking his test-drive, the car underwent a further, if only minor, facelift. A new, full-width screen had been fitted in place of the twin aero screens and another screen was fitted to the rear of the cockpit; passengers were not only shielded, to some extent, from the blast of on-coming air but also from the solid wall of heat from the exhaust fumes. The outing with Geoffrey Lloyd at the wheel was one of the last times the car was seen in public before it was sent to the London Science Museum on permanent exhibition. Before it left Solihull, however, it received a further design alteration when sidelights were installed immediately under the headlamps.

After Jabbeke Rover's Project Department 'C' was thrown headlong into gas-turbine research: already JET 1 had broken all records and the design team was set to continue its efforts to design the ultimate gas-turbine car. The main objective was to do something about the quite

After JET 1, Rover experimented with a front-engined gas-turbine saloon. The T2 prototype based upon the Cyclops P4 is pictured outside the Project Research department at Solihull.
(Courtesy BMIHT/Rover Group)

Following the aborted T2 programme, T2A had its engine installed over the rear axle. This is an early prototype; note the ugly battered tail fin/funnel.
(Courtesy BMIHT/Rover Group)

The rear quarters of T2A. Compare this picture with those opposite.
(Courtesy BMIHT/Rover Group)

alarming fuel consumption and, in this respect, the department strove to achieve an effective answer by means of finding a heat-exchanger which was both compact and efficient. Therein lay another problem: designing a suitable heat-exchanger was not only difficult but existing units were as large as the gas-turbine itself.

In a recent interview with Stan Johnstone and Matt White of the Rover P4 Drivers' Guild, Spen King was adamant that JET 1, despite its years in captivity, was quite capable of running again. In fact, the car had been taken out of retirement at the Science Museum in July 1963 for a spectacular 'gas-turbine race' at Silverstone and there certainly had not been a problem with the car then. Contemplating what would be required, Spen King detailed a plan of action: firstly the fuel lines would have to be cleaned out, then the oil drained from both the engine and oil tank; the fuel sprayers would need to be serviced and the starter motor checked and glow plugs tested. Given that an extra powerful battery was used, Spen King was quite sure the car would start perfectly well.

Cecil Bedford also had no reason to disbelieve that JET 1

MAC 273, the definitive T2A prototype car. The rear window has been extended to improve rearward vision and a huge air-intake has been mounted on the bonnet scuttle.
(Courtesy BMIHT/Rover Group)

Side profile of MAC 273. The fuel tank was situated under the bonnet with the oil reservoir and spare wheel.
(Courtesy BMIHT/Rover Group)

had alluded to such a development in his feature for *The Autocar* of July 4th 1952.

Further information on the proposed car is very limited. The T2, as the project was code-named, remained strictly in the secret file but it appears there were so many problems with the design that the car was virtually suffocated at birth. The philosophy behind the project was to allow the gas-turbine

could run again and reckoned that, given the chance, Spen King could have the car mobile and moving under its own steam within two hours. Recalling riding in JET 1 with Spen King at the MIRA test track, Cecil Bedford likened the feel of the car to an aircraft taxiing along a runway: with the throttle suddenly opened the car would roar away exhiliratingly.

The next phase: the T2 & T2A

Whilst the trials with JET 1 were catching the attention of the world's motor industries further research with a more meaningful purpose was being carried out at Solihull by the Project Department 'C' design team. The intention was to adapt the gas-turbine principle to a saloon-type car instead of the Bashford-designed experimental open-tourer. Behind the scenes desperate work continued in trying to fit the engine into the front compartment of a perfectly standard P4; Frank Bell

Gas-turbine installation on MAC 273 with funnel removed. The picture proves the T2A could never have been a practical car.
(Courtesy BMIHT/Rover Group)

In its final form and funnel in place. MAC 273 is by no means elegant: the turbine at the rear is very restrictive and the double bumpers give the car a very heavy appearance.
(Courtesy BMIHT/Rover Group)

principle to be modified to suit true production car use and it was therefore developed with a smaller power unit, the rating of which was approximately 120bhp.

A fundamental aspect of the T2 design was to exhaust the gasses through the rear of the car via the chassis sidemembers. This, alone, turned out to be disastrous as the build-up of gas had a tendency to self-ignite in the immense latent heat. It would have been necessary to install special lagging which, it was quickly realised, was far from practical. At least one trial run with the prototype car was made with

The T3 had graceful lines and aesthetic appeal. For all its 2-door coupé styling, evidence of the P4 remained.
(Author's collection)

dire consequences and the system was quickly abandoned.

What, in fact, then happened was that the T2 prototype car was completely dismantled and rebuilt, returning to the tried and tested rear-engine layout and code-named T2A. As with the T2, a saloon format was adopted for T2A and the car received the registration number MAC 273. Alas, good looks were

not one of the car's attributes: a large and unwieldy air-intake on the scuttle immediately ahead of the windscreen did little for the bonnet line, and at the car's rear-end the styling was positively abhorrent. With the gas-turbine installed in what was the boot, the exhaust stack was virtually level with the car's roof line and all but obscured any rearward vision from the cabin. To cover the engine unit and stack, an entirely new 'boot lid' had been designed, complete with a funnel which would have looked more in keeping on a ship. To compensate for the lack of rear vision a split back window was devised with a deep wrap-around extension which all but converged with the rear door pillars.

The turbine installation was responsible for completely destroying the P4 turbocar's aesthetics. There were further differences between this and the standard P4, the most obvious being the bumpers which were double-mounted, one on top of the other, giving the car a decidedly heavy appearance.

Rover was very reticent about publicizing the T2 or T2A and the cars remained very much on the secret list, although, at a later

date, some reference was made in a brochure detailing the gas-turbine development. All photographs of the cars were rubber-stamped 'confidential' and remained hidden away in company archives for many years.

For its transmission the T2A was fitted with the Land Rover gearbox, mounted in the usual position on the P4 chassis; drive was directed via a propeller shaft from the gas-turbine to the gearbox and a second propeller shaft took the drive back from the gearbox to the live rear axle suspended on semi-elliptic leaf springs. Unfortunately, there does not appear to be any data in respect of performance from T2 or T2A and the latter suffered a similar fate to that of its predecessor.

T3 – a new direction
Following the developments with JET 1, T2 and T2A, the gas-turbine episode appeared to go into decline when, in fact, the opposite was true.

In essence the T2A experimental car was the last gas-turbine prototype to be built in the exact image of the P4, but the story does not end here. Further serious and detailed work was carried out on the gas-turbine

project within the P4 era and many of the design principles that surfaced emanated from the P4 itself. Rover's ideas represented a two-direction policy in which gas-turbine units were to be built for both industrial and nautical use while, in utmost secrecy and on virtually no budget at all, a whole new breed of motor car was being devised.

As far as industrial and marine engineering was concerned Rover developed a complete series of engines code-named "Neptune" and designated model "IS/60". The engine's applications and the many uses to which it could be put were detailed to some extent in a company brochure which illustrated some of the models designed, all apparently working to some established efficiency.

As for automobile engineering, development seemed to go underground: there was no need for concern, however, as the project was very much alive. The reason for apparently confining work to the backroom was purely a matter of finance and the whole operation would have been in danger of collapse had it not been for the enthusiasm and conviction of Spen King, Peter Wilks, Gordon Bashford and Cecil Bedford.

Taking an overview of the gas-turbine development in the mid-1950s, it is clearly evident that, whilst a tremendous leap forward in technology had been achieved, there was something of a hiatus

about its commercialism. Apart from progress made in America there was also some claim to evolution of design from certain European car manufacturers with both Fiat and Renault leading a select band of companies demonstrating gas-turbine cars of their own. All the more apparent was that Rover, who had been successfully proving its prowess in gas-turbine design, had not received a single request to supply its product to a wider market. Considering the outstanding successes with JET 1 it would not have been out of the question to anticipate many potential orders or, for that matter, for Rover to adapt gas-turbine machinery for a particular use other than industrial applications such as stationary engines. Perhaps Rover had hoped that airlines, oil companies, railways and the world's armed forces would be queuing up to buy the gas-turbine concept. Alas, there were no customers. The answer, as seen by Spen King and Peter Wilks, was to produce the ultimate vehicle

with the widest possible appeal.

A particular concern of Frank Bell was that although Britain had a secure lead in the gas-turbine race with JET 1, there was the distinct possibility of America catching up and even overtaking in the race to put the first gas-turbine car into serious production. Fuel, too, was a particular advantage factor for the US in that paraffin, petrol or diesel could be used, and in America the lower cost of fuel made the gas-turbine car very attractive.

Responding to Frank Bell's theories Spen King – with support from Maurice Wilks – decided to develop a fourth gas-turbine car, the T3. His aim was that the car should demonstrate all the finesse and practicalities of an eventual production car. Most of Solihull's capacity, though, had been turned over to building the P4 as well as developing a new generation of production saloons in the shape of the P5 and the forthcoming P6 Rover 2000. There was little room,

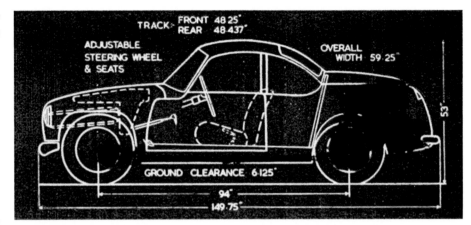

therefore, for what was considered such an extravagance as gas-turbine cars and its development was forced to take a back-burner stance.

Not happy at the possibility of the T3 project fading into obscurity the design room was transferred to Gordon Bashford's home. Without the overall support of Rover's design engineers, who were preoccupied with what was considered far more important diversification than turbocars, research and development of the T3 programme was relegated to a 'spare-time' activity, ending up on Gordon Bashford's dining-room table. At least three nights a week Spen King and Peter Wilks converged upon the Bashford household to do battle with the car's detail design. Another devoted Rover employee and a stalwart of the gas-turbine backroom, Cecil Bedford, should not be left out of the story; Cecil did much of the painstaking detail design in his own workshop at home, spending more hours than he dare admit to, working under the light of an angle-poise lamp. For all the gas-turbine team a social life was unheard of and wives suffered for the sake of the company and an experimental car. It is no romanticism to suggest the T3 was born by the light of midnight oil burnt over several months during the mid 1950s.

From the outset of the gas-turbine venture Rover experienced considerable difficulties in bettering fuel consumption. The Solihull engineers were not alone in this respect and strove to find a solution to the problem along with their American counterparts. Some of these difficulties were relayed to the motoring journals by Frank Bell, who still had a huge interest in gas-turbine development. The answer lay in designing a suitable heat-exchanger which was both efficient and compact. To a great extent the T3 design team also sought to overcome these traditional problems.

Rover did not officially announce the T3 until the autumn of 1956 when the prototype car was exhibited at the London Motor Show at Earls Court. The first clue as to the car's future design dates from early 1953 when Frank Bell, outlining some of the difficulties of turbocar design in *The Autocar*, cited a proposed layout planned to overcome many of the previous complications. With the article was an illustration of a proposed car, obviously based upon the P4 and significantly resembling the future T3. There were perceptible differences, however: Frank Bell's sketch outlined a 4-seat, 4-door saloon with exaggerated rear wings, whereas the T3 would be developed as a 2-door coupé, but the technology had a distinct affinity with the shape of things to come.

From its conception the Bashford-King-Wilks trio had opted for a rear-engine design for the T3. The technicalities involved in producing a front-engined car at that time were far too complicated and would undoubtedly have resulted in further disaster. This was a route the design team could ill-afford and it would certainly have been the death of the entire gas-turbine project and any future development. What did emerge from the make-shift design studio was a totally revolutionary machine, the design of which was way ahead of its time.

Leaving the P4 body styling to history, Bashford, King and Wilks enlisted the help of David Bache to devise the T3's shape which evolved as an especially pretty design, its sporting appeal enhanced even further by narrow pillars and large window area. In designing the car a lot of the old principles had been discarded to a certain degree and a decision was taken to use reinforced glass-fibre for the bodywork instead of steel. Specification of the T3 was impressive and included 4-wheel drive, all-round independent suspension and all-round Dunlop inboard disc brakes.

From the JET 1 prototype car T3 retained two-pedal control – an accelerator to make the car go and a brake to stop it. There was a complete lack of clutch, gear lever and gearbox yet, for all that, it enjoyed the total agility of 4-wheel drive possible, in the main, due to the car's power to weight ratio. By opting for 4-wheel drive it had been possible to develop a smaller engine which delivered extreme flexibility and sparkling performance as a result. For all its technical wizardry there were limitations though: as with JET 1 it had been necessary to install the fuel tank underneath the bonnet and, in the case of the T3, the spare wheel was located there as well, wedged between the nose of the car and between the front wheels. As a consequence the T3 had little room – the only space was a platform behind the rear seats against the engine bulkhead – for luggage, not that it was needed in a prototype car,

Ever since Rover had first toyed with the idea of gas-turbine cars, motoring magazines had had a heyday suggesting a plethora of designs and themes of their own, many of which were totally outrageous and beyond serious consideration. *The Autocar* published a series of avant-garde designs throughout the late forties and early fifties and in 1951 outlined a one-box streamlined machine with forward control. A mock-up of the car had been displayed at the Festival of Britain, only to be upstaged by an even more bizarre turtle-deck design in the Festival's 'car of the future' section in the transport pavilion. A myriad of space-age features were presented to complement the gas-turbine engineering: fully-enclosed wheels front and rear, forward control, ergonomic seats and pneumatic

suspension for good measure!

Although the T3 had evolved away from the instantly recognizable P4 shape, there were enough familiar features about the car to relate it directly to established Rover postwar styling. To give some idea of the prototype's forward-looking features it should be remembered that, at its debut, its sister car, the P4, had been launched only six years earlier and was still in relative infancy, production-wise. The overall dimensions of the T3 were noticeably smaller than the P4's, however, the compact styling ably demonstrating how the gas-turbine engine and its associated mechanical system could be shoe-horned into what was, after all, a neat and prettily designed coupé.

At 7ft 10in (2388mm) the wheelbase of the T3 was 17 inches (432mm) shorter than that of the P4; overall length, too, was considerably reduced by 2ft 4.25in (718mm), while the width was similarly trimmed down to 4ft 11.25in (1524mm) instead of the P4's 5ft 5 .62in (1677mm). Instead of the massive 200bhp of JET 1, T3 boasted a mere 110bhp, although information leaked in 1954 suggested the power would eventually be uprated to 120bhp. Performance was not impaired, however, and equalled that which could be achieved from a conventional 140bhp piston engine.

Put through its paces, T3 could fly from 0-60mph (0-96km/h) in 10.5 seconds and 0-80mph (0-128km/h) in 17.7 seconds. Fitted with its specially-

designed heat-exchanger fuel consumption improved dramatically and 14.3mpg (20 lts/100km) was easily attainable at a steady speed of 60mph (96km/h). Normal driving, of course, took a toll upon the car's overall fuel consumption but, even so, concern was stll expressed, especially when a comparable conventional car could be expected to return something like 33mpg (13.5lts/100km). The argument goes back then to the type of fuels used in gas-turbine cars, with paraffin being easily the most economically viable.

In October 1956 Rover produced a specially designed brochure to celebrate the T3's motor show debut at Earls Court. Development and performance were explained in depth as the car was considered representative of being a stage nearer to finding a definitive production road-going machine. As such, therefore, the T3's performance could not be expected to match that of JET 1, yet it was no slouch and lapped the MIRA test circuit at 102mph (163.2km/h) with plenty of power in hand.

T3 – impressive by all standards
For all its unique styling the T3 did bear an obvious family resemblance to the P4. The car's frontal appearance, although quite different to the P4's, had similar headlamp styling to that of the revised JET 1, and even the small dummy radiator grille was completely Rover. T3 received rave reviews when first shown to the

motor industry and the media, the car's ultra-modern image was both impressive and appealing and the design team had every right to be proud of its creation.

At the heart of the T3 was its engine, classified as 2S/100, a refined development of the Rover 1S/60 industrial gas-turbine which had been unveiled in 1953 for use mainly in stationary units such as water pumps and auxiliary power units for aircraft. In this form the engine's capacity amounted to 60 shaft horsepower but had been uprated to 100 shaft horsepower for use in motor vehicles. In essence, the engine comprised three main components. In the centre the gas-producer which, in itself, comprised the compressor, turbine and combustion chamber. Ahead of the main section, the power turbine, mounted upon a separate shaft with its own transmission gearing, was propelled by the hot gases which had driven the compressor turbine. At the opposite end of the engine, which housed the air-intake, another separate shaft drove the oil and fuel pumps, governor and starter.

In common with JET 1, starting was by means of a conventional 12-volt Lucas starter motor; in T3 this assisted in turning the compressor to 15,000rpm – its self-sustaining speed at which the starter motor was automatically cut out by

compressor pressure. The speed of the power turbine was enormous at 52,000rpm although at the road wheels only 1700rpm was all that was required. The reduction was achieved over three stages, the first of which was 6.3:1 via a helical pinion on the turbine shaft; then, in the second stage, helical spur gears provided a further 1.2:1 and, thirdly, a final reduction of 3.9:1 was effected via a crownwheel and bevel to the driving wheels.

Reverse gear was achieved via bevel gear differential on the second motion shaft and to engage it a simple lever was positioned between the seats. Pulled up the car moved forward, pushed down reverse

was engaged. The T3 forsook the shepherd's crook type of handbrake lever as revered on the P4; instead an 'umbrella' type could be found under the dashboard, similar in style to that on a number of cars. Instead of operating on the rear wheels the T3's handbrake operated on the transmission, an obvious connection with the Land Rover. Also, the Land Rover influenced the T3's system of 4-wheel drive which will be discussed later.

The T3 was registered VAC 905; the vehicle's first official outing had been on Sunday 16th September 1956 at the MIRA, Lindley proving ground, although the car had actually run as a chassis test-bed on the 4th January of that year. The next major event for the car was the London Motor Show where

T3 on a demonstration run. The overall P4 shape is discernible, despite the car's individual styling.
(Courtesy BMIHT/Rover Group)

it received universal attention and world-wide acclaim. Although the car had been put through its paces at Lindley it had not been pushed to its limits which, under the right circumstances, could easily be expected to be 115mph (184km/h).

The T3's profile had a definite sporting appeal with clean and well-balanced styling, the high 'boot' line contrasting nicely with the compact cabin and gently-sloping front bonnet. Only the tell-tale grilles on the engine compartment cover and rear wings indicated the engine was at the back. Once under power, the whine, absence of gear changing and smooth power were indicative of a gas-turbine engine.

Inside the cabin the T3 was pure Rover even though a touch of utility was in evidence due to the car being something of a test-bed. The controls, neatly grouped together in a single console, provided all the information the driver needed and included four matching large round dials. The rev counter, top left in the console, read up to 70,000rpm while the speedometer, opposite, showed a maximum of 120mph (192km/h); below, the jet pipe temperature was most important as the driver had to constantly check that exhaust gases did not exceed 580°C. The fourth dial contained three instruments: an ammeter and gauges for fuel and oil while the switches, four on either side of the cowling, operated lights, windscreen wipers and all the necessary electrical equipment.

Even the clock was in the Rover tradition, positioned on the fascia rail in the middle of the dash. The steering wheel had less of the Rover touch; gone was the horn ring to be replaced with a centre push in the simple two-spoke wheel.

Driving the T3 was unlike any other car; although rapid with a lively performance, there was something of a lag between accelerator and motion. Once at speed it was virtually a necessity to 'drive on the brake', especially on country roads, a technique that took a little time to get used to. The Rover freewheel, therefore, played an important role in providing an overrun between the front and rear wheels, again something to get accustomed to and all part of the car's all-wheel drive.

Drive to the rear wheels was via a crownwheel on the third motion shaft. For the front wheels a bevel pinion in the assembly provided the drive to a two-piece propeller shaft which incorporated a centre bearing to iron out any vibration. A second crownwheel, identical to that at the rear and containing the differential, produced the driving force for the front wheels. Between the two differentials the freewheel allowed the front wheels to overrun the rear, reducing the possibility of wheelspin but allowing, at worse, skidding when the turbine developed full torque.

The drive assembly, incorporating driveshafts with single Hooke joints at each end, also provided the means of suspension, utilizing basic wishbone units with telescopic dampers and coil springs. Completing the transmission system the Dunlop inboard-mounted brakes with 10 inch (254mm) discs provided the all-important stopping power.

So, what was the T3 like to drive? Ronald Barker, experiencing T3 for *The Autocar* some eight years after the car had first taken to the road, commented that it handled like a thoroughbred sports racer – a true driver's car. There were two ways in which to propel the car into motion; gradually let the turbine, acting as a torque converter, glide the car to the desired Rover's 'Roverdrive'), or by the jet-propelled method, which produced exhilarating results. By letting the turbine develop almost full power, holding the car against its considerable power on the handbrake and then releasing the brake, the car would thunder away, reaching 60mph (96km/h) in 10.5 seconds and 70mph (112km/h) in just over 18 seconds; standing to the quarter mile post (0.4km) could be covered in a mere 20 seconds.

The T3 never made it as a production vehicle; its purpose was to demonstrate the advance in gas-turbine engineering and pave the way for the future. T3 has reserved itself a unique place in automobile history and illustrates what can be achieved on a shoestring.

T3 was registered VAC 905 and was unveiled at the 1956 London Motor Show. This picture appears to date from 1963 – the tax disc expires at the end of December that year – the occasion probably the gas-turbine event at Silverstone.
(Courtesy BMIHT/Rover Group)

T4 – almost there

Rover's gas-turbine story would not be complete without mentioning the T4, the all but definitive gas-turbine car. Whilst not directly connected to the P4, its development stemmed firmly from the P4 era and a direct involvement with JET 1 and subsequent models.

Development of T4 – Rover's fifth prototype gas-turbine car – started in 1957 with a revised version of the 2S engine arriving in 1959 as the 2S/140. For all the background work, though, T4 very nearly did not materialize at all: the T3 programme had shown there were still difficulties in obtaining anything like satisfactory fuel consumption and, if the truth be known, interest in gas-turbine work was beginning to wane.

T4 was jolted back into life when it was realised that American technology had almost caught up with Solihull's and Chrysler unveiled its Turboflite car at the Paris Salon in the early sixties. If all the other Rover gas-turbines had offered little in the way of real hope for an expedient volume production alternative to the piston-engined car, the T4 was different.

Following the aborted attempt with the T2 at putting a gas-turbine into the front of a car, Rover had returned to the relative safe method of installing the engine at the rear for the T2A and T3. For the T4 it was all change again: not only had the decision been taken to place the engine up front but also, quite radically, upon front-wheel drive as well.

T4, the last of the gas-turbine cars. When launched it was generally not appreciated that this was the forerunner to the P6 Rover 2000. T4 differs from JET 1 and T3 by having a front-mounted engine.
(Courtesy Science Museum/Science & Society Picture Library)

Side by side, JET 1 and T4. The side lamps on T4 which, according to David Bache, probably came from the Austin A35, do nothing for the car's appeal.
(Courtesy BMIHT/Rover Group)

The design and engineering behind the new 2S/140 engine was the work of Noel Penny, who eventually replaced Spen King as head of the turbine department in 1961. Spen King took on the role of chief engineer of new vehicles – a position he immensely enjoyed – before becoming director of engineering of both Rover and Triumph when the two concerns merged.

When the T4 was unveiled in 1961 its long, sleek styling and sporting saloon features were considered sensational. Those close to the British motor industry, and Rover in particular, knew of the company's plans to develop the P6 – the Rover 2000 – and were aware of the decision taken in October 1960 to put the car into production. As it happened, the Rover 2000 did not appear until 1963 but here, two years ahead of schedule, the T4 revealed the shape of the future car. Unveiling the T4 – and, indeed, the 2000 – in this manner was most unprecedented, even if generally the relationship between the two cars was not appreciated by the majority of people.

The emergence of the T4 came about through Spen Kings's insistence that a gas-turbine option for the future P6 be retained: almost as a measure of sheer panic to not let the competition overtake in turbine development the project was thrust forward two years ahead of its time.

The P6's initial design was the work of Gordon Bashford and Robert Boyle. Several prototypes were constructed between March 1959 and the definitive P6 but it is the tenth experimental model that was suddenly projected towards an unsuspecting public in the guise of Rover's latest, and most advanced, gas-turbine car.

Whilst the definitive shape of the P6 was wholly evident, the T4's overall styling reflected contemporary Rover design department thinking. The T4 had been planned as a front-engined car from the outset, the design of the suspension system allowing far greater room under the bonnet than would normally have been the case in a conventional car. Bristling with features, the T4 set new standards in gas-turbine technology. The air-intakes formed an integral part of the front wings, only the twin headlamps

disguising the fact; the engine was constructed with an integral heat-exchanger which at last brought fuel consumption a little nearer to normal, and the exhaust gases were expelled through twin pipes housed in a central tunnel within the platform floor of the car that emerged from underneath the boot.

Disc brakes all round as designed on the T3 were used on the T4, whilst fully independent suspension on all four wheels provided a ride second to none. Two-pedal control was provided, the reverse selector being positioned on the dashboard to the right of the instrument housing. Between the front seats the handbrake held the car against its residual power which had been markedly reduced to approximately 4bhp, somewhat less – by a third – than on the T3.

The T4 was presented to the media with a double set of instruments which allowed engineers, sitting in the passenger seat, to fully evaluate the vehicle. On starting the engine the gas-turbine noise increased from a faint whine to one of rushing air emanating from somewhere beneath the body of the car. Once on the move the turbine would reach a high frequency noise level which was, nevertheless, no louder or obtrusive than that of a sports car of that era.

On its trials T4 recorded an average of 16-20mpg (18-14 lts;100km) but it was considerably faster than the T3, managing rest to 60mph (0-96km/h) in just 6

T4 leads JET 1 onto the race track for a demonstration run. (Courtesy BMIHT/Rover Group)

seconds using a full throttle take-off. Light-up occurred at approximately 35,000rpm when the engine settled down to idle but normal driving would send the rev counter spinning round to 50,000rpm plus and a top speed of 115mph (184km/h). For all the hype, though, the T4 was still not ready as a viable production car and an alternative to a conventional piston engine. Rover was under some pressure to say when gas-turbines could be safely fitted to its cars. Their reply was to fudge the issue by saying maybe three years, probably four. As to the price, a gas-turbine car could be expected to be at least double that of a normal production car, perhaps £3000-4000, when the P4 100 was selling at £1500.

In April 1962 Maurice Wilks sent the T4 off to the New York Motor show to demonstrate to the world what Rover could achieve. Accompanying it went faithful old JET 1, representing the P4 which, of course, was still in production. Wilks could only admit, though, that whilst Rover had until now led the world-

What might have been ... T4 with a collection of prototypes from Rover's experimental and design department. NMT 395E is a rear-engined sports coupé. (Photo: Stan Johnstone)

LE MANS '63

The original styling of the Rover/BRM gas-turbine car. The machine caused quite a sensation at Le Mans in 1963. (Author's collection)

wide gas-turbine car development, Chrysler had caught up.

The T4 was still a prototype, although many of the teething troubles associated with gas-turbine cars had been ironed out. Throttle-lag on the T4 had been almost eliminated and the next stage would have been the development of a two-speed automatic gearbox to improve the car's performance still further. There was more acclaim in store for the T4 at the Le Mans race circuit and its appearance resulted

in a further development for the Rover gas-turbine department in the shape of one of the most exotic sports cars of all time, the Rover-BRM.

Rover BRM – the ultimate gas-turbine

The Rover-BRM was quickly developed – initial drawing to the very first practice took just three months. The idea for such a car had materialized when the T4 was put through its paces at Le Mans in

1962: Sir Alfred Owen, who owned BRM, and William Martin-Hunt, now Rover chairman, discussed such a project and from there on it was all systems go.

Owen had appreciated the immense development that had taken place with gas-turbine cars over the years and considered his BRM company right for using Rover's expertise on the race track. He brought in Graham Hill and Richie Ginther to the talks as prospective drivers.

By early January 1963 the first designs were ready. Rover, in the meantime, had carried out extensive work on the 2S/140 engine, further refined it and classified it as the 2S/150. For their project, Rover and BRM had reverted to a rear-engine design with the turbine sitting neatly in the tail, a heat-exchanger being unnecessary due to the plain scroll engine casing. The chassis of the car was typical of that used for Formula 1 cars and by the end of February an all-out effort was underway in preparation for the first trial run.

After extensive tests and getting the whole car together, the first public trial was held on 2nd April 1963 at the MIRA proving ground. It was not the car's first outing, though, this had been at Rover's own test track at Gaydon. Although not entirely happy with the engine's performance, the car was pushed up to 133mph (213km/h) but had the power unit been in top form there was no doubt the car could have achieved at least 140mph (224km/h).

There had been a lot of criticism over the car's shape, which certainly was distinctive with its hugely prominent wings, the front incorporating the headlamps and the rear the air-intakes. To infer the car was ugly is unfair and it was mainly the fact that the car was not ideally aerodynamic which influenced the decision to smooth the outline somewhat. David Bache started work on re-modelling the car for the 1964 season.

It was, therefore, a newly-streamlined Rover-BRM that appeared on the test-track: the car's front end was completely smoothed off to let it dart through the air like an arrow. By 1965 the Rover-BRM was performing to perfection at Le Mans, clocking up an impressive 142mph (227km/h) along the Mulsanne straight.

1965 is significant in Rover gas-turbine history with the Le Mans event in particular, as it constituted the last serious outing for this and any other Rover turbine.

Jackie Stewart and Graham Hill at the wheel of the Rover/BRM gas-turbine car at Le Mans, 1963. Note the design of the car has been modified since its 1963 appearance. (Author's collection, courtesy Les White)

Certainly JET 1, T3, T4 and the Rover-BRM performed the odd spectacular event, for posterity and publicity, but to all intents the gas-turbine affair was over. As for the Rover-BRM, probably its final outing was in 1993 at the Gaydon circuit when the car was given a final blasting before going on permanent exhibition. The event was recorded by the BBC and will, no doubt, become an archive motor sport favourite. For its swan song at Gaydon a host of Rover dignitaries gathered to say farewell to the Rover-BRM and the gas-turbine team that had gone before it. Watching the car thunder around the circuit were Spen King, Noel Penny and chief gas-turbine fitter, Sidney Hill.

Although Rover's gas-turbine era was effectively over work in this area did continue in the commercial vehicle sector. In retrospect, development of the gas-turbine for production cars had reached an acceptable level; Rover engineers smiled when they remembered how the exhaust gasses could melt a bicycle's tyres at 20 feet and when, on the Rover-BRM, a brand new engine disintegrated after only a few yards on the race track – on April Fools' Day, too!

The final blow was delivered with the British Leyland takeover. On the first day of the new regime Cecil Bedford was working at his bench when he was told to put down his tools; there was no money for such research and the gas-turbine era was no more.

Looking back over past issues of all the motoring magazines, there was an underlying doubt as to whether the gas-turbine car would ever achieve the success to which it aspired. More bluntly, there were those who foresaw it would never reach production.

The last word has to be left to Spen King when interviewed for *Overdrive,* the magazine of the P4 Drivers Guild:

"Some people believe there will be gas-turbine cars in the future. The myth that the exhaust gases would melt the tyres of the car behind is nonsense as, with a heat-exchanger, the gases coming out of a turbine are cooler than that of a piston engine. As for emissions, a gas-turbine today with all the advances in technology could be cleaner than a piston engine."

The Rover/BRM car in striking contrast to the buses in the streets of Coventry. (Courtesy BMIHT/Rover Group)

The staff of S.H. Howard Ltd. look on with some amusement at the Rover/BRM car outside their shop. (Courtesy BMIHT/Rover Group)

IV

MARAUDERS, COUPÉS AND SPECIALS

The establishment Rover P4 is probably the most unlikely postwar car ever to lay claim to sporting aspiration, yet the seeds were sown to develop what was a quintessentially staid, stolid and reliably comfortable saloon into something which, by comparison, was wholly daring.

The sporting versions of the P4 – apart from the record-breaking gas-turbine car – were not directly attributable to Rover itself but to the much smaller and almost unheard of concern of Wilks, Mackie and Co., founded in January 1951, whose sole product was the Marauder sports tourer.

If the name of Wilks and Mackie is not instantly recognizable as a car manufacturing company, the individuals behind the concern certainly are well known and there is little need to explain that a connection with the Rover company existed. The association of the Marauder name may not be quite so apparent but this will be explained in the following paragraphs. What is not obvious from the company name is that a third party – Spen King – played a hugely prominent part in the company's establishment.

To get to the heart of the Wilks, Mackie and Marauder connection it is first necessary to return to pre-P4 days, when three young men who were totally involved to the point of obsession with both the motor industry and motor racing realised their ambition to compete in motor sport. At the time, all three – Peter

George Mackie (left) and Peter Wilks with the Marauder sports car. The rear styling of the P4 75 is clearly evident. (Courtesy Rover P4 Drivers Guild)

Wilks, George Mackie and Spen King – were working at the Rover company, when they decided to build their own racing car and enter into competitive sport.

Enter the Rover Special
The chance to build and race a car of their own occurred during the immediate postwar period when the Wilks, Mackie and King trio unearthed the remains of a Rover Ten in a disused store. The car, which had been dismantled and hidden away, could have suffered the fate of disposal had it not been discovered by the trio. Finding the Ten turned out to be much more significant than was originally understood: not only had the car survived the war, it materialised that it had been built as a prototype for the postwar P3, having been built in 1939 and designed as a test-bed for the new car's suspension. The car had been used throughout the war period by Maurice Wilks, who had succeeded in clocking up a hefty mileage in it.

The prototype chassis represented an intriguing aspect of Rover history. It had been built to the design of Adrian Lombard, who eventually rose to the technical directorship of Rolls-Royce, and the engine, a 1.6-litre 4-cylinder affair, held the key to the future Rover 60 power unit. Also of interest was the gearbox, an experimental 4-speed unit.

Had Wilks, Mackie and King not stumbled across their treasure it would have, more than likely, quietly rotted away in an obscure store until finally relegated to the scrap heap. Gripped by a spirit of adventure and enthusiasm, the trio dragged the chassis out of its hiding place, and purchased it for the princely sum of £20.

Originally the idea was to transform the Rover Ten into a single-seat club racer, but the 1600cc sloping-head engine was eventually changed for a 2-litre, 6-cylinder unit which, in itself, was a prototype for the forthcoming P4 engine. The Special had been run with its 1600cc motor up to around 1948 but the urge for extra performance proved too much of a temptation.

Problems were encountered immediately as the engine was by far too large for the then Formula 2 racing category. Jack Swaine was brought in to help sort the engine out and down-rate it to a fraction under 2-litres.

In order to stiffen up the Ten's chassis, the 2-litre engine was bolted directly to it; installing the engine further back than it originally had been helped improve somewhat the car's weight distribution and the decision to use a pre-selector gearbox provided an all-important refinement in driving and handling characteristics. Pre-selector gearboxes were by no means a novelty in motor racing – ERA had been using them very successfully – the ratios on the Ten Special, while not absolutely perfect, were good enough for the required purpose.

Most of the work was carried out away from the Rover factory in a lock-up garage during evenings, weekends and any spare time that could be legitimately found. Spen King spent a lot of time redesigning the Special's rear suspension, which proved quite instrumental in guiding the way towards the De Dion system which was used on the P6 Rover 2000. In Rover history, therefore, the racing Special was particularly significant.

The Ten Special behaved itself impeccably throughout the 1949 season and brought about a double success. So good was the car's performance that Rover considered entering into competitive sport with its own works team. This at least allowed Wilks, Mackie and King to move out of their lock-up garage and take over premises adjacent to the Rover works which had been owned by J W Gethin, the same Rover agency that offered the unique floor gearchange for the early P4s.

The height of the 1949 season's success was George Mackie's second placing in an Easter handicap meeting; throughout the rest of the period, however, the trio were happy to enter sprints and hillclimbs. The results included an impressive 49.41 seconds on the old course at Prescott. Peter Wilks' prowess at Shelsley Walsh was also mentioned in despatches by *The Motor* and *Autocar*.

The **M A R A U D E**

The **M A R A U D E**

For Fast Touri

It is a tribute to both the car and the engineering skills of the Wilks, Mackie and King trio who built it that the car has survived to the present day. The Ten Special was acquired by Frank Lockhart in 1963 and almost immediately he changed the engine for the short-stroke 2-litre unit that had been designed in 1950 by Spen King. This unique car has always been happy thundering up to and beyond 'the ton' and has been a regular visitor to all the best-known circuits.

From the Rover Special to the Marauder

The success of the Rover Special

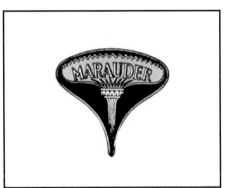

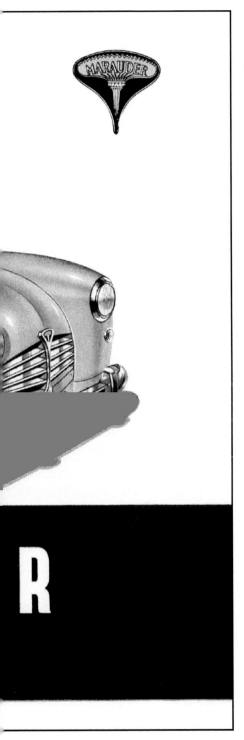

The Marauder badge.
(Author's collection)

led to a series of developments that changed the career course of both Peter Wilks and George Mackie, in the short term, at least.

Having built their own racing machine by trial and error, together with their Rover expertise and sundry scrap materials which had more often than not been begged or borrowed, the thought of building single-seat racers to their own design appeared wholly attractive to the pair. These desires eventually manifested themselves into a planned 2-seat sports racer with a lightweight body and mudguards more in keeping with cycle-car design.

All this was at the time the P4 was under serious development, having adopted the full-width styling features of the Raymond Loewy-designed Studebaker. George Mackie at once saw some potential for producing a sporting version of the P4 prototype design and helped stop Peter Wilks going headlong into the sports racer concept, as had first been contemplated.

At the same time as Mackie and Wilks decided to produce their own cars, Spen King joined the Rover company from Rolls-Royce to build up Project Department 'C'. George Mackie had taken on the post of continental factory representative and was spending considerable amounts of time in Brussels. Peter Wilks was active in the company's technical department where he eventually reached the position of technical director. His initiation into the motor industry was an apprenticeship with tool-makers, Alfred Herbert Ltd. of Coventry, and he also did five years military service before starting in the 'family business' at Solihull.

With the appearance of the P4 75 Peter Wilks and George Mackie decided to design and build a sports machine of their own, based upon the P4's overall design and using many of its components. Assurances had been given by both Spencer and Maurice Wilks that necessary components could be made available – albeit on a very small scale. This was made possible, without doubt, because of the family connection and constant badgering by Peter Wilks. Most important was the availability of suitable premises in which to build the cars and these were eventually found adjacent to the coachbuilding concern of Richard Meade.

To set up the business of building specialist sports tourers it was necessary to raise a minimum capital of £3500. Spen King had decided not to enter the partnership; he was too occupied designing gas-turbines. Instead, he offered capital

profusion of weeds growing there! After clearing it sufficiently to make it look like a proper workshop and putting on a new roof, work started in earnest in developing the car to their own specification.

The Marauder takes shape

The single-seat racer concept was finally abandoned after George Mackie had sent Peter Wilks a sketch for an idea of a car loosely based on the design of the Ferrari 166. Mackie had fallen in love with the new Italian car after spotting an example whilst working in Belgium. The smooth lines of the car excited him to the extent that he obtained an advertisement illustration for

investment and as much time as he could afford. Peter Wilks and George Mackie terminated their employment with Rover and threw in £2500 between them – Wilks putting up £1500 and Mackie £1000. Some of Wilks' investment came from a compensation payment after a motor cycle accident, while the remaining £1000 was received from Peter Wilks' father, G N Wilks, and Spen King, who placed £500 each.

It really was no accident that the business, known as Wilks, Mackie and Co., was founded alongside Richard Meade's workshops. Wilks and Mackie both knew Richard Meade who they found sympathetic to their cause and willing to participate in their venture. Liking what they saw of Meade's work, they considered him a very useful ally in the coachwork department. The premises, however, left a lot to

be desired, a faulty roof allowing the rain to get inside to water the

the newly announced P4, cut off the drawing at the roof line and drew in a hood emulating somewhat the style of the Ferrari. When Peter Wilks received Mackie's sketch not only did he share the excitement, he wanted to get started on a project of similar style without further delay!

As far as Wilks and Mackie were concerned the entire prospect of starting production of their sports car was looking decidedly good: not only had Spen King agreed to provide something in the way of financial backing, he had also offered technical help on a part-time basis. Furthermore, there was a glimmer of interest from a small but not insignificant group of Rover agents who agreed to sell the car on a franchise basis.

The Marauder name was chosen only as an afterthought. Originally, the intention was to call the car the 'Viking' in order to establish some connection with the Rover company, but this was changed after the patent agents foresaw some difficulty and proposed Marauder instead.

The design complete, the Rover parentage was there for all to see, especially at the rear. Features of the P4 were clearly in evidence, especially in the Marauder's similarly curved lower body line where it joined the chassis. At the rear, instead of an opening boot, a small locker provided access to the spare wheel and tool kit. Luggage space, although in the tail, could be accessed via the folding squabs of the seats, in the style of sports tourers of the era.

The final weeks of 1949 and the beginning of 1950 were all-important for the Marauder: Spencer Wilks managed to get the agreement of the board of directors to release twenty-one sets of chassis and components to Wilks, Mackie and Co. in December 1949 and the new company opened its doors for business on 1st January 1950 at Poplar Row, Dorridge, Birmingham.

Production of the Marauder did not start until March of that year when the first of the P4 chassis arrived from Solihull on the 9th of the month. Spen King recalls that the basic idea behind the Marauder design was to use the back end of a P4 after shutting off the rear doors. The front of the car, which was totally re-made, was the work of coachbuilder Richard Meade. To accommodate the Marauder's body the P4 chassis had to be shortened by 9 inches, achieved by cutting the frame ahead of the rear axle; the second and third crossmembers were subsequently moved farther forward. By locating the front engine mountings upon the main frame members and the rear mounting, which was under the gearbox, upon the third crossmember, it was possible to sit the engine 19 inches farther back and 2 inches lower than that of the saloon.

There were further modifications: the position of the second chassis crossmember which, of course, was farther ahead than on the production saloon, enabled the ball joints of the front wheel radius rods to be placed inside the box section of the crossmember. The steering, too, was modified: by lengthening the drop arm the number of turns lock-to-lock was reduced from four turns to two and a half. The steering box was mounted more towards the rear and a universal Hardy-Spicer joint made adjustment of the column for rake and driver comfort possible.

The Marauder's independent front suspension remained virtually unaltered from that of its P4 cousin and allowed an anti-roll bar to be fitted. At the rear, however, the front anchor points of the half elliptic springs were below the main frame and therefore mounted lower than the Rover's. Also, the springs – rated the same as the saloon car – were flatter and controlled by Woodhead-Munroe dampers. These inclined inward and projected up through the rear crossmembers, helping to transversely locate the axle.

The clutch and gearbox – exactly the same as for the P4 – were fitted onto the Marauder chassis without alteration apart from a shortened propeller shaft; the free-wheel was also retained but could, as an option, be replaced by an epicyclic overdrive which conveniently fitted into the same position as the free-wheel device. A point of interest is the Marauder's gearshift, which forsook the P4's column change arrangement in favour of a floor

change lever offset by some 6 inches from the centre towards the driver. It may well have been this floor change system which gave Gethins the idea for the floor change option for the P4 saloon, especially as Peter Wilks later joined the company before eventually returning to Solihull. The handbrake, too, had the touch of the rebel about it. Gone was the shepherd's crook; in its place a horizontal floor lever much in the style of that found on 1954 P4s.

Wilks and Mackie retained Girling's hydro-mechanical braking system for the Marauder although it received some refinement to take account of the sports car's different weight distribution. Essentially, the Marauder was built from well tried and tested components, its sporting appeal was unpretentious and it should have been assured of success especially with its distant but inbuilt pedigree.

The Marauder – 'for fast touring'

The brochure for the Marauder is a timeless classic: quite different to anything Rover ever produced, the front cover heralded the sports tourer with all the flair and vigour of the Italian super-cars. Only one picture adorned the brochure; no other was necessary as the vivid-red open tourer more than adequately portrayed the hot-blooded Latin spirit. There is no doubt the shape was sensual: the 2-door tourer with its cockpit only just ahead of the rear wheels had a vast bonnet sweeping down to the smoothest of frontal

designs flanked by contoured wings in the finest sporting tradition. Even the radiator grille badge, the design of which is attributed to George Mackie's wife, Rosemary, echoed the car's evocative styling with its distinctive motif suggesting the Olympic torch.

Like the P4, the Marauder's weight was kept to a minimum with the use of aluminium for the doors, bonnet, scuttle, cowl and spare wheel cover. The rest of the car was steel. Performance was all part of the package as the brochure text implied: 80mph (128km/h) was easily attainable with overdrive but push the car to its limits and it was good for well over 90mph (144km/h).

Wilks and Mackie completed their first Marauder by July 1950 and, to celebrate, they took time off from building car number 2 to take the prototype on a European tour to Switzerland, calling at Belgium and Luxembourg on the way. The ten-day trip was a good test for the car, which completely lived up to all expectations and suffered only one minor problem, that of gearbox lubrication.

While in Switzerland showing the car to the Rover agents, who greeted the Marauder with huge enthusiasm, Wilks and Mackie were invited to display a car at the Geneva Show the following season. Offers such as that did not happen often and the two left for Britain in a somewhat euphoric state. Happily, the car, registered KAC 313 and

featured in *The Autocar* of August 1950, survives to this day.

While life returned to some normality and production of Marauders continued, Wilks and Mackie were happy to hand over the Marauder prototype to Bernard Willmott, who put the car through its paces in motor sport events. Willmott had a well-known Rover agency at Bognor Regis and lost no time in entering the car in the "1000 Miles Rally" sponsored by the *Daily Express*. Willmott and the Marauder were well-placed, coming second in their particular class.

Other rally successes followed and Peter Wilks enjoyed particular success with another car competing against Mike Hawthorne at a meeting at Goodwood in June 1951. Car number 1101, which was registered as MBP 2, was also rallied by Willmott and entered for the Isle of Wight rally in the Spring of 1951.

The motoring press quickly latched on to the Marauder as a car with a difference and it was not long before orders were dropping through the letterbox at Poplar Road, keeping the staff of five constantly busy. After Richard Meade built the first four bodies Wilks and Mackie transferred the contract to Abbey Panels who were based in Coventry. Meade was not left out entirely as the bodies which had been completed by Abbey Panels were sent back to him for painting and trimming. Strangely, the Abbey bodies, apparently

identical in every respect to the earlier cars, weighed considerably more and added something like 100 kilos to the car's overall weight.

Following their initial success with the Marauder, Wilks and Mackie developed some new ideas for future production. From March 1951 power was increased by using a 100bhp engine as an option and even more power could be extracted by installing triple carburettors. The more powerful engine was the result of boring out the 75 engine to 2.4-litres and installing the pistons from the P3 60 engine. All this was a trifle academic as it appears only two cars were ever so equipped. There were other minor changes; access to the luggage compartment was improved by redesigning the seats so that they were more manoeuvrable and separate seats were fitted in place of the original bench seat which had allowed the claim that the Marauder was a three-seater.

A year after the first Marauder had left the little factory at Poplar Road the future looked quite rosy. So good were the prospects, in fact, that Wilks and Mackie decided to move to larger premises at Common Lane, Kenilworth, and rename the company the Marauder Car Company. The move was made in the early part of 1952 and no sooner had they started production when the British economy took a tumble. Materials were difficult to obtain due to the Korean war and the government of the day imposed restrictions on bank loans,

making it virtually impossible to expand businesses. The most swingeing imposition was the 66. 66% purchase tax on all new cars costing over £1000 which, of course, drastically affected the Marauder, putting its price up to over £2000. This sounded the death knell for the car as it made it far too expensive.

Henly's of London took delivery of the last Marauder to be built on 26th March 1952. George Mackie and Peter Wilks realised they could no longer compete in a depressed market and neither would they be able to meet their bills. Under such circumstances they finally closed the business in the middle of 1952. Both Mackie and Wilks returned to Rover, Peter Wilks having taken up an appointment with Gethins, the Midland-based Rover agent.

Between 1950 and 1952 15 Marauders had been built, the majority of which have survived to this day. At least 12 cars have been accounted for which include a delightful fixed-head coupé and car number 11, which is in America and was built to the 100bhp specification. There is some irony about the 'American' Marauder as this was originally built as a left-hand-drive model in anticipation of demand from Europe and the USA. In the event it was left unsold where it had been on show in Paris for several months. Eventually the Marauder was sent back to Wilks and Mackie where it was converted to right-hand-drive and promptly

sold to an American who took the car to the United States. George Mackie owned car number 1107 which is registered HFY 330.

Less than a year after the first reports had appeared in the motoring journals, *The Autocar* featured a much more revealing examination of the Marauder. For this, car number 1106, which was registered KWD 111, was used, the same car that had appeared at the 1951 Geneva Motor Show and was subsequently modified to the 100bhp specification, sporting three carburettors.

The fixed-head coupé was built to special order and has an altogether different appeal and appearance to the other Marauders. There is more than a hint of BMW and Bristol about the car's frontal styling. It has been suggested that George Mackie quite disliked the car which is a shame as it bears all the hallmarks of a true sporting grand-tourer.

Registered MOE 645, the fixed head coupé was the fifth Marauder built and was numbered 12004. Apart from its frontal styling the car had far more of a Rover resemblance than any of the other cars – a point in particular being the boot which was accessed externally via a normal P4 opening lid. This was almost wholly due to the fact that a great number of standard P4 panels were used in its construction.

The Marauder, therefore, has remained one of the enigmas of the British motor industry. It should

Possibly the most coveted P4 of all. This Tickford drophead is a remarkable car with an even more remarkable history. Now belonging to Bill Henderson, LOK 918 has been the subject of a 9-year restoration project. (Photo: Bill Henderson)

have been a success and, had not fate played a hand, there would almost certainly have been a healthy market for the car. Possibly the most fitting tribute to the Marauder is car number 5, OUG 777, which completed the 1994 Monte Carlo Challenge.

Fixed and drophead coupés

There is clear evidence that Rover was keen to proceed with variants of the P4 in the style of fixed and drophead coupés to provide a viable alternative to the standard Cyclops 75 saloon. The fact that the Marauder venture was allowed to get underway using Rover chassis and components was another sign that the company was keen to expand its model range. What is doubtful, though, is whether Solihull had the capacity to produce the cars in any volume, hence an approach to the Tickford concern of Newport Pagnell

to produce a couple of prototype cars.

Whilst the existence of the two drophead coupés was known of, the actuality of a fixed head coupé was less certain. The only clue to the car's existence is a pencil note in the Rover despatch records now held at the British Motor Industry Heritage Trust at Gaydon, Warwickshire. The proof that the car did actually exist arrived in 1964 when an advertisement for it appeared in the 'for sale' columns of the *Exchange and Mart,* where it was described as a 'normal' P4 Cyclops model.

The Tickford-bodied fixed head coupé was registered LAC 447 on 18th May 1951 after having been built in November 1950. The car did not leave Solihull until September 1951 when it was delivered to Henly's of London. The car was distinctive for its two

large doors and extra large rear window – more in the style of the 1955 saloon models – but it had chromed joining strips rather than the rubber of the later cars. The rear side windows were designed to wind down in an arc which was pivoted at the leading bottom edge. The roof was also different to that of the saloon cars and was covered in a rubberised canvas material; the quality of the covering was not completely perfect and quickly wore away exposing the bare metal beneath it. A further feature of the car was the dashboard panel which had circular dials at a time when the normal Cyclops 75 had rectangular instruments.

The car's interior had the luxury that was to be expected of such a coachbuilt car: the front bench seat was retained but the seat back was divided and hinged to allow access to the rear seats.

THE ROVER '90' IN SMOKE BLUE FINISH

To expand the model range for 1954 Rover introduced a variant of the P4 either side of the existing 75. The 60 received a 4-cylinder, 2-litre engine and the 90 a 6-cylinder, 2.6-litre unit. No less comfortable than the 75, the 60 was the ultimate motor car at a 'budget price'. The 90, however, provided even more luxury and soon attracted a loyal following. (Author's collection)

THE ROVER '75' IN DUO-TONE GREY FINISH

THE ROVER '60' IN BLACK FINISH

Changes to the interior of the P4 included replacing the
original rectangular instruments with round dials, as
these were considered more in keeping with the car's
character. The column gearchange gave way to a floor-
mounted lever, so positioned as to allow three people to sit
on the front bench seat. Note also the plain leather seats
and wing-top sidelights. The rear window was increased
in size to a 3-piece unit and the boot redesigned.
(Author's collection)

One of Britain's Fine Cars

Close-up of the front suspension. According to Rover, rubber bushes eliminated road noise and the need for greasing. King pins had their own oil reservoir and the long radius arms afforded a superlative ride. (Courtesy Matt White)

The 'non-slip, easily located jack – finger-light in operation, rigid and absolutely safe on any surface' – which was provided with the car. (Courtesy Matt White)

Dated March 1952, this majestic brochure illustration depicts the revised frontal styling of the P4.
(Courtesy Matt White)

The **ROVER** *Seventy Five*

The P4 is a handsome car and its controls reflect the straightforward approach to commonsense engineering.

The two engines fitted to 6-cylinder cars. The Rover 75's had a capacity of 2103cc (later increased to 2230cc), whilst the 90 had a 2638cc unit. (Courtesy Matt White)

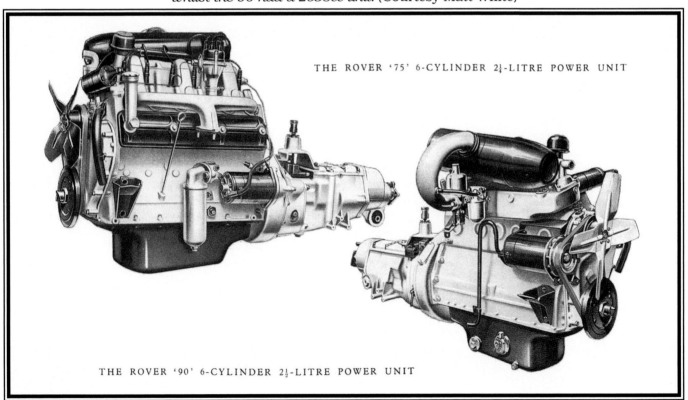

THE ROVER '75' 6-CYLINDER 2¼-LITRE POWER UNIT

THE ROVER '90' 6-CYLINDER 2¼-LITRE POWER UNIT

'One of Britain's Fine Cars'. The Rover range for 1954 was expanded to include two new models: the 4-cylinder 60 and the 6-cylinder 90. In this brochure illustration the P4 sports a duo-tone colour scheme. (Courtesy Matt White)

Right: Early styling changes resulted in the disappearance of the Cyclops grille. Note the box-shaped headlamp fairings, small rear window and sharply-raked boot. (Author's collection)

Drawings in this style were popular during the mid-50s. In this picture of the 60 in what appears to be a Swiss scene, note the ladies' fashions and obligatory pipe-smoking gent. (Courtesy Matt White)

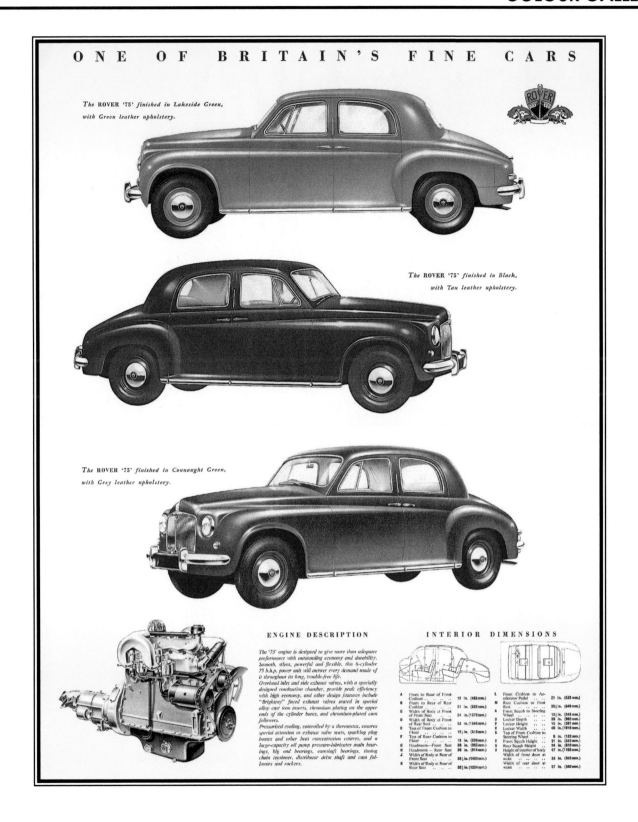

ONE OF BRITAIN'S FINE CARS

The ROVER '75' finished in Lakeside Green, with Green leather upholstery.

The ROVER '75' finished in Black, with Tan leather upholstery.

The ROVER '75' finished in Connaught Green, with Grey leather upholstery.

ENGINE DESCRIPTION

The '75' engine is designed to give more than adequate performance with outstanding economy and durability. Smooth, silent, powerful and flexible, this 6-cylinder 75 b.h.p. power unit will answer every demand made of it throughout its long, trouble-free life.

Overhead inlet and side exhaust valves, with a specially designed combustion chamber, provide peak efficiency with high economy, and other design features include "Brightray" faced exhaust valves seated in special alloy cast iron inserts, chromium plating on the upper ends of the cylinder bores, and chromium-plated cam followers.

Pressurised cooling, controlled by a thermostat, ensures special attention to exhaust valve seats, sparking plug bosses and other heat concentration centres, and a large-capacity oil pump pressure-lubricates main bearings, big end bearings, camshaft bearings, timing chain tensioner, distributor drive shaft and cam followers and rockers.

INTERIOR DIMENSIONS

A	Front to Rear of Front Cushion	19 in. (483 mm.)
B	Front to Rear of Rear Cushion	21 in. (532 mm.)
C	Width of Body at Front of Front Seat	54 in. (1372 mm.)
D	Width of Body at Front of Rear Seat	53 in. (1346 mm.)
E	Top of Front Cushion to Floor	12½ in. (318 mm.)
F	Top of Rear Cushion to Floor	15 in. (330 mm.)
G	Headroom—Front Seat	38 in. (965 mm.)
H	Headroom—Rear Seat	36 in. (914 mm.)
J	Width of Body at Rear of Front Seat	55¼ in. (1403 mm.)
K	Width of Body at Rear of Rear Seat	52¼ in. (1334 mm.)
L	Front Cushion to Accelerator Pedal	21 in. (532 mm.)
M	Rear Cushion to Foot Rest	25½ in. (648 mm.)
N	Front Squab to Steering Wheel	13½ in. (343 mm.)
O	Locker Depth	38 in. (965 mm.)
P	Locker Height	15 in. (381 mm.)
R	Locker Width	40 in. (1016 mm.)
S	Top of Front Cushion to Steering Wheel	8 in. (152 mm.)
T	Front Squab Height	21 in. (532 mm.)
U	Rear Squab Height	24 in. (610 mm.)
V	Height of interior of body	47 in. (1193 mm.)
	Width of front door at waist	33 in. (838 mm.)
	Width of rear door at waist	27 in. (686 mm.)

The ROVER "75"

Ivory finish, with
Red leather upholstery.

The boot has an unobstructed floor, and is automatically lit; a separate compartment houses the spare wheel. The petrol filler flap is locked from inside the boot.

An automatic reversing light, brought into action by engagement of reverse gear, makes light of night-time reversing.

A comprehensive, well laid out tool kit is carried in a neat rubber-lined drawer beneath the front seat.

Door panels, bonnet cover and spring-balanced luggage boot lid are all of strong, rustless aluminium alloy.

No other car has quite so many good points as the Rover Seventy-Five ; in no other car has the search for perfection in its class been quite so unremitting. Silent running, smooth power, perfect control and finish have always been Rover characteristics. The latest model has all these, and much more, in generous measure. The interior offers luxurious comfort for a full passenger complement, with all seats well within the wheelbase. Upholstery is hide on foam rubber, and there are massive central folding and side armrests, a built-in 3½ kw. heater, front and rear interior lights operated by opening the doors, and rear pull straps. The exterior is immaculately styled and finished, with door panels, bonnet cover and luggage boot lid in rustless aluminium alloy. The rear window extends to almost the full width of the car. The 6-cylinder 75 b.h.p. engine, described elsewhere, provides ample smooth, silent power. Controls are finger-light, and in all situations the Rover handles delightfully. Independent front suspension and variable rate rear springs give the same unruffled ride irrespective of road or load, and stabilisers front and rear ensure freedom from sway and provide superb road-holding. The popular Rover Free-wheel gives clutchless gear changes. The spare wheel is housed in a separate compartment, giving extra luggage space, rubber is used even more extensively to simplify maintenance — the body is now rubber-mounted — and for all those *hidden values* essential to pleasurable motoring the Rover remains unique.

Left, top: Individual illustrations detail the 75's finer points. (Author's collection)

Left, bottom: The P4's sumptious interior is clearly shown in this brochure illustration. The seats are pleated and have improved springing and the position of the gearchange lever permitted passengers to sit three-abreast on the front bench seat (meaning the car could be classified as a full 6-seater). Note the grab handles and reading lamps on the rear pillars and enlarged rear window. (Author's collection)

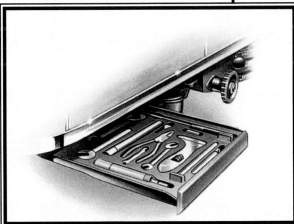

Above & left: Placing the spare wheel underneath the boot floor increased boot space but, even so, capacity was never that good. The tool tray under the fascia is a reminder of the thoughtful accessories incorporated into the P4. (Author's collection)

Below: Cutaway drawings were always a feature of Rover publicity and this particular example clearly shows the essential workings of the P4. (Author's collection)

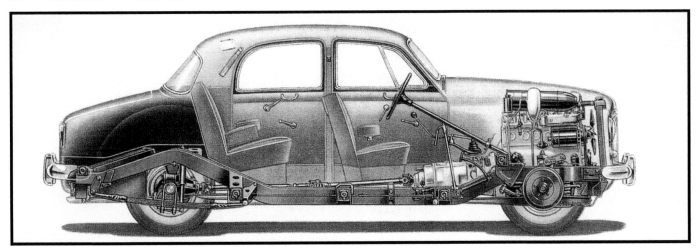

THE ROVER *75*

The Rover Seventy-Five is a car of great distinction and silent, effortless movement. Beautifully equipped for luxurious motoring, it may be optionally fitted with automatic overdrive. This replaces the normal free-wheel and gives greater economy with exceptional smoothness at high cruising speeds.

The Seventy-Five is powered by a six-cylinder engine developing 80 b.h.p. and possessing many special features to ensure complete reliability and long life.

THE ROVER *9*

When introduced the 90 represented the ultimate in Rover luxury. Rover finery is portrayed in this brochure illustration, which also exemplifies the styling modifications introduced by David Bache. (Author's collection)

The 75 in this charming brochure picture illustrates quite clearly the styling changes for 1955 implemented by David Bache. (Author's collection)

The Ninety is a luxury car by any classification and combines an outstanding performance with supreme comfort and impressive smoothness and silence. Even when travelling at maximum speed passengers may relax in the well-furnished interior and talk in normal tones. Power is provided by a six-cylinder engine of 2,638 c.c. capacity developing 93 brake horse-power and operating with commendable economy. This economy may be further improved by the fitting of automatic overdrive which is available as an optional extra.

Above: The P4 appears quite at home in these gracious surroundings. (Courtesy National Motor Museum)

Left: Was it really possible to get all that luggage in the boot of a 1955 P4? (Courtesy National Motor Museum)

The 105R was unfairly regarded as slow and complicated, when it should have been the P4 flagship. A special de-luxe model was also available, the only difference being that it had a cigar lighter! (Courtesy National Motor Museum)

The 105S had overdrive fitted as standard. This luxuriously appointed variant was capable of over 100mph (160km/h).

Rover retained its aggressive image for the cover of the 1956 brochure with a hard-hitting illustration that is particularly effective. (Courtesy Matt White)

Considerable artistic licence was taken with automobile publicity material and this example is no exception!
(Courtesy National Motor Museum)

Artistic licence at work again! Frontal styling here looks more like that of the P5; it's certainly much wider than it should be.
(Courtesy National Motor Museum)

Left: The Cyclops design seen on the Studebaker may have influenced the incorporation of a central fog lamp on the P4. The Tucker also had a similar feature. (Photo: N. Wright, National Motor Museum)

Below: The Wilks brothers were infatuated with Studebaker's designs. Two cars were shipped to Solihull and the body of one was mounted on a Rover chassis. The 'Roverbaker' was a common sight at the factory for several years. The Studebaker shown here is the 1950 champion. (Photo: N. Wright, National Motor Museum)

A trio of Cyclops P4s pictured at a Rover event in the mid 1990s. (Author's collection)

When the Tickford car was discovered in 1964 it already had something like 150,000 miles on the clock. The new owner put on another 50,000 before handing the car over to a relative who, unfortunately, did not appreciate its worth. Finished in light grey paint and trimmed with red leather upholstery, the car was quite unique and it is something of a shame that it remained in almost total obscurity throughout its life and even more so that it ended up at the breaker's.

At about the same time as the fixed head coupé was built Tickford was preparing the two dropheads for Rover. The decision to market the drophead may have been influenced somewhat by the appearance of the gas-turbine car, JET 1. There is no doubt the turbine was a handsome car but it had been so designed not out of vogue and desirability but from pure necessity and practicality. To have a coachbuilt variant of the P4 saloon was one thing, but to emulate the sporting qualities of the turbine car was far more prestigious.

Although the exact date is unknown, the two dropheads were built during 1950 but the first was not registered until 11th October that year. One of the two cars made an unscheduled appearance at the London Motor Show at Earls Court in the early 1950s, and additionally, the P4 was awarded the *concours d'élégance* Grand Prix in Monto Carlo in 1971. Nevertheless, the car made quite an impact with its striking lines and luxurious appointment.

In common with the fixed head coupé, the two dropheads were built as two-door cars which gave the vehicles their particular sporting penchant. The standard P4 windscreen and surround was retained, the rear side windows were made to drop in the manner of the fixed head coupé and the hood, manual in operation rather than power-operated, had three positions. An interesting point is that an electrically-operated hood was not considered due to Spencer Wilks' dislike of being reliant upon a power-operated mechanism.

The reasons for Rover not continuing with the drophead are unclear, although there may well have been several. For example, Rover might have been happy for Wilks, Mackie and Co. to take over this market using Rover chassis and components and keeping the project 'in the family' as it were; price may well have had an influencing factor, as did the question of the quality of the hood material.

As well as the Tickford cars Rover also approached Farina to prepare a coachbuilt variant and there is some evidence that Mulliner was also involved. As in the case of the aborted M-type and Road Rover projects, it may well be that the ideas finally ran out in the preoccupation with building saloon cars for sale and profit. Certainly there is reason to suggest that one of the two cars sold to Sir Martin Lyndsay suffered from problems concerning the quality of the hood material, the entire hood having to be replaced three times in the two and a half years he owned the car.

Both cars were sold directly from the Solihull factory and Sir Martin Lyndsay, who was Member of Parliament for Solihull from 1945 until 1964, bought his for £1000 at the time the standard 75 Cyclops cost £1106. Spencer Wilks and the Rover company enjoyed a healthy relationship with Lyndsay and it is very likely that Wilks was more than happy to have his MP driving around in a constituency company's prestigious product. There is some confusion as to the original colours of the cars: Sir Martin recalled both were finished in black with a khaki hood whilst Cliff Petts, who remembers the cars at Tickford where he worked as a coach finisher and a pattern maker, remembers one of them being a maroon colour.

Sir Martin Lyndsay's car, KNX 518, was delivered to him on 27th October 1950, having been registered two weeks earlier. The second drophead was registered LOK 918 on 19th July 1951. KNX 518 was sold by Lyndsay through Henly's of London in 1953; little is known about what happened to this car although it is rumoured it was sold to a north London solicitor who ran it for several years but returned the car to Henly's on several occasions for routine servicing.

Almost beyond restoration: the Tickford drophead, as found, is so rotten the front wings, suspension and running gear have all but disintegrated. (Photo: Bill Henderson)

A drophead for £20

Out of the three Tickford cars produced, only one has survived. It is known that the fixed head coupé was relegated to the scrap yard in the early 1970s and relatively little is known about KNX 518. It was only by chance that the third car, LOK 918, was saved from a fate similar to that of LAC 447, and for a time there was some doubt whether it could be salvaged due to its dire condition.

LOK 918's owner, Bill Henderson, was not particularly looking for a Rover when he discovered the car in 1985. True, he was looking for a classic convertible but had more in mind a Riley as he had enthused over the cars for many years. Not having too much experience in Rover history he was at first unaware at what he had found but knew it was a car worth saving. The car was in a pretty sorry state when he found it, its previous owner having rescued it from a scrapyard in 1964 for just £20 and partly restored it to have some fun with. It appears LOK was used to tow the family caravan on holidays to Scotland but in 1969 was left to slowly rot in peace.

When found, LOK had lost most of its floor and the sills were almost non-existent; the wings were missing from the car although the remains of one them was discovered nearby, and the front suspension dangled in a quite useless fashion. The rest of the car was very much in the same tatty condition, the boot had rotted through and the rear wings were full of rust; although the seat frames were still intact the upholstery had long given up the ghost as it had been exposed to all weathers. As for the instruments, the original Rover dials were still intact although in need of renovation and the engine, although seized, was capable of working again with some tender loving care, such was the ruggedness of the unit. The original engine had been changed at some point after 1955 in favour of the 90 unit and it was decided to leave it there until an original engine could be located.

Determination to get the car back on the road meant there was only one solution: a ground-up restoration. Stripping the car down to the barest of essentials revealed the chassis to be in surprisingly good shape, considering the rest of the vehicle's condition. The brakes had to be completely renewed but it was a stroke of luck that at some stage the original hydro-mechanical system had been updated in favour of the Girling all-hydraulic system as found on post1951 cars.

The bodywork was the cause of Bill Henderson's greatest difficulties: instead of being made from Birmabright the panels beyond the doors were formed out of

130

Getting there! Front wheels have been fitted, the floor cut away and an improvised seat is in place.
(Photo: Bill Henderson)

steel, which meant they had to be completely reformed, with the rotten areas cut away and new steel welded in, and painstakingly shaped to perfection. Two further differences to the saloon cars was the length of the drophead variants, which were six inches longer, and the rear panels, which were built upon an ash frame. Fortunately, the wooden structure was in remarkably sound condition which, ultimately, helped save the car.

Although he had the drophead professionally resprayed, Bill Henderson carried out all the surface preparation himself, often working into the small hours to achieve the perfect result. Luckily,

In all its restored glory, the Tickford P4 poses on the ramparts of Alnwick Castle.
(Photo: Bill Henderson)

LOK 918

Bill Henderson's Tickford cabriolet in good company with the fifth Marauder to be built and which competed in the 1994 Monte Carlo Challenge. (Photo: Stan Johnstone).

frequent visits to autojumbles and constantly searching for anything connected with the P4 resulted in finding most of the remaining body panels and trim. When at last the surface was ready the car was painted in its present blue cellulose.

Once the bodywork had been sorted out it was time to get started on the car's interior. Local craftsmen in Bill's native Northumberland were employed on the project and they replenished the African walnut where required. An upholsterer completely re-made the leatherwork to perfection from the finest quality hides and also undertook extensive repairs to the hood while Bill's wife helped make the new worsted hood lining. The wiring, too, was in total disrepair and much of it had to be replaced.

Now complete, LOK 918 is a superb motor car, a tribute not only to its owner's tenacity and perseverance in rescuing it from the dead, but also to original Rover engineering. As a piece of motoring history the car is unique but it is

not destined for a museum. In a feature about the car in *Overdrive*, Bill Henderson told Matt White, the journal's editor: "I believe that a car should be used, this one isn't going to be mothballed. You will be able to find a smear of oil in the engine bay and it will do a job of work".

The Farina episode and the Italian connection

A further development in the quest to produce an alternative variant of the P4 came about when Spencer and Maurice Wilks invited Farina to produce two prototype cars for them, a drophead coupé based on the Rover 75 and a fixed head coupé using the 90 chassis. The Tickford affair had not progressed further than the three cars already produced.

Farina's reputation was such that Rover would have little difficulty marketing the cars and two chassis were eventually despatched to Farina's workshops at Turin. The Italian *carrozzerie* had flourished in the 1930s and it was fashionable for respectable car makers to be

knocking at its door in the search for individual bodies for their discerning customers. Even the Marauder episode with a design very much in the style of Enzo Ferrari's 166 creation may have influenced the Wilks brothers to look further afield than British designers, but, whatever the reason, the outcome was glorious.

Farina's offerings were devastatingly gorgeous and the drophead coupé, with its gold metallic paint and majestic finery, was displayed at the 1953 Earls Court Motor show. There is no doubt the car stole the show, the luxurious beige leather upholstery and deep red hood epitomising sheer elegance. The car caught the eye of the Duke of Edinburgh who opened the show and it is said he would have liked it for his personal transport.

The fixed head coupé, which was finished in an attractive green metallic paint, was just as elegant but Rover considered the drophead to have the greater appeal. The Rover parentage remained quite obvious,

Sheer elegance: Pininfarina produced two coupés based upon the P4. Here, the drophead displays its exquisite styling. (Courtesy Rover P4 Drivers Guild)

In the finest Italian tradition Pininfarina's fixed-head coupé transforms the P4 into a luxury sporting machine. (Courtesy BMIHT/Rover Group)

Pictured at Solihull, the Pininfarina drophead was lavishly appointed. (Courtesy BMIHT/Rover Group)

although the frontal treatment had been somewhat modified and the basis of the eventual P5 styling can be seen. The Farina cars were 12 inches longer than the production P4s, the sculptured vestigial rear wings were retained and the two large doors gave the whole car a distinctly graceful appearance. In his *Rover Story* Graham Robson makes the point that the design had a great deal in common with the Rolls-Royce Corniche of almost twenty years later.

The sleek lines of the Farinas were emphasized by slim screen pillars and steeply-raked windscreens, the frameless side windows, both front and rear, wound down fully into the doors while the hood on the drophead folded neatly into a purpose-built well behind the rear seats. As for the drophead, the lines of the car were enhanced with the hood in the lowered position; the same can be said of the Tickford cars.

Just as was to be expected the cars were luxuriously appointed with map reading lamps, a light in the boot and even the drophead had a lamp built into the hood frame. The seating was sumptuous with a split bench seat at the front but, curiously, the driver's seat was six inches narrower than the passenger's. Full instrumentation was provided in the specially designed fascia which, instead of being made from African walnut, was finished in painted metal. The convertible retained the column gearchange as seen in the Rover 75 but the fixed head coupé was fitted with a floor-mounted gearchange. There were other little touches of luxury: the boot lid was operated from a lever in the front seat squab but the tool tray was relegated to fit vertically inside the rear wing.

Whilst impressed with the Farina cars, Rover commissioned the Mulliner company to investigate the possibility of producing a similar car. Mulliner duly presented the Solihull company with an example which was registered RNX 10 and put to exclusive use within the company fleet. There is evidence the car was eventually sold but since then records of the car have been lost. The project to build the Mulliner cars was abandoned due to the prohibitive costs and difficulties of manufacture.

As for the two Farina cars, the drophead coupé was sold between 1955 and 1956 to W A Apperley, a director of a Liverpool Rover dealership. It appears that Apperley continually pestered to buy the car from Rover until finally an agreement was reached. Ironically, the car was later badly damaged when a lorry collided with it in Lode lane, Solihull, and it now, having received various modifications over the years, sports a Bentley Continental boot lid in place of the original item.

The fixed head coupé suffered a similar fate. The car was sold to a Rover concessionaire in Spain but was damaged before it arrived there. The owner's chauffeur involved the car in an accident near to the same spot in Lode Lane where the drophead was damaged. After it had been repaired and safely delivered to Spain, it is said the car's owner suffered a heart attack at the wheel of the car and that it was again badly damaged. Reports abound that the car was eventually sold but for the moment there is no clue as to its whereabouts. As for the Farina drophead, this is now safely in the hands of a Dutch Rover enthusiast.

Although the Farina variant was never put into production the design found favour with two Italian car makers, Fiat and Lancia. The Fiat 1900 of 1952 used Farina's overall styling to influence the Gran Luce and Torpedo versions, while Lancia produced its idyllic B24 Aurelia Spider in virtually the same guise as the would-be Rover. In the case of the Lancia most left-hand-drive cars were exported to America.

Whilst the coachbuilt P4 variants never materialised the prototype cars serve as an important episode in Rover history. Those cars that have survived are all the more valuable for demonstrating what might have been, as well as enriching the company record.

The striking lines of the Pininfarina fixed head coupé are clearly evident. The car had been newly delivered to Solihull and created a huge sensation. The rear styling is reminiscent of the Bentley.
(Courtesy BMIHT/Rover Group)

The Irish connection

From the very beginning of P4 production Rover found a market for locally assembled cars and, from 1950, began supplying CKD kits to Ireland. Rover agents, Lincoln and Nolan, provided the assembly service on behalf of Solihull and were well known for their extremely generous working conditions which, in the 1950s, were the among the best in Europe.

Rovers were not the only British cars to be assembled in Ireland from CKD kits: Citroëns from the British plant at Slough were also sent to the Irish Republic for local assembly and sale, although hardly on the same scale.

By the mid-fifties relatively large numbers of cars were being sent to Lincoln and Nolan: in 1955 alone 62 kits of the model 90 and 14 model 60s were despatched.

The Irish cars used different colour schemes to that of the Solihull-produced cars and were delivered as duo-tone models with quite different paint specifications to the British produced cars. Whereas duo-tone models delivered from Solihull had the colour-break at roof level, the Irish cars used the waist line as the dividing point. It is therefore unwise to associate the colour schemes shown in the appendices of this book with a car known to have been assembled in Eire.

Royalty and the P4

The association between Land Rover and the British royal family is one of long-standing, just as it is with the P5 models. The P4s were seldom seen in service with the royal household although there is some evidence that two cars were prepared for HRH Princess Margaret. According to the Crown Equerry the two cars, which were based upon the 105R, were specially supplied with 3-litre engines. These engines, in fact, appear to be the normal P4 engines bored out to 3-litres and fitted with pistons from the Rover 60 unit.

Little is known about these cars from Rover's records, which suggests that the cars were built to particular specifications by a coachbuilder. However, it can be confirmed that the cars were in service with the Royal Motor Fleet between 1959 and 1963. In his book *The post war Rover P4 and P5*, James Taylor claims that both cars had an 8 inch panel inserted aft of the B/C post; this suggests the cars had a lengthened wheelbase and gives rise to the supposition they were coachbuilt. It is known that the earlier car was fitted with a bench-type front seat but little is known of the second car.

In 1963 two further cars were delivered but these were based upon the P5 and were loaned to the British Motor Industry Trust as long-term exhibits in the late 1980s.

Along with the Road Rover, experiments were carried out to find an all-purpose estate car variant of the P4. Inspired by the Chevrolet, this scale model never made the grade. (Courtesy BMIHT/Rover Group)

What might have been

Had the P4 been allowed to continue after 1964 power-assisted steering would, more than likely, have been obligatory. There is another option which was evaluated but in the event did not come about – a diesel engine.

Faced with the prospect of winning an order for a fleet of taxis destined for Brazil, the availability of a diesel engine was seriously considered and, it appears, much work was done in this respect. Early experiments were undertaken with the 2-litre Land Rover diesel unit but this was not considered refined enough. A 2286cc engine was then tested on a Rover 90 which was registered NAC 514; the engine was very similar in dimensions to the late P4 petrol units but, again, a long-term test did not produce results that met with Rover's demand for engineering quality. It appears the sale of taxis never materialised and the diesel project was dropped.

There is also some question as to why an estate car version of the P4 was never made. There is no evidence that Rover ever considered such a proposition other than allowing the apprentices to build a prototype model. Known as "Woody", the car was built in the finest shooting brake tradition and has been acquired by Bill Henderson.

Some of the experimental work carried out on the Road Rover project appears to have been concentrated upon an estate-type car, for which a Chevrolet was used as a model. A prototype vehicle was built but there is no evidence it was any more successful than the Road Rover itself.

Possibly the most innovative of all Rover engineers was Gordon Bashford and his sketch books display a host of intriguing ideas. Not least was a tear-drop design, years and years ahead of its time, which was no doubt influenced to a certain extent by some of the

stylist ideas that abounded in the early 1950s with the appearance of the gas-turbine car. The Road Rover has already been discussed but, suffice to say, that had the project been allowed to come to fruition it would have been the ultimate vehicle in people-carrying and would surely have pre-dated all other go-anywhere combi-vehicles except for, perhaps, the Land Rover.

There were, no doubt, considerably more projects worked upon behind closed doors. Some prototypes would have been built but never shown outside the experimental department. Many of these research vehicles have, sadly, been lost forever but occasionally the odd snippet of information arises and even more interestingly a previously unrecorded vehicle is discovered. The occurrence of these occasional 'finds' makes automobile history all the more interesting.

Rear view of the Chevrolet-based Road Rover. Only one prototype model exists. The lines of this scale model are remarkably advanced for the era.
(Courtesy BMIHT/Rover Group)

Below: Road Rover variant based upon the Chevrolet takes shape in the experimental department at Solihull. Note the Citroën 2CV hammock-type seat, not part of the original specification!
(Courtesy BMIHT/Rover Group)

P4

V

LIVING
WITH
A P4

The sight of a majestic Rover P4 in sparkling condition being driven on the roads of today is enough to stir the emotions of any motorist. The 'Auntie Rover' is evocative of the not-so-long-ago grandeur of another era and P4 enthusiasts delight in being part of the aura the car so readily exudes.

It is hardly surprising that with such a pedigree the P4 commands a deep sense of loyalty from those that share their lives with it, brought about by the car's inbuilt longevity of useful service and the resultant long association owners enjoy with their cars. Kept in good order with plenty of tender loving care there is no reason why a car, whether it be 45, 50 or 55 years or more old, should not still be capable of providing reliable every day transport.

Gordon Bashford always insisted the P4 was never 'over-engineered' but 'properly-engineered' and as a result it is easy to find many pre-1959 cars easily maintaining regular day-to-day transport. Many cars of the same era are now relegated to classic car events only, their owners never

Stan Johnstone's 95. (Author's collection)

Specialist events such as the Beaulieu Autojumble can offer the right car at the right price. This particular P4 may warrant close inspection: the bumpers have been painted and the wheels are a different shade to the body. A reasonable P4 can be purchased for £1500 but expect to spend some money restoring the car to the desired condition. (Author's collection)

dreaming of using their car as a daily workhorse.

The P4 is in many respects the forgotten classic car. For all this, though, it is best remembered as being the archetypal quality postwar British saloon, the choice of the discerning motorist and professional classes who looked for a high degree of workmanship over and above popular fashion and a turn of speed. Not that a P4 is by any means slow; drive it properly and it will still show many a modern car a clean pair of heels!

Many classics have achieved cult status, with prices spiralling accordingly; not so the P4 which remains an affordable classic with loads of character that has retained its supreme comfort and upmarket appeal. To a certain extent the build quality and thorough design has been the P4's downfall in the classic stakes: because of its inherent longevity and zest for long service a vastly higher proportion of cars have survived than usual.

In getting to grips with living with a P4 I was pointed very definitely in the direction of Stan Johnstone and Matt White. Stan is a leading personality within the Rover P4 Drivers Guild and his engineering prowess stems from an early age when many hours were spent building models from Meccano sets. This early training with a spanner and screwdriver stood him in good stead for looking after his first P4, a 1953 Rover 75, which he bought in 1966 for the

princely sum of £100.

To Stan, £100 in 1966 was a lot of money, especially as he was about to get married. The Rover 75 was to be the car for life and, in a way, it has been as Stan has never owned anything else except P4s.

Today, there are two cars in Stan's life; a 100 and a pristine burgundy 95 which he enjoys driving 363 days a year – Christmas Day and Boxing Day are its only two days off. The 75 is not forgotten and is the subject of an on-going restoration.

Although a 1963 car this fine example, which has been restored to a very high standard, reveals its age by its styling which includes a high bonnet line, narrow windscreen and heavy wheelarches.
(Author's collection)

A lesson in Rover history: from left to right, 95, P3 75, early series 75 and 110. (Photo: Stan Johnstone)

Matt White also uses P4s as his everyday transport and, when not at the wheel of his superb 90, enjoys the luxury of a relative rarity: a 105R. A professional photographer, Matt White obviously appreciated the photogenic qualities of the P4. Testimony of this is *Overdrive* which he has edited and produced with enthusiasm.

Owning and buying a P4
One of the fundamental aspects of living with a P4 is the confidence owners have in their cars. Built-in obsolescence was never considered when the car was designed and this is borne out by the quality and sheer belt and braces attitude to components. Stan Johnstone showed me a selection of parts: king-pin sets, wheel bearings and the clutch thrust mechanism, all of which were built to last and take exceptional wear and tear.

It is quickly apparent that P4 owners are jealously loyal towards their cars, and for good reason. Providing, of course, that a P4 is properly looked after it will return a degree of reliability second to none. Unlike many classic cars the situation concerning the supply of spare parts is happily no problem; the two owners' clubs – the Rover Sports Register and the Rover P4 Drivers Guild – have the benefit of members who have sourced parts and remanufactured where necessary so there is no reason for a car to be off the road due to mechanical failure.

To find out just what P4 ownership is all about I was invited to go along for the ride in Stan Johnstone's 95, a car with quite a difference to modern Rovers. The P4 is a car that is stepped into, more like a carriage, and not one that has the human body doing contortions

in order to sit down in low-slung seats which are even more difficult to climb out of. The leather seats of the P4 are sublimely comfortable – more like grandad's armchair – not squashy but supportive and upright, allowing easy vision over the impressive bonnet line.

From the driving seat it is possible to see the tops of both wings, a feature associated with the latter cars but not so earlier models. A valid criticism of the early series of P4s is the limited all-round view but the raised front wings of David Bache's design modification improved matters considerably. Working under the sole direction of Maurice Wilks this was one of Bache's first consignments, together with the early designs for the P5. What is generally not so well understood is that David Bache's influence on the P4 was something of a sideline; to all intents the P4 was

an established model that merely required updating from time to time in order to bring the car within the current Rover corporate image. As a digression, it is worth recounting the story of David Bache's arrival at Solihull: in those days he drove a Jaguar XK which did not please Spencer Wilks one little bit. It was three years before Bache owned his first P4 ...

A few hundred yards in a P4 is convincing enough that the car is not quite the stuffy and ultra-staid vehicle it is often perceived to be. On the contrary, it is a willing and spirited performer, although older and less well preserved cars than Stan's 95 will make rather more of a fuss about things. Stan is a perfectionist; his car is in tip-top condition and he insists on driving it the way it was designed to be driven – using all its potential while understanding its limitations and keeping within its capabilities.

This particular 95 is something rather special; its sister-model, the 110, was fitted with overdrive as standard while the 95 was not in order to keep the specification and price at a premium. On Stan's 95, however, overdrive has been fitted and what a difference it makes to the car's performance! Stan admits to installing the overdrive on his 95 simply because he could not get on without it, having been used to it on his 100 for something like 17 years. The differential has also been changed from a 3.9 to the 4.3

unit so that, in essence, his car is equivalent mechanically to a 100 but with 95 trim and dashboard.

Once on the open road a flick of the overdrive switch on the steering column is all that is required to settle the revs down. The engine, although barely audible, keeps the Rover rolling along in a relaxed state, maintaining an easy high cruising speed. Country lanes with twisting bends and sudden hills are no problem: flicking the car out of overdrive is all it takes to unleash a surge of power that takes the car safely and quickly through the meandering bends. For sheer performance – Rover-style, at least,

– a quick change down from top to third, automatically knocking out overdrive, is all that is needed to pin you firmly into the back of the driving seat while the P4 accelerates with alacrity.

Stan reckons that a lot of P4 owners do not always get the optimum performance from their Rovers and are quite content to let their car potter along, rather than giving it its head. He would never expect his car to be in the situation where it might be in the way; certainly he would never have a queue of frustrated motorists trying to pass him. Although it is a forty-five year old car Stan drives his 95

The outline of the P4 changed relatively little over its 14 year production span. On this 95 can clearly be seen the raised front and rear wing line common to all the David Bache modified models. (Author's collection)

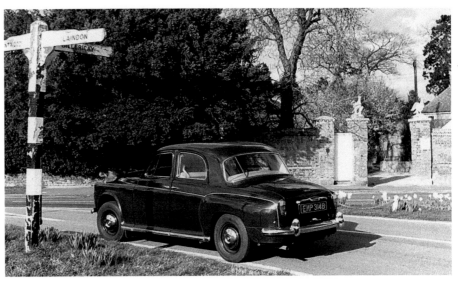

Bearing number 158, STM 1 storms along mountain roads whilst participating in the Monte Carlo Rally.
(Courtesy BMIHT/Rover Group)

as he claims it should be driven but remembers two vital factors: not only has the car to be carefully positioned at the right speed and in the correct gear for spirited driving on a twisty road, it also has to be in perfect condition.

When new, P4s were fitted with crossply Avon tyres and there are owners who still insist on fitting them. Most enthusiasts, however, are very happy to use radial tyres: heavier steering at low speeds and a slight increase in road noise is a small penalty to pay for more agile handling and reduced wear. On later cars radial-ply tyres look completely acceptable but on the Cyclops and early models appear strangely out of place.

When Matt White first became acquainted with Stan Johnstone he considered he treated his car too harshly when driving. Stan would agree that he does not drive with a light right foot but argues this is perfectly possible as long as the car is well maintained and in good mechanical condition. He knows that as he is driving along, all the oils are new and clean and doing their job; he knows the brake pads have got lots of life in them and that the rear brakes are sliding and the slave cylinders are operating on the back plate. Moreover, it is a matter of having confidence in the car, knowing that everything has been attended to, such as replacing all the old brake pipes with copper examples.

Spen King shares Stan's view that the P4 is an extremely tough car and most fun when it is driven with vigour. Spen should know, of course, his experience with JET 1 is testimony to that. Part of the secret of putting a P4 through its paces is not being frightened to rev the engine: it is one of the best things for the car as Rovers like to be worked.

Colin Blowers' 110 flanked by 2 Cyclops models, both of which have the 8-bar grille. For the first-time buyer it is recommended a late car be chosen in preference to an early model. (Photo: Stan Johnstone)

Apart from the gas-turbine cars, motor sport has not been a particular forte of the P4. Certainly enthusiasts such as Frank Lockhart have raced and rallied P4s to some effect and the sight of a P4 in full flight lumbering around Silverstone is a somewhat awesome spectacle. The car is, of course, much more at home being driven with some dignity although it is by no means without performance.

For somebody buying their first P4 it is more likely to be a late model, ie post-1959/60, rather than an early example that will be chosen. Later cars benefit from greater comfort, better all-round vision and enhanced styling; the superb engineering of the P4 will enable more chance of a robust car being found that is in need of less attention both mechanically and cosmetically. Earlier P4s, that is the 75, 60 and 90, will be immediately identified by the box-shape headlamp fairings and sloping boot; needless to say the Cyclops is quite obvious to identify.

A 95 or 110 will have the benefit of trim and instrumentation from the P5, and the 110 will have the best performance of all the P4s, but watch out for those cars with all-steel panels which have a tendency to rot a lot quicker than those manufactured from Birmabight. Many owners of late 95s and 110s have decided to forsake the steel panels in favour of alloy, which means reduced weight and better insurance against rusting. A point to be aware of when looking at a P4 is that cars that should have aluminium panels may have had steel panels fitted if the car has been involved in an accident.

An issue the first time buyer might wish to ponder is the braking systems fitted to P4s over the years which fall into three categories. Early cars, that is before mid-1955, had a basic all-drum system although it will be appreciated that initially the Cyclops model employed the Girling hydro-mechanical system before Rover felt confident enough to rely upon fully hydraulic brakes. Between mid-1955 and mid-1959 the brakes were upgraded, retaining all-round drums but assisted by a servo unit. Servo assistance was at first limited to the 90 and 105 models but was not fitted to cars with the free-wheel device on grounds of safety. As the new generation of P4s arrived, ie the 80 and 100, 95 and 110, so front disc brakes became universal although drums were retained for the rear wheels and the whole system had the benefit of a servo unit.

There is more likelihood of choosing a 6-cylinder engined car than a 4 as only two models were produced with 4-cylinder engines, the 60 and 80, the latter's unit being derived directly from the Land Rover engine. The 60, a 2-litre unit which

143

P4s on parade! From left to right: an early post-Cyclops car; Cyclops P4 with 8-bar grille; 95 and 100. The remaining cars appear to date from around 1955. (Photo: Stan Johnstone)

retained the inlet over exhaust principle and had more in common with the original 6-cylinder engine block, is now something of a rarity, having been first introduced for the 1954 season with a little over 9000 units built over a five year period. It is true that the 80's engine is not quite as smooth as a 6-cylinder

The 60 provided all the usual Rover refinement at a budget price. The 2-litre, 4-cylinder engine, although considerably lighter than the 6-cylinder, was, however, no more economical when worked hard.
(Courtesy BMIHT/Rover Group)

The 80 superseded the 60 as the range's 4-cylinder variant. Using the Land Rover engine meant a little finesse was lost, although the 80 is a willing worker. (Courtesy BMIHT/Rover Group)

unit but it definitely should not be overlooked for that reason. It is also true that there is a strong model loyalty within Rover circles but it is a sad indictment when there are those who consider that a 4-cylinder P4 is not in the same league as the sixes.

The 60s and 80s do have their dedicated enthusiasts; the cars are every bit as charismatic as, say, a 90 or 100; the same finesse is evident and handling is that much lighter due to the saving of weight over the front wheels. The 80 may have a distinctive growl compared to the more familiar whine of a six but, as for driving enjoyment, there is little difference.

The advantage of the 80 engine is its strength which is to be expected due to its Land Rover ancestry; to class it as 'agricultural' is, in fact, more of a compliment than a criticism. The most economical P4 is the 60 but do not expect the 80 to show any economical advantage over a 6-cylinder car. Although something like 13% smaller in capacity than a 2.6-litre car, the 80's ohv engine arrangement does not have the thriftiness of an inlet over exhaust layout. Whereas the 100, 95 and 110 are adept at high speed cruising, the 80 is more at home being put through its paces on minor roads.

The 60, with its frugal fuel consumption, can quite easily squeeze up to 28-30mpg (approximately 10 lts/100km) from its 11.5 gallon (52.325 litres)

fuel tank and makes an excellent everyday car, but do not expect it to be an out-and-out performer. It is at its best taking secondary roads in its stride and on the motorway is happiest at an easy 60-65mph (96-104km/h). When first introduced its price was kept down by a lower level of specification but, for all that, it was an excellent car with a pedigree second to none.

For the P4 enthusiast buying their first car, what is the ideal model to look for? Knowing that if I posed this question to six Rover enthusiasts I would probably receive six different answers, I asked Stan Johnstone for his advice. The message was quite clear: go for the 100. The reason for his choice is that, in his opinion, the 100 represents singular P4 engineering complete with all the benefits of the later cars' specification, including overdrive but without the complications of the Weslake head as fitted to the 110.

The same reply came from Richard Stenning who has been associated with P4s for a long time. His preference of models also includes the 90, the stalwart

of the earlier cars which sold in remarkably large numbers. The later 75s – together with the 90's successors, the 105 and 105S which shared the same basic engine design – all have their devotees who consider their cars to be the ultimate in P4 development. The 105R is in a class of its own and, as such, deserves special mention later.

When the P4 was first announced a particularly attractive feature of the car was its free-wheel device. With the progression of time, together with general driving conditions and the advancement in transmission systems, this aid to economy and driver fatigue lost much of its usefulness. As overdrive units became available so the free-wheel became less favoured until it was phased out altogether. There is no question that it served its purpose at the time but eventually became impractical. There were numerous occasions when the question of safety was raised: in theory, of course, the car was constantly in gear and Rover somehow managed to get away with specifying the free-wheel device. The economy benefits of using the free-wheel are obvious

The family resemblance between these three Rovers can be clearly seen. The P5 is flanked by what appears to be a 100 on the right and an 80 on the left. (Courtesy BMIHT/Rover Group)

but whether the savings Rover claimed could actually be achieved is a matter of opinion.

For sheer individuality there is nothing to beat the original Cyclops 75 with all the character of its rectangular instruments and column gearchange. Driving a Cyclops is rather different to a late P4, of course; it is somewhat slower but nonetheless an excellent performer and quite capable of maintaining reasonable speeds, certainly up towards 70mph (112 km/h) under the right conditions. Whether the engine of the early 75 is as strong as that of the 90 and the other middle period cars is arguable; certainly the white metal bearings of the first series suggest more preventive maintenance may be needed as well as a more cautious driving approach.

The original Cyclops cars are now quite difficult to locate and have become a serious collectors' item. Due to the problems caused through overheating, very few of the original cars fitted with the 15 bar grille exist and only two are registered with the Rover P4 Drivers Guild.

Anthony Rowland's car is one such example. Built in 1950 and registered KLJ 188, the car has amassed only around 80,000 miles (112,000km) in its 52 years. Owned originally by an estate agency in Liverpool, it had two further owners before Anthony purchased it in 1982. He had spotted the car parked outside a MoT test station; the vehicle looked tired although obviously in a solid condition. Above all, it was intriguing to see the Rover had retained its original grille.

Learning that the car was for sale the decision to buy it was quickly made. The first impression of the Cyclops was that it felt more like a P3 to drive than the later P4s such as the 100 and 110, both of which Anthony has owned. Over a period of time an entire overhaul of the car was completed culminating in a bare metal respray in the original ivory colour, together with an interior retrim in green leather.

Now that the necessary restoration is complete – and it is worth stressing that the engine required only a top-end overhaul: the bottom-end, gearbox and rear axle

did not have to be touched – the car currently covers approximately 3000 miles (4800km) a year. Anthony does all the maintenance himself but there are particular areas that require special attention. The hydro-mechanical braking system can go out of balance and on one occasion the cause was eventually traced to a faulty wheel cylinder. The gear linkages need systematic inspection and regular lubrication to avoid unnecessary wear on the bushes; finding the original oil filters is something of a problem but, luckily, Anthony has a good store of them, picking them up at autojumbles whenever he can.

With a host of awards collected both at home and abroad, Anthony has every right to feel proud of his Cyclops: "Forget winking indicators, forget safety belts and forget motorways; when I drive this car I put the clock back 50-odd years and enjoy the unique combination of leather settee, column change, free-wheel, valve radio and non-motorway driving."

Owning an original Cyclops has its lighter moments. Whilst

146

Owners new to the P4 will enjoy the unashamed luxury of best quality leather and finest African walnut. Note the shepherd's crook handbrake, adjustable gearchange and the free-wheel device to the left of the heater controls. (Author's collection)

One of the few remaining 8-bar Cyclops with rectangular instruments. Despite its age, the car provides regular transport. (Author's collection)

Above: Cyclops P4s always attract attention at shows and events.
(Authors collection)

at a Rover enthusiasts meeting a so-called expert proclaimed to his companion: "Of course it's a 90 with the badges taken off and customised front!"

Talking to Rover enthusiasts it's clear the most understated P4 is the 105R. Given the P4's style and market level, history shows Rover managed to miss a specific opportunity with this car, allowing its demise after what was not really a fair sales trial. For some reason the motoring press at the time did not like the car; certainly, it was a trifle slower than its sister models and, granted, fuel economy was less thrifty, but this was little loss compared to the relaxed and sublimely comfortable motoring the car offered.

Maintenance was of the essence where the 105R was concerned

Left: Tony Rowland's beautifully restored Cyclops model. The car is very much original and sports the 15-bar radiator grille which caused so much concern in respect of over-heating that a modification had to be devised.
(Photo: Matt White)

and, if the truth be known, Rover specialists knew precious little about the car. With hindsight, the servicing arrangements of the 105R were much more involved than the 105S. Quite possibly more than a few cars suffered from unknowing neglect by mechanics not properly briefed in servicing procedures. Correctly set up, however, the 105R is a very rewarding car to drive and has in recent times been appreciated as possibly the most classic of all production P4s.

What to pay for a P4

The P4's undisputed longevity is a tribute to the car's basic engineering excellence. Due to the relatively high number of surviving vehicles the value of the cars is relatively low.

Forget the price guides in some of the classic car magazines though; they tend to be rather lower than what cars actually change hands for. Prices are all relative, of course, in as much as a car is only worth what the purchaser is willing to pay for it. Rarity and age factors all have their part to play but, whatever the model, a start has to be made somewhere.

Living together. Les White with his trusty 95 which provides comfortable and totally reliable everyday service. (Author's collection)

At the time of writing a car in running condition, quite usable and with a current MoT test certificate can be obtained for between £2000 and £2500. Some work will obviously be necessary but without too much difficulty the car can be transformed into something worth considerably more with a further £2000-£3000 being spent on it.

A car in a thoroughly presentable condition and mechanically reliable

Matt White's pristine early 90 has a 95 (right) and 110 (left) for company. When introduced, the 90 was the ultimate P4. (Photo: Stan Johnstone)

would fetch more than £6000, while a super-concours P4 could easily cost in excess of £8000, depending on the model. Imagine finding a pristine or concours 105R: such a car could be worth around between £9000 and £10,000.

Cars can be bought for relatively little money, £2000 or less, but invariably extensive work will be necessary to bring the car up to an acceptable condition. If a restoration project is required and the would-be purchaser is prepared to undertake a ground-up rebuild, a car can be had for as little as £750.

P4s do find their way onto the forecourts of purveyors of classic vehicles so, if buying from this source, be prepared to pay slightly over the odds. The dealer may have undertaken some work on the car and it is naturally very important to know what exactly has been done.

What not to do to a P4! The P4 does not take kindly to customizing. The frontal treatment of this particular car is slightly reminiscent of the American style of Cyclops models, where the central fog lamp was removed for safety reasons and replaced with a large star. Note the lack of sidelights and the non-standard sun roof. (Photo: Stan Johnstone)

Having decided life is no longer tolerable without Auntie, where are the best places to go looking for a suitable P4? Certainly there the usual papers, journals and classic vehicle magazines containing the normal plethora of classified advertisements. There are, of course, the two clubs which cater for the Rover enthusiast and both the Rover Sports Register and the Rover P4 Drivers Guild magazines carry members' adverts. Alternatively, try some of the P4 specialists, who may well know of particular cars currently for sale. Most importantly, don't trust to luck and, if you can, take along a P4 enthusiast who knows what to look for in a car.

The down-side: foibles & weaknesses

• CHASSIS AND BODYSHELL
However well engineered the P4 is, it does still have weaknesses. For the many cars that are in sound condition there are a whole lot more which have not been so well maintained.

These vehicles are instantly recognisable and will have rust and corrosion around the leading edge of the front wings, leaving the indicators and sidelights in a bed of rotten metal. The area beneath

At the Beaulieu Autojumble enthusiasts come to haggle, reminisce or just browse. This 100 was for sale at the time and it looks as if it might have just found a new owner. (Author's collection)

The Rover '90' chassis frame is of welded box section construction—light in weight and immensely strong and rigid. The '90' engine is a 6-cylinder unit with a 2.875-in. (73.025 mm.) bore, 4.134-in. (105 mm.) stroke and a capacity of 2,638 c.c. (161 cu. in.). Maximum b.h.p. of 90 is developed at 4,500 r.p.m. The same robust frame is used on the '75' and on the '60'.

According to Gordon Bashford the P4 was "properly engineered", rather than being over-engineered as said by a number of commentators. Depicted here is the 90 chassis frame which has welded box-section construction. (Rover publicity material, Author's collection)

the headlights is also an easy target for the rust bug; wheelarches will appear tatty and the bottom of the doors, especially those made from steel, will seem in a sorry state.

The doors have built-in drain holes and, if future damage is to be avoided, it is important these are kept clear. Birmabright panels also have their own problems and, apart from denting easily, are susceptible to salt with the result that paint will flake off leaving white deposits of aluminium oxide. As a guide, remember that cars were fitted with steel panels from March 1963. Wings suffer too and the areas most vulnerable are the lower-rear section at the front and the lower-front section of the rear.

As for the chassis, this is a hefty-enough affair but can in time show serious problems in extreme cases. It is claimed that later cars were built with a slightly thinner gauge steel which could account for rot forming around the swept-up section adjacent to the rear axle. There is only one effective way to examine the condition of this area and that is to remove the rear wheels.

Other areas of the chassis to check most carefully are the six outriggers which support the bodyshell: extensive corrosion here could affect the jacking points, result in an MoT test failure and, even worse, raise the question of whether the car is actually

worth repairing, especially for the inexperienced owner.

Further evidence of fatigue in this area relates to the front offside outrigger which supports the handbrake lever: should this corrode extensively it is likely to put the parking brake mechanism in jeopardy of complete failure. Another tell-tale indication of chassis and floor corrosion is the boot: by lifting the matting on the boot floor it is possible to check for rust which is likely in this area. Any holes here will allow water and road dirt to penetrate the fuel pumps. The rear valance can show evidence of corrosion; this area is particularly vulnerable and, as it supports the hatch to the spare

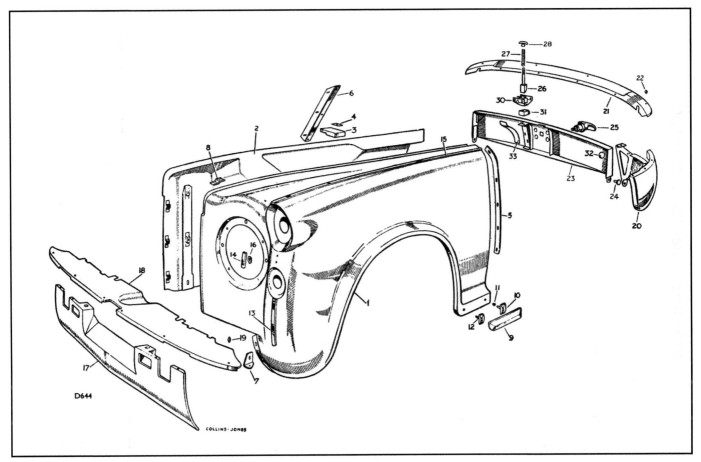

1 Front wing top & side	17 Front bumber valance
2 Front wing valance	18 Front apron panel
3 Robber seal, wing to dash	19 Rubber buffer for front apron
4 Retaining strip, wing to dash	20 Rear bumper valance
5 Angle for front wing mounting	21 Rear apron panel
6 Angle for wheelarch front mounting	22 Rubber buffer for rear apron
7 Stiffening bracket, front wing to	23 Spare wheel lid panel complete
chassis frame	24 Special rivet, plain washer
8 Cover plate for drain hole in wing	25 Handle for spare wheel lid
9 Moulding for front wing, rear bottom	26 Lock bolt for spare wheel lid
10 Retainer for moulding, plain	27 Spring for bolt
11 Tubular clip	28 Handle for spare wheel lid lock
12 Retainer for moulding	29 (not listed)
13 Trim strip for front wing nose, bottom	30 Guide bracket, spare wheel lid lock
14 Trim strip for front wing nose, centre	31 Striker for spare wheel lid lock bolt
15 Trim strip for front wing, top	32 Buffer for spare wheel lid
16 Clip pop rivet	33 Steady spring for spare wheel

Front wing assembly of the P4. The leading edge and area under the headlamp can be susceptible to rot and need to be regularly checked. (Author's collection courtesy Rover P4 Drivers Guild)

wheel housing, should be examined carefully.

One of the assets of the P4 when new was the car's separate chassis in an age when unitary construction had become the norm. A particularly attractive feature was the filling of the box section members with a sound-proofing material which helped give the car its air of refinement and quality. This is perfectly fine until water is allowed to reach the material, transforming it into a massive sponge – a possible recipe for accelerated rot and damage.

Open the doors of a P4 and the inner sills which really are a type of running board are readily evident. Although an attractive feature of the car they really are not of great strength and can deteriorate surprisingly quickly. While the doors are still open, check the bottom of the A-post as corrosion can work quickly but quietly here causing extreme damage if not checked. The base of the central pillar can be a weak spot and door hinges, too, have a habit of wearing.

• OIL – THE LIFEBLOOD OF THE P4
In conversation with Stan Johnstone it quickly becomes very plain that attention to oiling and

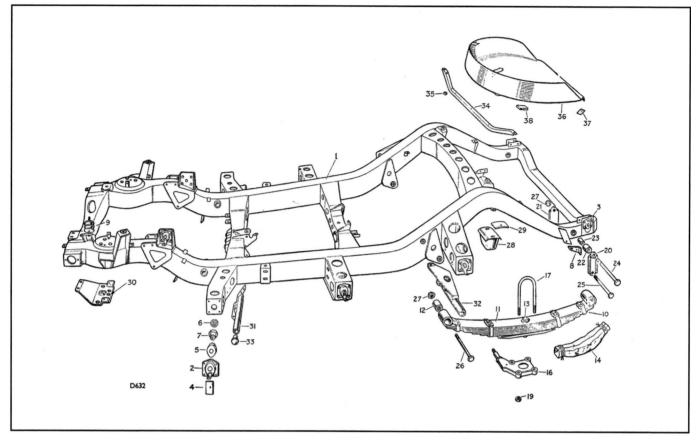

Chassis construction of the P4 is explained in this diagram. Note the three outriggers on each side and detail of the rear suspension. (Author's collection courtesy Rover P4 Drivers Guild)

1	Chassis frame	20	Shackle plate for spring, plain, outer
2	Housing, front & intermediate for body mounting rubber	21	Shackle plate for spring, taped, inner
		22	Bearing for shackle plates
3	Housing, rear; fixing housing to chassis frame	23	Distance piece for shackle bearing
		24	Shackle pin, plate to bearing
4	Shim for body mounting	25	Shackle pin, spring to plate
5	Body mounting, rubber, large	26	Shackle pin, spring to front brackets
6	Body mounting, rubber, small	27	Self-locking nut for shackle pins
7	Centre piece for body mounting, rubber	28	Bump rubber for rear axle
8	Stop bracket for shackle	29	Packing piece for rear axle bump rubber
9	Front engine mounting		
10	Road spring, rear	30	Jacking bracket, front centre
11	Main leaf for spring	31	(not listed)
12	Bush for spring	32	Jacking bracket
13	Dowel for spring	33	Plug for jacking bracket
14	Grease sleeve for rear springs	34	Support for spare wheel housing & petrol tank
15	(not listed)		
16	Bracket for shock absorber mounting	35	Rubber packing for support
17	'U' bolt	36	Housing for spare wheel
18	(not listed)	37	Insulation pad, thin
19	Nut, locknut	38	Insulation pad, thick

oil changes cannot be taken too lightly. In an age when changing the engine oil is done at seemingly huge intervals, the oil change requirements of the P4 appear stringent.

To keep the engine in good condition it is essential to drain the engine oil every 3000 miles (4800km). For cars with very low mileages, or those used for short journeys when the oil never really gets the chance to thoroughly warm up, oil changes are even more important and should be carried out every 1000 miles.

Under normal usage it is quite usual for a P4 to use oil at the rate of approximately 250 miles

(400km) per pint. On an engine showing signs of age and wear oil consumption can increase to as much as 100 miles (160km) per pint and, in extreme cases, to 50 miles (80km) per pint.

A feature of the P4 engine is the amount of oil squirting everywhere from the moment the starter turns the engine over. A

problem associated with irregular oil changing can take the form of worn camshafts, caused by gritty oil.

The Achilles' heel of the IoE engine is the 'O' rings, or rubber oil seals, on the inlet valves. These harden with wear and age and allow oil to be drawn into the combustion chambers and burnt. The solution

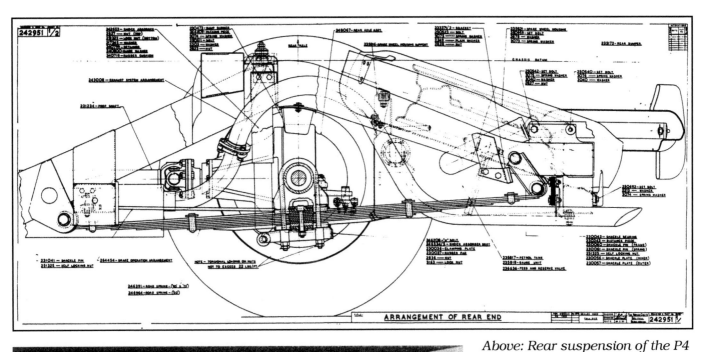

ARRANGEMENT OF REAR END

Above: Rear suspension of the P4 shown in graphic detail. (Author's collection courtesy Rover P4 Drivers Guild)

Left: For a short period the shepherd's crook handbrake was replaced by a floor-mounted lever alongside the driver's seat. The mechanism was fitted below the car as shown in the photo. (Photo: William F.Scott, courtesy Rover P4 Drivers Guild)

Although perhaps least refined of the P4 engines, the 4-cylinder 80 unit is extremely strong and has few weaknesses apart from timing chain rattle, which is more annoying than troublesome. The Solex carburettor as fitted may well have been replaced by a Weber unit which gives improved economy and does not deteriorate like the original equipment.

Gearboxes on the P4 have proved very robust considering the basic design dates back seventy years. Characteristically there is a whine from 1st gear; this is quite normal and adds to the charm of the car. The main cause for concern, however, is the layshaft bearing together with the front pinion

is to replace the seals but to do this the cylinder head has to be removed. While undertaking a top-end overhaul it is probably wise to inspect the valve guides which also tend to wear.

Pre-1960 IoE engines have another weakness in as much as the cam follower design causes wear not only to the cam follower pads but the camshaft itself. A symptom of wear

here is noisy valve gear which can be recognised by a distinct tapping sound from the engine's top-end. On post-1960 cars the problem is less severe but does exist to some extent. Whilst smoother in operation and with roller cam followers on the limit of the pushrod, with age and wear the similar tapping symptom may be detectable. Engine rebuilds on a P4 can be expensive, so beware.

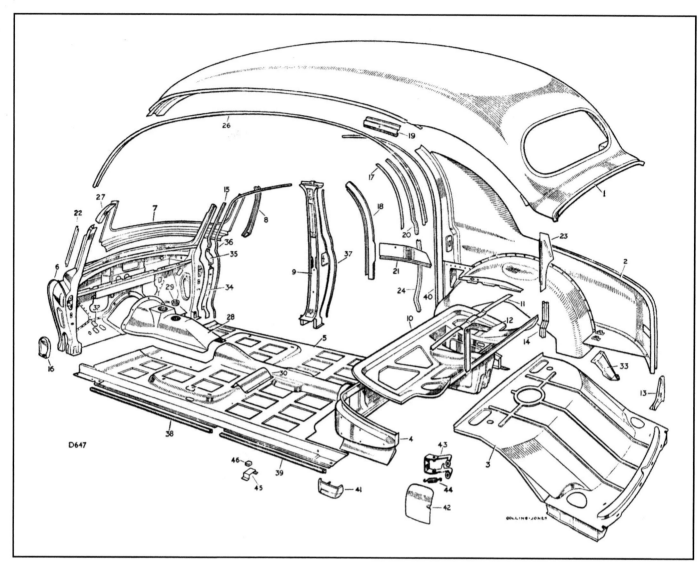

The component parts of the P4 floorpan and bodyshell are shown in this exploded view. Apart from the very last cars, boot, bonnet and doors were formed from Birmabight aluminium. (Author's collection courtesy Rover P4 Drivers Guild)

bearing. On high mileage cars these will almost surely rattle. Late cars, the 95 and 110, have a heavier duty unit with larger bearings which Rover considered might alleviate further problems. Over the long term period the problem was not resolved as wear is virtually the same.

1	Roof panel
2	Tonneau panel
3	Boot floor panel
4	Heelboard panel
5	Floor & sills
6	Shroud complete
7	Windscreen lower panel & sides
8	Spacer, windshield opening
9	'BC' post complete
10	Rear seat panel complete
11	Angle, rear squab support
12	Brace, rear seat squab
13	Gusset, spare wheel floor
14	Boot lid hinge support
15	Retainer for rubber seal on 'A' post
16	Access panel on dash side
17	Drip moulding, 'D' post
18	Reinforcement 'D' post upper
19	Reinforcement, side header, centre; support plate 'D' post reinforcement to roof frame
20	Retainer for rubber seal 'D' post, upper
21	Reinforcement 'D' post to back light
22	Drip moulding 'A' post
23	Closing plate, rear squab
24	Retainer for rubber seal
25	(not listed)
26	Drip moulding
27	Filler for 'A' post, top
28	Cover for gearbox
29	Rubber grommet for gearbox cover
30	Footrest panel
31	(not listed)
32	Cover plate for foot control holes & dip-switch hole
33	Splash plate for rear wing
34	Angle, rubber retainer 'A' post
35	Angle, rubber retainer 'A' post
36	Sealing rubber for 'A' post and top
37	Sealing rubber front & rear 'BC' post
38	Sealing rubber, front sill
39	Sealing rubber, rear sill
40	Sealing rubber 'D' post and top
41	Moulding for 'D' post
42	Petrol filler lid
43	Hinge, complete, for filler lid
44	Spring for hinge
45	Support bracket for floor
46	Rubber packing, floor to chassis

156

Getting to grips with a P4 engine. Stan Johnstone, technical adviser to the Rover P4 Drivers Guild, gives advice on how to tackle an overhaul at a regular Guild 'workshop meeting'.
(Photo courtesy Stan Johnstone)

The 105R with its Roverdrive automatic gearbox is particularly attractive even though it was not so popular as the manual box. Servicing the Roverdrive, although not a problem, did present particular difficulties which may have been the result of a communication problem between Rover and its agents. In short, Rover garages did not completely understand the design of the unit.

Difficulties centred around the torque converter which shared its lubrication system with that of the engine. In addition to the 16 pints (9 litres) of engine oil, a further 10 pints (5.7 litres) were required in the torque converter and it was essential this oil was drained at the same time as that in the engine sump. The process of changing the torque converter oil was not at all clear and many garages were unaware of this procedure. Due to the time and labour intensity of the operation it is quite possible less scrupulous garages conveniently ignored the task ...

At the bottom of the torque converter housing a large brass nut gave access to the mechanism itself. With assistance from a second mechanic, the engine would have to be turned slowly until a drain plug came into view, whereupon the mechanic working under the car could, by using an extension socket, undo the plug and let the oil drain. At this stage the job was only half complete as a second plug,

at 180°, had also to be undone and the remaining oil drained. Failure to change the oil meant that the torque converter bearing eventually wore to the extent that a serious oil leak developed. A 105R could, therefore, often be identified by the puddle of oil left on the ground underneath the gearbox.

The Lacock overdrive unit is generally trouble-free. In the case of it failing to engage, the fault can usually be traced to the solenoid, which has a habit of sticking. Servicing an overdrive unit can be quite easily undertaken as exchange units are normally available from Rover P4 specialists.

Although early cars featured grease nipples on the track rod ends the only other grease nipples to be found on the chassis are on the propeller shaft. If grease nipples are found on the king pins it is a sure sign that undue wear will have occurred which will almost certainly mean new king pin sets will have to be fitted.

The king pins on a P4 have a reservoir of oil and, if correctly maintained by oiling every two or three months, will last for an indefinite period. Unfortunately, in the past many mechanics did not appreciate this and, considering greasing was necessary, screwed grease nipples into the air release

holes. Pumping in grease did nothing for the king pins at all except allow the bushes to dry up and, of course, wear quite rapidly.

Oiling is also essential on the steering box and idlers but is often neglected with resulting steering wander. Wear on the bushes will eventually mean replacement but this is not a big problem as new bushes can be obtained relatively easily.

• PREVENTATIVE MAINTENANCE
The idea that P4 Rovers are so well built they run for ever is only partly correct. Certainly the cars are well built, very well built, in fact, but like any motor vehicle will only provide good service if properly looked after. If not given tender loving care even a P4 will wear out in time.

The key to efficiency and long life is preventative maintenance and thorough lubrication. Open the bonnet at least once a week, check the oil and water levels but, above all, check the brake fluid level.

P4s do not like being unused and left standing for excessively long periods and the brakes, along with the servo unit, can seize up. The piston in the servo tends to stick to the side of the unit, as do the seals, and if unused for long periods can be torn and damaged when activated for the first time, with the result

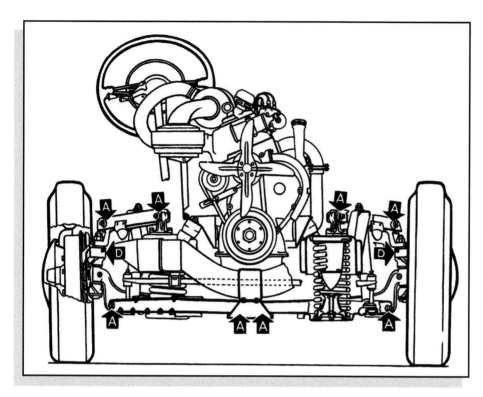

Front end assembly of the P4. 'A' denotes rubber bushes while 'D' denotes the king-pin oil reservoirs. (Courtesy BMIHT/Rover Group)

that fluid can pass unchecked. A tell-tale sign of trouble here is the presence of white smoke from the exhaust as brake fluid leaks from the servo into the inlet manifold. Callipers have a habit of sticking on later cars if the vehicle has been stored but, luckily, reconditioned units and repair kits are available.

Seizing of the braking system will not normally occur except in the case of lack of use. The engineering of the braking system is such that should the brake adjusters seize it is highly unlikely they would ever break off. Squirt some lubricant around the area and after a short time they will be doing their work again. Little 0.25in adjusters will never be found on a P4; instead are fitted chunky 0.44in square adjusters in the finest Rover tradition.

Hardworked cars may well suffer from tired suspension and rear springs will sag, especially if they are used for towing. Most suspension components are readily available although original equipment dampers may

be difficult to find. The front suspension is one of the hardest-working parts of a P4 and requires routine checking of the top link rubber bushes. Cars driven high mileages with unchecked shock absorbers are contenders for a front suspension overhaul before the annual MoT test.

Worn front suspension can usually be detected by a ragged edge around the bushes at the point where they are squeezed between the links and the top anchor; there will also be some excessive movement between the links and the chassis. In replacing the bushes it is probable the metal sleeve inside the bush may have become rusted to the pin. If the pin shows signs of corrosion it, too, will have to be replaced. Replacement of the top link bushes is essentially quite straightforward if the right lifting equipment is used – remember the P4 is a heavy car.

Stan Johnstone does not mince his words when it comes to the subject of owners maintaining their cars. He reckons that regular

maintenance should never be a nuisance, regardless of whether it is done by the car's owner or a specialist.

The P4's interior and electrics have few foibles: the worst is possibly removal of the windscreen and leaks from the rear window, especially on the later cars with three-piece assemblies. The front screen does have a habit of leaking and it is important that the carpets are kept dry if a musty smell is to be avoided. Water can also enter the car around the transmission tunnel and at the base of the handbrake. These areas should be checked carefully when choosing a car.

Although normally a quiet car in operation, the P4 can suffer from wind noise, especially around the front quarterlights. This can be easily rectified by fitting remanufactured quarterlights which are available through the Rover P4 Drivers Guild. The quality of the interior trim is second to none but, even so, the wood and leather can deteriorate if not looked after or allowed to get damp.

Early P4s were fitted with front bench seats, individual seats arrived in 1956, as did pleated seats which offered greater support. Reclining seats were available on the 95 and 110. Hide food is easily obtainable and the effort of applying this to the seats is well rewarded by soft and supple leatherwork. There is nothing more pleasing than to ride in a car with polished wood trim and soft fragrant leather.

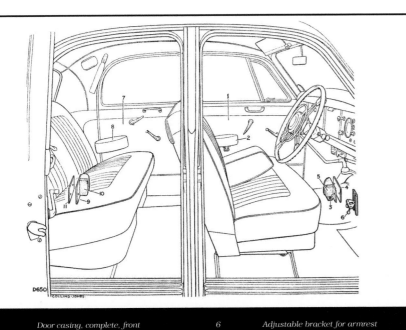

Interior components of the P4. The model shown represents the 80 and 100 models. (Author's collection courtesy Rover P4 Drivers Guild)

1	Door casing, complete, front	6	Adjustable bracket for armrest
2	Side armrest, complete, front	7	Door casing, rear
3	Bracket for side armrest	8	Side armrest, complete, rear
4	Backplate for armrest, drive screw fixing plate	9	Bracket for side armrest
		10	Rubber interior for side armrest
5	Rubber interior, backplate for front armrest bracket	11	Backplate for armrest bracket

The appendices in this book carry a list of known P4 specialists, some of whom provide a dedicated parts service. Parts are no longer offered through Rover agents,

A particularly authentic piece of equipment offered as an optional extra is the radio which, on earlier cars, happened to be of the HMV valve type. These do provide some extra character to the car even if they are somewhat cumbersome. Remember, though, that the aerial was always roof-mounted.

• SPARE PARTS AVAILABILITY

The P4 enthusiast is lucky enough to have access to an excellent spares organisation. Where older cars are concerned there will undoubtedly be cases of scarcity of parts, especially for items of trim. In the main, mechanical parts present little problem, even for the Cyclops 75, as there has been considerable work carried out in the remanufacture of components where necessary.

Detail of the driving position. The split front seats were initially optional although standard on the last models. (Author's collection, courtesy Rover P4 Drivers Guild)

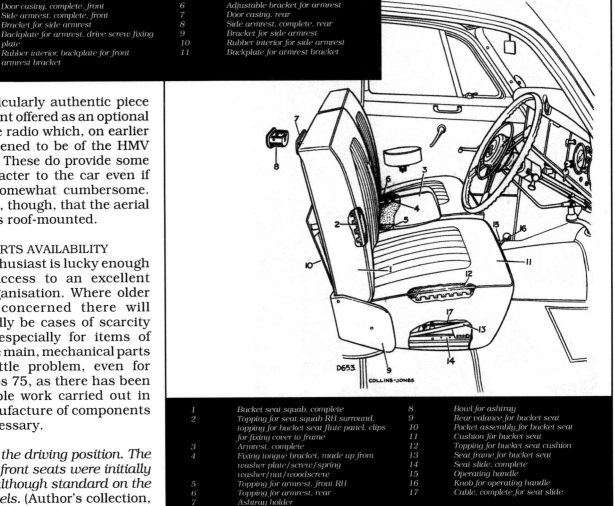

1	Bucket seat squab, complete	8	Bowl for ashtray
2	Topping for seat squab RH surround,	9	Rear valance for bucket seat
	topping for bucket seat flute panel, clips	10	Pocket assembly for bucket seat
	for fixing cover to frame	11	Cushion for bucket seat
3	Armrest, complete	12	Topping for bucket seat cushion
4	Fixing tongue bracket, made up from	13	Seat frame for bucket seat
	washer plate/screw/spring	14	Seat slide, complete
	washer/nut/woodscrew	15	Operating handle
5	Topping for armrest, front RH	16	Knob for operating handle
6	Topping for armrest, rear	17	Cable, complete for seat slide
7	Ashtray holder		

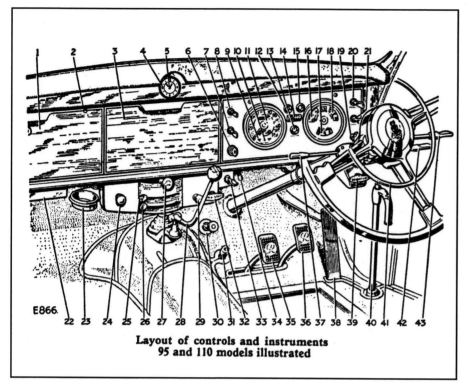

1. Outer glovebox lid*
2. Interior light switch*
3. Centre glovebox lid
4. Clock
5. Clock adjustment knob
6. Ignition & starter switch
7. Fuel reserve switch
8. Main lamp & parking switch
9. Direction indicator arrows
10. Headlamp warning lamp
11. Speedometer
12. Cold start control warning light
13. Ignition warning light
14. Handbrake & fluid level warning light
15. Oil pressure warning light
16. Water temperature indicator
17. Fuel & oil level indicator
18. Ammeter
19. Windscreen wiper switch – on 110 models also windscreen washer switch
20. Instrument panel light switch
21. Oil level switch
22. Tool tray
23. Ashtray
24. Backlight heater switch (optional 95 & 110 models)
25. Heater 'screen' control
26. Heater 'heat' control
27. Fresh air control
28. Gearchange lever
29. Car heater fan switch
30. Windscreen washer knob (80, 95 & 110 models only)*
31. Headlamp dipper switch*
32. Cold start control
33. Fog lamp switch (optional)*
34. Speedometer trip knob
35. Clutch pedal*
36. Brake pedal*
37. Overdrive control switch (80, 100 & 110 m models only)*
38. Accelerator*
39. Bonnet lock control
40. Handbrake*
41. Horn ring*
42. Headlamp switch*
43. Indicator control*

Layout of controls and instruments 95 and 110 models illustrated

Layout of controls and instruments on the 95 and 110 models.
(Author's collection)

The instrument panel complete, and items marked *, are transferred to the opposite side on left-hand-drive cars

although those components common to Land Rover *can* be obtained through the usual dealer network.

Membership of one of the enthusiast clubs is virtually essential as up-to-date information on spares availability is given in the clubs' magazines. Technical advice can also be obtained through the clubs and, in the case of the Rover P4 Drivers Guild, technical workshop demonstrations are a feature. Further details of the clubs can be found in the appropriate appendix.

Many P4 owners will want to carry out all their own servicing of the car. Those owners who don't want to or are unable to may want to entrust their P4 to a particular specialist. It is important that a

P4 ownership is all about enjoying the car and what better place to do this than in these wonderful surroundings! (Courtesy Stan Johnstone)

A fleet of P4s. All the cars shown here are later models. (Photo: Stan Johnstone)

measure of confidence is established between owner and specialist before entrusting a car to anybody and it is useful to discuss requirements personally. A visit to the workshop will confirm a lot about the concern – don't be sorry after the event.

Lastly, living with a P4 is all about getting enjoyment from the car. It is a car that needs to be driven and used to its full potential; it will not provide satisfaction sitting in a garage, slowly deteriorating, and neither is it a museum piece. To appreciate the P4's fine qualities it will need constant care and attention, it will become part of the family and, as such, will provide unlimited pleasure.

This chapter has looked at ownership of the P4 from a objective point of view. Every car has its weaknesses and the P4 is no exception although it possibly has fewer than most postwar production vehicles. It is important that the cars' weaknesses are understood and accepted: with this in mind car and driver will enjoy a long and happy relationship.

Publicity and the P4

For such a refined car it seems only right that Rover should have taken immense care to produce for the P4 what can only be described as an elaborate series of brochures. Throughout the car's production Rover sales catalogues subtly captured the charm and sophistication of 'One Of Britain's Fine Cars' and purposely latched

Side by side, Riley and Rover at Alexandra Palace. Both companies were eventually joined under the giant BMC/BL umbrella. In the days of the Cyclops pictured here, it was a different matter. (Photo: Stan Johnstone)

on to it's obvious upper class appeal.

The first of the 75 Cyclops brochures carried delightful drawings illustrating the car's sumptuous, full-width interior, bench seating and column gearchange; other features such as push-button door locks, concealed petrol filler and the telescopic jack were also graphically shown. The open boot showed the luggage space packed with cases and the almost compulsory golf bag, suggesting cavernous proportions which were, in fact, sadly lacking.

All this was in complete contrast to the P3 brochure which bore all the hallmarks of postwar stoicism with its photogravure pictures printed on austere paper.

For the P4 75's official launch a special edition brochure was splendidly presented with a greyish blue card cover. The publication was made all the more appealing by the profile illustrations of two cars which not only featured the latest and attractive Connaught green and pastel blue body colours, but also enhanced the car's already engaging design.

By Appointment to the late King George VI. Manufacturers of Land-Rovers. The Rover Co. Ltd.

One of Britain's Fine Cars

THE ROVER COMPANY LIMITED · SOLIHULL, BIRMINGHAM also DEVONSHIRE HOUSE · LONDON

This artist's impression depicts the Rover P4 as being considerably larger than it actually was. (Author's collection)

magnificent and cleverly combines charmingly detailed drawings with creative photography. Large format brochures were a speciality of Rover, again, artistic renderings predominated, giving the publications and the products they featured a feeling of elegance. Most famous of all the illustrations must be the curious 'Midget Chauffeur' packing the boot of a car who was so drawn in an effort to make the P4's rather less than adequate luggage space seem more generous.

The artwork of the mid-fifties Rover brochures is a particular joy and suggests a certain innocence. It is always summer, the women femininely appealing and the men always smoking pipes! Happy families abound and the Rover is part of the family scene. This is, of course, what sold cars: artistic licence was allowed much greater freedom then.

Overall, Rover maintained a high degree of sophistication in its advertising, at home within the pages of *Autocar* and *Motor* or gracing the inside covers of *Country Life*. The brochures themselves are a work of art, now very collectable, and symbolize the best of engineering in One of Britain's Fine Cars.

Fifty years on

Although it is more than forty years since the last P4 left the production line at Solihull, there remain some examples in everyday service. Luckily, many cars have fallen into

Slightly less lavish brochures followed in the wake of the launch catalogue, although a similar format was retained. Dated January 1951, a revised style of brochure was evident: the cover featured an artist's impression of the Cyclops P4, complete with 8-bar grille and reduced chrome trim. The evocative front cover had everything to do with selling cars and depicted the P4 in uncharacteristically aggressive mode, the trilby-hatted driver only just discernible. Inside the brochure charismatic artists' sketches remained – gone were rectangular instruments; round dials had arrived.

By the mid-1950s Rover had decided on a plush and opulent approach towards publicity: the 1954 brochure is nothing short of

A number of constabularies specified the P4 for police work. This retired example was used in the Heartbeat television drama series. (Author's collection

On the beach – a charming period piece of Rover advertising. (Author's collection)

One of Britain's Fine Cars

"On very few cars . . . will one find such intelligent planning coupled with such a fine standard of workmanship and finish."

The Motor, January 20th

ROVER

SIXTY · SEVENTY-FIVE · NINETY

THE ROVER COMPANY LIMITED · SOLIHULL, BIRMINGHAM also DEVONSHIRE HOUSE · LONDON
CV3-233

enthusiastic hands and stand a good chance of being preserved for many years to come.

At last the faithful P4 is being recognised as the classic it undoubtedly is, remembered and desired not only for its quaint upper class appeal but also its honest and straightforward approach to motor engineering.

Cars have survived in the most

RWD 576 makes a fine picture in the mid-1950s. (Courtesy BMIHT/Rover Group)

unlikely of places. From Solihull the P4 was despatched to all corners of the earth: India, Thailand, America, Australia and New Zealand, to mention but a few countries where the Rover tradition has been carried on. In these countries, as in Britain, enthusiasts unite to cherish their cars for the benefit of another generation.

Profile of a P4 enthusiast

It seems somewhat unfair to single out one particular enthusiast from the hundreds of devoted P4 owners but this feeling is quickly dispelled upon meeting Bill Henderson, as it is quite evident he is no ordinary Rover enthusiast.

Bill's collection of cars is something like the contents of Aladdin's Cave. Not only is there

a couple of 110s and a 95, there are also three very special P4s: 'Woody', the sole factory-built estate car, the quite astonishing Tickford drophead coupé as described in an earlier chapter and the remarkable P4 2.6-litre Cyclops prototype car, the only example to survive out of 30 cars built.

The drophead was, in Bill's terms, "thrown together", although it did take nine years to complete the restoration. For a Cyclops, this machine is a real flyer and Bill loves taking the car out on a fine day – just to drive it as intended, with the hood down.

'Woody' is in the frustratingly long process of restoration; fragments of the car's wooden-framed body are so rotten in places that only dust remains. Nevertheless, salvageable parts have been carefully stored away to either reuse on the car or as a pattern for remanufactured parts.

The one special P4 in Bill's collection is undoubtedly the 2.6-litre Cyclops prototype. The fact it has survived at all is a miracle as it should have been returned to Rover after its test and evaluation period at Rolls-Royce. For a long time no one at Rover would admit

the car existed until proof of the engine and chassis numbers finally convinced the company.

Before I visited Bill the engine of the prototype was minus its sump and essential components but a chance to show the car off was a treat too good to miss. Working hard right up to the Easter 1994 weekend, Bill managed to get the car together in time for Easter Sunday and was determined it should have its first outing of the year after its winter break.

When I met Bill on Easter Sunday the British weather lived up to all expectations: rain, hail, snow and sun. Not to be deterred Bill insisted we should take the car on a tour of Northumbria but not before a look at the photographs of the car when he found it. To most people the restoration of a vehicle in such a condition would be totally unthinkable and, in the garage, work complete, the car is a tribute to Bill's patience and painstaking dedication. There is no doubt the car was in a pretty sorry state when he bought it; rot prevailed throughout the car as a whole and the front and rear wings had virtually disintegrated.

The cost of such a project hardly comes into it – as a commercial venture it would be wholly impractical and the car would have been scrapped. Luckily, real enthusiasts never consider the cost and therefore cars survive.

With a pull of the starter the 2.6-litre experimental engine burst

Rot! This is how Bill Henderson's 2.6-litre prototype looked before restoration.
(Photo: Bill Henderson)

into life and after a short time began to settle down. With a few miles under its belt in the most dreadful weather the elderly Auntie gave up making any fuss and negotiated the hills and bends of England's north-east corner with a brisk keeness. The free-wheel, properly used – not for the novice – is effective enough, saving on fuel and, at the same time, allowing clutchless gearchanges.

The prototype's interior is a delight: Bill was able to use the original grey leather seats, the bench seat providing far greater comfort and support than expected. The instruments – rectangular, of course, – are completely in vogue with the car and it seems a shame that opinion was largely responsible for their demise in favour of round dials. The American influence seemed quite apt considering the car's Studebaker roots. The gearchange is another matter and has a habit of jamming up, usually at a road junction with at least a dozen cars behind all trying to get into the flow of traffic. Bill has the 'box mostly sorted out now but, even so, it catches him out on the odd occasion.

It is not until the car is seen on the open road that the Cyclops lamp and the frontal design is fully appreciated. Although later P4s have a much smoother appearance there really is nothing quite like a Cyclops for pure style and character. Bill, of course, is well known in his native Nothumberland for his love of old Rovers although he can also lay claim to a particularly attractive Riley RMA. On most weekends when he is not buried deep in a restoration project, he is happiest taking to the hills and moorlands in one of his P4s.

Looking at Bill Henderson's restored cars it is hard to believe that his expertise is self-taught. In his own words, he knew he wanted to save the Rovers and to do so he just had to get on with the job, solving all the problems as he went along. The result is a tribute

Bill Henderson with the 2.6-litre prototype on its first outing of 1994. 30 cars were built for test purposes and all were returned to Rover except one, which was lost by Rolls-Royce. (Author's collection)

to Bill's thoroughness and tenacity and, of course, to Rover design and engineering in the first instance. When 'Woody' is complete it will be just as excellent as the drophead and 2.6 prototype.

APPENDIX I

ORIGINAL SPECIFICATIONS
AND
GENERAL DATA

Rover 75

The 'Cyclops' 75 was the first all-new postwar Rover. In replacing the P3 model which retained the overall prewar styling of the P2, it made its debut at the 1949 London Motor show at Earls Court. The 'Cyclops' name came about as a result of the car's centrally-positioned foglamp which, together with a number of other features, reflected American styling.

The engine, an inlet over exhaust (IoE) 6-cylinder unit, had a capacity of 2103cc and produced 75bhp at 4200rpm. Transmission was via a 4-speed gearbox and a column-mounted change lever. Instruments were initially rectangular but, from 1951, were changed to round dials partly due to public opinion and demand; at the same time other modifications were also made.

From 1952 the car's frontal appearance altered when a new radiator grille was introduced featuring vertical slats – the Cyclops lamp also disappeared. Further changes were made in 1955 when a larger engine, 2230cc, was introduced which pushed the power up to 80bhp at 4500rpm.

Engine:	6-cylinder in-line 2103cc IoE, output 75bhp at 4200rpm. 6-cylinder in-line 2230cc IoE, output 80bhp at 4500rpm. Bore and stroke 65.2 x 105mm (2103cc); 73.025 x 88.9mm (2230cc). Compression ratio 7.25:1 (2103cc), 6.95:1 (2230cc). 2x SU Carbs. (2103cc), single SU carb. (2230cc). Sump 15pts (7.5lts).
Transmission:	4-speed gearbox and 9 inch single dry plate clutch. Gearbox oil 3.5 pts (2lts); rear axle 3pts (1.75lts).
Cooling system:	21 pints capacity (12 litres).
Fuel system:	SU electric pump, tank capacity 11.5 gals. (52.325 litres).

Brakes:	Drums all round, Girling hydromechanical.
Tyres:	6.00 x15.
Weight:	27.75-28.5 cwt/3108-3,19lbs (1412kg/ 1451kg).
Performance:	Max. speed 82mph (132km/h); average fuel consumption 25mpg (11.9 litres/100km).

Rover 60

In an effort to popularize the P4, Rover introduced the 60 model in 1953 for the 1954 season. Instead of the 6-cylinder engine a 4-cylinder unit was developed. This shared the same dimensions as the Land Rover engine but furthered the design of the inlet over exhaust principle.

The body and chassis were almost identical to that of the 75 but with a slightly lower trim level. The 60 never enjoyed the success it deserved and only in its last two years of production did it outsell the 75. Rover sales literature referred to the car as the 2-litre 60.

Engine:	4-cylinder in-line inlet over exhaust, 1997cc. Bore and stroke: 77.8x105mm, output 60bhp at 4000rpm. Compression ratio 6.73:1; single SU carburettor. Sump 10pts (5.6lts).
Transmission:	4-speed gearbox, 9 inch single dry plate clutch. Gearbox oil 5.5pts (3.1lts) with overdrive, 3pts (1.75lts) without overdrive. Rear axle 3pts (1.75lts).
Cooling system:	17 pints capacity (9.25 litres)
Fuel system:	SU electric pump, tank capacity 11.5 gals. (52.325 litres).
Brakes:	Hydraulic, drums all round.
Tyres:	6.00x15
Weight:	26.25cwt (1336 kilos).

Performance:	Max. speed 79mph (127.1km/h). Average fuel consumption: 28.7mpg (9.8lts/100km).

Rover 80

Introduced in 1959 the 4-cylinder 80 replaced the 60, Rover's only other 4-cylinder version of the P4. Identical in appearance to the 6-cylinder 100, the 80's engine has its origins in the Series II Land Rover. Its 2286cc overhead valve engine produced 77bhp.

Top speed was in excess of 85mph (136km/h) but the car was more happy at its cruising speed of 70mph (112km/h). Total production amounted to 5900 cars and price on introduction was £1163.

Engine:	4-cylinder in-line, 2286cc with overhead valves. Bore and stroke: 90.47 x 89.9mm; output 77bhp at 4250rpm; compression ratio 7.0:1. Single Solex downdraught carburettor. Sump 12 pts (6.5lts) after replacing filter.
Transmission:	9 inch single dry plate; 4-speed gearbox with overdrive. Gearbox oil 5pts (2.75lts) with overdrive; rear axle 3pts (1.75lts).
Cooling system:	17.5 pints capacity (9 litres).
Fuel system:	Mechanical fuel pump; tank capacity 11.5 gals (52.325 litres).
Tyres:	6.00 x 15.
Brakes:	Girling hydraulic, servo-assisted with discs at front and drums, rear.
Weight:	3304lbs (1502 kilos).
Performance:	Maximum speed 82-85mph (131.2-136km/h); Average fuel consumption: 19.8mpg (14.3lts/100km).

Rover 90

By introducing the 90 in 1953, Rover was seen to be expanding the choice of models as well as offering a 'top of the range' alternative. More power was available from the 6-cylinder engine, which had repositioned cylinder centres to allow larger bores, 2638cc and 90bhp.

The 90 arrived with a larger rear window and trim modifications; '90' decals were fitted to the bonnet sides whilst a fog lamp was fitted to the nearside front.

Instantly successful, the 90 mostly outsold both the 75 and 60 combined during the 6 years of its production, ie 1954-59.

Engine:	6-cylinder in-line, inlet over exhaust, 2638cc. Bore and stroke: 73.025 x 105mm, output 90bhp at 4500rpm; compression ratio 6.25:1. Output 93bhp at 4,500rpm, compression ratio 6.73:1; compression ratio 7.5:1 also available with 93bhp at 4500rpm. Single SU carburettor. Sump 16pts (9lts) after replacing filter.
Transmission:	9 inch single dry plate clutch, 4-speed gearbox and overdrive available for 1956 season. Gearbox oil 3.5pts (1.75lts); rear axle 3pts (1.5lts).
Cooling system:	21 pints capacity (11 litres).
Fuel system:	SU electric pump; tank capacity 11.5 gals. (52.325 litres).
Brakes:	Lockheed hydraulic, drums all-round, servo-assisted from 1956 season.
Tyres:	6.00 x 15.
Weight:	3108lbs (1412 kilos).
Performance:	Maximum speed 82mph (131.2km/h); 91mph (146.5km/h) with overdrive. Average fuel consumption 20.3mpg (14 lts/100km); 23.4mpg (12.12lts/100km) with overdrive.

Rover 100

Together with its sister model, the 80, the 100 was introduced as a result of some rationalisation of the P4 range in 1959. The engine, a 6-cylinder 2625cc unit, was, in effect, a short-stroke version of the 3-litre power unit in the P5 models.

For many enthusiasts the 100 was the ideal P4 as it followed the model's tradition but enjoyed such modifications as servo-assisted braking with discs at the front, overdrive in place of the free-wheel and the re-designed front-end styling.

Throughout its production span, over 16,000 examples of the 100 model were produced, making it the most popular of the later P4s.

Engine:	6-cylinder in-line inlet over exhaust, 2625cc. Bore and stroke; 77.8 x 92.075mm, output 104bhp at 4750rpm. Compression ratio 7.8:1, single SU carburettor. Sump 16pts (9lts) after replacing the filter.
Transmission:	9 inch single dry plate clutch, four-speed gearbox with overdrive as standard. Gearbox oil 5pts (2.75lts) with overdrive. Rear axle 3pts 1.75lts).
Cooling:	23.5 pints capacity (13.5 litres).
Fuel system:	Twin SU elctric pumps, tank capacity 11.5 gals. (52.325 litres).
Brakes:	Girling hydraulic; servo-assisted with discs at front and drums at rear.
Tyres:	6.00 – 6.40 x 15.

| Weight: | 3332lbs (1515 kilos). |
| Performance: | Maximum speed 92.1mph (147km/hr); average fuel consumption 20.26mpg (13.7 lts/100km). |

Rover 105R, 105S & 105

The 105 series of cars was introduced in the autumn of 1956 and displayed the new frontal styling designed by David Bache. The cars were equipped with a range of features which included a Girling brake servo.

The 105R was the first Rover to be fitted with an automatic gearbox and the only P4 so equipped. Performance was a little more languid than the manual P4 and sales disappointing; the model was withdrawn after less than 3500 examples had been built.

The 105S was claimed by racing driver Raymond Mays to be 'the best value car anywhere in the world' and offered a 'performance' version of the P4 with its twin-carburettor engine and overdrive as standard. Trim specification was generous which helped make the car particularly attractive and it sold in relatively high numbers throughout its two year production span.

The 105, which was built for just one season, was identical to the 105S apart from a slight variation in trim detail. Counting all 105 models, production amounted to 10,700 cars.

| Engine: | 6-cylinder, in-line, inlet over exhaust, 2638cc (all); bore and stroke 73.025 x 105mm (all), output 108bhp at 4250rpm, compression ratio 8.5:1 with 7.5:1 optional. Twin SU carburettors. Sump 25pts (14.00lts) 105R, 15pts (8.5lts) 105 & 105S. |
| Transmission: | 105 & 105S 9 inch single dry plate, 4 speed gearbox with overdrive. 105R – 'Roverdrive' automatic, 2 speeds plus emergency low ratio. Gearbox |

	oil 4pts 105R (2.3lts), 5.5pts with overdrive (3.1lts) 105 &105S. Rear axle 3pts (1.75lts).
Cooling:	21 pints capacity (10.75 litres).
Fuel system:	SU electric pumps, tank capacity 11.5 gals (52.325 litres).
Brakes:	Girling servo-assisted, drums all-round.
Tyres:	6.00 x15.
Weight:	3472lbs (1578 kilos).
Performance:	Maximum speed – 105 & 105S- 100mph (160km/h);105R – 94mph (150.4km/h). Average fuel consumption – 105 & 105S – 18.5mpg (15.3 lts/100km); 105R – 20.1mpg (14.1 lts/100 km).

Rover 95

Another rationalisation of the P4 range saw the introduction of the 95 in 1962, which was designed as a direct replacement for the 4-cylinder 80 model. Based on the 100, the 95 was fitted with the 2625cc, 6-cylinder engine which produced 102bhp at 4750rpm. In an effort to keep cost and specification lower, the 95 was not fitted with overdrive.

Together with the 110, the 95 was the last of the production P4s; in March 1963, a few months after launch, the car was fitted with steel panels instead of alloy as on all previous cars. The last P4 to roll off the assembly line was a 95 on 17th May, 1964.

| Engine: | 6-cylinder, in-line inlet over exhaust, 2625cc; bore and stroke 77.8 x 92 mm. Output 100bhp at 4750rpm (export models) and 102bhp at 4750rpm (home market). Compression ratio 7.8:1 (export) and 8.8:1 (home |

market). Single SU carburettor. Sump 16pts (9.0lts) after replacing filter.

Transmission:	9 inch single dry plate clutch, 4-speed gearbox. Oil capacity 3 pts (1.75lts). Rear axle 3 pts (1.75lts).
Cooling:	23.5 pints capacity (13.5 litres).
Fuel system:	Twin SU electric fuel pump; tank capacity 11.5 gals. (52.325 litres).
Brakes:	Girling hydraulic, servo-assisted; discs front, drums at rear.
Tyres:	6.00 x 15 front, 6.40 x 15 rear.
Weight:	3399lbs (154.5 kilos).
Performance:	Maximum speed 94 mph (150.4 lts/100km). Average fuel consumption 20.25mpg (14 lts/100km).

Rover 110

Introduced at the same time as the 95, the 110 was fitted with the same basic engine but developed 123bhp at 5000rpm. The usual Rover traditions were maintained: full luxury specification as well as overdrive, which had been omitted on the 95. Steel panels were fitted to the 110 as well as to the 95 in March 1963, making the car considerably heavier and more prone to rot than earlier cars.

Engine:	6-cylinder, in-line inlet over exhaust, 2625cc; bore and stroke 77.8 x 92mm, compression ratio 8.8:1 (7.8:1 export market cars). Output 121bhp at 5000rpm (export) and 123bhp at 5000rpm (home market). Single SU carburettor. Sump 16pts (9.0lts) after replacing filter.

Transmission:	4-speed gearbox with overdrive, single dry plate clutch. Oil capacity 5pts with overdrive. Rear axle 3pts (1.75lts).
Cooling:	24.5 pints capacity (14 litres).
Fuel system:	Twin SU electric fuel pumps; tank capacity 11.5 gals. (52.325 litres).
Brakes:	Girling hydraulic, servo-assisted; discs at front and drums at rear.
Tyres:	6.00 x 15 front, 6.40 x 15 rear.
Weight:	3463lbs (1574 kilos).
Performance:	Maximum speed 105 mph (168km/h); average fuel consumption 18.4mpg (15.2 lts/100km).

Marauder

Not a Rover, the Marauder was an adventurous 2/3-seat sports tourer built by Wilks, Mackie & Co. The relationship between the Marauder car company and Rover was so close, however, that the car has become part of Rover P4 history.

With styling based very much on the Italian idiom of the era the Marauder used P4 running gear on a modified 75 chassis. Output from the Marauder factory was restricted, with 21 cars originally planned, but production ceased after only 15 units had been delivered. The majority of Marauders have survived and an example completed the 1994 Monte Carlo Challenge, one of the most prestigious classic car events.

The Marauder is amongst the most desirable and interesting classic tourers of the fifties.

Engine:	6-cylinder, in-line, inlet over exhaust, 2103cc; 2390cc. Bore and stroke 65.2 x 105mm (2103cc); 69.5 x 105mm (2390cc). (See also details of Rover 75). Compression

One of Britain's Fine Cars

	ratio 7.6:1. Output 80bhp at 4200rpm.
Transmission:	9 inch single dry plate clutch; 4-speed gearbox with overdrive or free-wheel.
Cooling:	21 pints capacity (12 litres).
Fuel system:	11.5 gals. tank capacity (52.325 litres), SU electric fuel pump.
Brakes:	Drums all-round, Girling hydro-mechanical system.
Tyres:	6.00 x 15.
Weight:	2800lbs running weight (1273 kilos).
Performance:	Maximum speed 90mph (144km/h); average fuel consumption 23-25mpg (18-16 lts/100km).
Dimensions:	Wheelbase 8ft.6in. (2,591mm); overall length 13ft.10in. (4217mm); overall width 5ft.6in (1677mm).

All models
(Apart from Marauder, gas-turbine cars and coachbuilt versions).

Dimensions:	Overall length 14ft. 10in.(4523mm)
	Overall width 5ft. 5 62in. (1670mm)
	Overall height 5ft. 3.75in. (1621mm)
	Wheelbase 9ft. 3in. (2821mm)
	Turning circle 37ft. (11,285mm)

Tyre pressures (original specification tyres):

75/80/90/95/100/105:
Front 28lbs/sq.in (1.9kg/cm)
Rear 24lbs/sq.in. (1.7kg/cm) 60:
Front 25lbs/sq.in. (1.75kg/cm)
Rear 24lbs/sq.in. (1.7kg/cm) 110:
Front 28lbs/sq.in. (1.9kg/cm)
Rear 26lbs/sq.in. (1.8kg/cm)

The above figures relate to normal conditions only; for fully laden cars increase front pressures by 2lbs/sq.in. (0.14kg/cm) and rear pressures by 6lbs/sq.in. (0.42kg/cm). In the case of sustained high speed driving in later cars, pressures should be adjusted as follows:

105, 105S:	Front 34lbs/sq.in. (2.4kg/cm) Rear 30lbs/sq.in. (2.1kg/cm)
105R:	Front and Rear 34lbs/sq.in (2.4kg/cm)
80, 95, 100:	Front 34-36lbs/sq.in. (2.3-2.5kg/cm) Rear 30-36lbs/sq.in. (2.1-2.5kg/cm)
110:	Front 32lbs/sq.in (2.2kg/cm) Rear 30lbs/sq.in (2.1kg/cm)

APPENDIX II

AT-A-GLANCE CHRONOLOGY

1949: P4 75 launched at Earls Court. Identifying features included 15-bar radiator grille, Cyclops foglamp, rectangular instruments and column gearchange.

1950: Revised instruments introduced with circular dials. Rover's gas-turbine car makes its debut. Marauder launched. Work starts on drophead models.

1951: Further detail changes to mechanical specification of 75. Drophead development continues.

1952: Drophead coupé shown at Geneva Motor show in March. New frontal styling to 75 with disappearance of Cyclops lamp; new rear window on 75. Jabbeke trials for JET 1.

1953: Two new models announced: 60 and 90; 75 continues. Floor gearchange replaces column change and 2nd gear receives synchromesh.

1954: Styling changes for '55 season announced; redesigned rear lights, new rear shape improves boot space. 75 receives short-stroke 90 engine.

1955: Rover proving ground opens. Servo brakes for 90 introduced.

1956: Overdrive optional in place of free-wheel. T3 shown at Earls Court.

1957: 105R and 105S introduced and shown at Motor Show autumn 1956. 105R has Rover's own automatic gearbox, 105S has twin carbs. and servo brakes. 60 and 75 available with either overdrive or free-wheel.

1958: Detail changes to 105R. 105R discontinued. 105S continues as 105.

1959: 80 and 100 models introduced in autumn. 60, 75, 90 and 105 models deleted. 80 fitted with Land Rover engine. Free-wheel discontinued.

1960: Front brakes standard.

1961: 80 and 100 models known as mark IV models.

1962: 80 and 100 models discontinued. 95 and 110 models introduced. Both new cars have 6-cylinder engines but 95 without overdrive. T4 shown for first time.

1963: All-steel panels fitted to 95 and 110. Rover / BRM appears.

1964: P4 production ceases after 130,342 cars. Last car, a 95, was built on 17th May.

APPENDIX III

PRODUCTION FIGURES

Model 75

Year built	Number produced	Price on introduction (£)
1950	3563	1106
1951	8821	1106
1952	8090	1487
1953	9224	1487
1954	4037	1269
1955	3220	1269
1956	3178	1374
1957	1087	1416
1958	1418	1446
1959	1039	1479

Total 43,677

Model 60

1954	1997	1163
1955	1488	1163
1956	1807	1261
1957	828	1299
1958	1498	1326
1959	1643	1350

Total 9261

Model 90

Year built	Number produced	Price on introduction (£)
1954	5957	1297
1955	8728	1297
1956	9870	1419
1957	3299	1465
1958	4167	1500
1959	3870	1539

Total 35,891

Model 105 R

1957	1889	1650
1958	1610	1688

Total 3499

Model 105 S

1957	1504	1596
1958	3667	1633

Total 5171

Model 105

1959	2030	1624

Total 2030

Model 80

1960	2797	1365
1961	2483	1365
1962	620	1438

Total 5900

Model 100

1960	6873	1538
1961	5878	1538
1962	3870	1598

Total 16,621

Model 95

1962	3	1373
1963	2387	1373
1964	1290	1237

Total 3680

Model 110

1963	2802	1534
1964	1810	1382

Total 4612

GRAND TOTAL 130,342

Survival of the fittest

The Rover P4 Drivers Guild, has over the years, maintained comprehensive records of all known surviving P4 models.

The following table, which represents home market cars, is reproduced here courtesy of Colin Blowers, the Guild's membership secretary.

Model	No. built	Surviving cars	%
75	24,380	409	1.68
60	8501	244	2.87
80	5364	442	8.24
90	24,772	467	1.89
95	3297	536	16.26
100	13,990	1400	10.01
105R	2681	88	3.28
105S	4384	111	2.53
105	1736	87	5.01
110	4348	804	18.49

A list such as this can, of course, never be fully up-to-date as previously unknown cars are continually being discovered.

APPENDIX IV

P4
COLOUR
SCHEMES

Model 75

1950-51:	Black; Ivory; Pastel Blue; Lakeside Green; Connaught Green.
1952:	Black; Ivory; Pastel Blue; Light Green; Sage Green; Connaught Green: Dove Grey; Dark Grey.
1953-4:	Black; Ivory; Pastel Blue; Light Green; Sage Green; Dove Grey; Dark Grey.
1955:	Black; Ivory; Pastel Blue; Smoke Blue; Sage Green; Dove Grey; Dark Grey.
1956-7:	Black; Ivory; Smoke Blue; Sage Green; Dove Grey; French Grey; Dark Grey.
1958:	Black; Ivory; Parchment; Smoke Blue; Pale Green; Sage Green; French Grey; Smoke Grey; Dark Grey; Fawn.
1959:	Black; Dark Blue; Shadow Green; Rush Green; Light Grey; Dove Grey; Smoke Green; Light Brown; Heather Brown.

Model 60

1954:	Black; Ivory; Pastel Blue; Light Green; Sage Green Dove Grey; Dark Grey.
1955:	Black; Ivory; Pastel Blue; Smoke Blue; Sage Green; Dove Grey; Dark Grey.
1956-7:	Black; Ivory; Smoke Blue; Sage Green; Dove Grey; French Grey; Dark Grey.
1958:	Black; Ivory; Parchment; Smoke Blue; Pale Green; Sage Green; Dove Grey; French Grey; Smoke Grey; Dark Grey; Fawn.
1959:	Black; Dark Blue; Shadow Green; Rush Green; Light Grey; Dove Grey; Smoke Grey; Light Brown; Heather Brown.

One of Britain's Fine Cars

Model 90

1954:   Black; Ivory; Pastel Blue; Light Green; Sage Green; Dove Grey; Dark Grey.

1955:   Black; Ivory; Pastel Blue; Smoke Blue; Sage Green; Dove Grey; Dark Grey.

1956-7:   Black; Ivory; Smoke Blue; Sage Green; Dove Grey; French Grey; Dark Grey.

1958:   Black; Ivory; Parchment; Smoke Blue; Pale Green; Sage Green; Dove Grey; French Grey; Smoke Grey; Dark Grey; Fawn.

1959:   Black; Dark Blue; Pale Green; Shadow Green; Rush Green; Light Grey; Dove Grey; Smoke Grey; Light Brown; Heather Brown.

Models 105R & 105S

1957:   Black; Smoke Blue; Sage Green; Dove Grey; French Grey; Dark Green.

1958:   Black; Parchment; Smoke Blue; Pale Green; Sage Green; Dove Grey; French Grey; Smoke Grey; Fawn.

Model 105

1959:   Black; Dark Blue; Shadow Green; Rush Green; Light Grey; Dove Grey; Smoke Grey; Fawn; Heather Brown.

Model 80

1960:   Black; Dover White; Dark Blue; Shadow Green; Rush Green; Light Grey; Dove Grey; Light Brown; Heather Brown.

1961:   Black; Ivory; Norse Blue; Royal Blue; Shadow Green; Rush Green; Light Grey; Dove Grey; Smoke Grey; Light Brown; Heather Brown.

1962:   Black; Ivory; Pine Green; Light Navy; Burgundy; Storm Grey; Medium Grey; Smoke Grey; Slate Grey

1963:   Black; Ivory; Burgundy; Storm Grey; Smoke Grey; Slate Grey; Medium Grey; Shadow Green; Pine Green.

Model 100

1960:   Black; Dover White; Shadow Green; Rush Green; Light Grey; Dove Grey; Smoke Grey; Light Brown; Heather Brown.

1961:   Black; Ivory; Norse Blue; Royal Blue; Shadow Green; Rush Green; Smoke Grey; Storm Grey; Slate Grey.

1962:   Black; Ivory; Light Navy; Pine Green; Shadow Green; Medium Grey.

Model 95

1962:   Black; Ivory; Light Navy; Pine Green; Shadow Green; Rush Green; Smoke Grey; Medium Grey; Storm Grey; Slate Grey.

1963:   Black; White; Dark Blue; Steel Blue; Juniper Green; Pine Green; Charcoal; Marine Grey; Stone Grey; Burgundy.

1964:   Black; White; Light Navy; Steel Blue; Juniper Green; Charcoal; Marine Grey; Stone Grey.

Model 110

1963:   Black; White; Dark Blue; Steel Blue; Juniper Green; Pine Green; Charcoal; Marine Grey; Stone Grey.

1964:   Black; White; Light Navy; Steel Blue; Juniper Green; Pine Green; Charcoal; Marine Grey; Stone Grey.

Duo-tone colours – models 80 & 100

Exterior colours	Interior trim	Carpets	Headlining
Shadow Green over Pine Green	Green Tan Light Grey	Green Tan Med. Grey	Light Grey Biscuit Light Grey
Medium Grey over Burgundy	Red Light Grey	Red Light Grey	Light Grey Light Grey
Medium Grey over Pine Green	Green Light Grey Tan	Green Med. Grey Tan	Light Grey Light Grey Biscuit
Medium Grey over Light Grey	Blue Light Grey Tan	Blue Med. Grey Tan	Light Grey Light Grey Biscuit
Slate Grey over Light Navy	Light Grey Blue Tan	Med. Grey Blue Tan	Light Grey Light Grey Biscuit

APPENDIX V

ROVER P4
SPECIALISTS

The following list of specialists represents those who have been recommended by individual owners and enthusiasts of P4s. Their inclusion is not a guarantee of quality or performance.

Scotland, Ireland & Northern England

M.H. Annable & sons
Unit 20, Darley Abbey Mills
Darley Abbey
Derby
DE22 1DZ
Tel: 01332 346299
General servicing & repairs, parts

Jon Backhouse
Higher Moorhead Farm,
High Cross Moor, Quernmore,
Lancaster LA2 0QS
Tel 01524 792740
Rebuilt spares plus windscreen wiper components

David Beswick Coach Trimmers
Unit 19, Robinson Industrial Estate
Shaftesbury Street
Derby
DE23 8NL
Tel/fax: 01332 292122
Coachtrimming

Stephen Grundy Coachtrimming
60 Church Road
Warton
Preston
Lancashire
PR4 1BD
Tel: 01772 633143
Coachtrimming and upholstery

J.P. Restorations
Holt Mill, Lloyd Street
Whitworth
Lancashire
OZ12 8AA
Tel: 01706 854017
Restorations, service and repairs

John Mann
5 Nevis Close
Lourdsley Green
Chesterfield
Derbyshire
S40 4NS
Tel: 01246 271036
Parts for all classic Rovers from 1948

Viking Restoration
Unit 11, Deanfield Mills
Asquith Avenue
Morley
Leeds
LS27 9QS
Tel: 0113 238 1558
Mobile: 07768 298164
E-mail:
Richard.stockwell@btopenworld.com
Servicing & repairs, body repairs, parts etc

John Wearing Rover Parts
Oxford Mill Garage
Victoria Street
Clayton-Le-Moors
Lancashire
BB5 5HH
Tel: 01254 386935
Fax: 01254 388955
Parts for P4s and Land Rover

Wales & Central England

Colin Blowers
32 Arundel Road, Luton
Bedfordshire
LU4 8DY
Tel: 01582 572499
Engine repairs and other mechanical work

Classic Car Restorations
Unit 2 Newman Road
Rackheath, Norwich
NR13 6PN
Tel: 01603 720550
Engine and mechanical repairs, welding

Complete Automobilist
Tel: 01692 406510
Fax: 01692 406465
Website:
www.completeautomobilist.com
Accessories

Dragon Restorations
Unit 5, Foxoak Enterprise Centre
94 Foxoak Street
Cradley Heath
West Midlands
B64 5DP
Tel: 01384 635557
Mobile: 07989639214
Repairs and restorations

Ely Service
17a Lancaster Way
Ely, Cambridgeshire
CB6 3NW
Tel: 01353 662981
Fax: 01353 667679
Restorations, bodywork, mechanical, paint and parts

Carl Haworth
7 St Helen's Road
Retford, Notts
DN22 7HA
Tel: 01777 705503
Restoration and supply of Rover instruments, plus can source many obscure fittings, clips and hoses.

Richard Hedger
3 Ireland Farm, Marsh Lane,
Algarkirk, Boston
Lincolnshire
PE20 2AY.
Tel: 01775 821684/
01205 260227/07860 655986
Supplier of reconditioned parts

Tim Hodgekiss
Mack Cottage, Broad Road
Worstead, North Walsham
Norfolk
NR28 9RU
Tel/fax: 01692 535802
Electical parts and accessories

Humphrey's Garage
Anderson Road
Bearwood
Smethwick
West Midlands
B67 5DR
Tel: 0121 429 1741
Complete service to P4 owner

Page Vehicle Repairs
Norwich Road Garage
Strumpshaw
Norfolk
Tel: 01603 712010
Mechanical work only and MoTs

Rimmer Bros
Triumph House, Sleaford Road
Bracebridge Heath, Lincoln
LN4 2NA
Tel: 01522 568000
Fax: 01522 567600
Website: www.rimmerbros.co.uk
E-mail: sales@rimmerbros.co.uk
Restorations, servicing, repairs and parts. British Motor Heritage Specialists

J.R. Wadhams Ltd
45 Valley Road, Stourbridge
West Midlands DY9 8JG
Tel: 01384 891800
E-mail: jrwadhams@boltblue.com
website: jrwadhams.co.uk
Spares for classic Rovers 1950-1977; callers by appointment only

Ray Weekley
Ryland, Main Road, Wrangle
Nr Boston, Lincolnshire
PE22 9AT
Tel: 01205 870805
Fax: 01205 871805
Website: www.roverclassics.co.uk
Parts, technical support, servicing and repairs

Woolies
Whitley Way
Northfields Industrial Estate
Market Deeping, Peterborough
PE6 8AR
Tel: 01778 347347
Fax: 01778 341847
Email: info@woolies-trim.co.uk
website: www.woolies-trim.co.uk
Trim, upholstery & fittings

Southern England

B.J.Ashpole
Southmill Road
Bishops Stortford
Hertfordshire
CM23 3DJ
Tel: 01279 653211
E-mail: bjashpole@btconnect.com
General repairs

Family Repair Service
Beales Close
Andover
Hampshire
SP10 1HT
Tel: 01264 323144
Fax: 01264 364209
Website:
www.familyrepairservice.co.uk
Interior work, door trims, carpets, window channels etc

Grants of Bath
108 London Road west
Batheaston
Bath
BA1 7DB
Tel: 01225 858147
General servicing and repairs

Lavender Motors Ltd
40 Sussex Road
Haywards Heath
Sussex
RH16 4EA
Tel: 01444 440 100
E-mail:
ryanandrews@dsl.pipex.com
General servicing and repairs

Mend-All Services
Units 1-2 Blatchington Road
Seaford
Sussex
BN25 2AN
Tel: 01323 896649
Engine and mechanical repairs

Mongers Garage Ltd
77 King Street
Maidstone
Kent ME14 2QE
Tel: 01622 751258
Servicing and engine repairs

Sussex Classic Car Parts
Unit 28 Huffwood Trading Estate
Partridge Green
Horsham
West Sussex RH13 8AU
Tel: 01403 711551
Fax: 01403711319
Website:
www.sussexclassiccar.co.uk
Parts

C.A.Upton & Son
5 Armstrong Close
St. Leonards-on-Sea
East Sussex TN38 9ST
Tel: 01424 853899
Interior and upholstery

APPENDIX VI

CLUBS

In the United Kingdom there are several Rover clubs but only two which offer membership facilities for the P4 owner and enthusiast.

The Rover Sports Register is open to owners of all Rover cars, from the very earliest to the latest models. The RSR has an excellent technical information service and regular meetings are held throughout the year. The P4 is well represented within the Register and the club's magazine *Freewheel* features news of members' cars as well as general articles on the marque.

Further information on Rover Sports Register can be obtained from:
John Holford,
Mill Wood,
Wethersfield Road,
Finchingfield
Nr Braintee,
Essex
CM7 4NS
www.thersr.co.uk

There is only one club devoted entirely to the P4. The Rover P4 Drivers Guild is an extremely active organisation which was formed in 1977 and now has approximately 2000 members. The Guild offers a comprehensive service to the P4 owner and enthusiast, and as well as operating a spares support scheme, keeps in touch with members through *Overdrive*, a particularly attractive magazine which is published bi-monthly. As well as news concerning club events, technical features are aimed at helping members get the best from their cars, whether they carry out their own servicing and repairs or not. In addition, a useful and informative yearbook is also published.

Guild meetings are held nationally and locally throughout the year with regional sections offering a wide range of events. An impressive technical information and support system is available which includes tool hire, workshop manuals and insurance and valuation advice.

The Guild's membership secretary will be delighted to provide further information. Website: www.roverp4dg.org.uk

Clubs for P4 owners exist throughout the world, to include Denmark, Holland, Australia and New Zealand. For up-to-date information concerning these organisations, it is advisable to consult the internet; alternatively the aforementioned UK-based clubs may be able to provide details.

APPENDIX VII

BIBLIOGRAPHY

Rover Memories – Richard Hough and Michael Frostick. Published by George Allen and Unwin Ltd. (Out of print but may be found at specialist bookshops).

The Automobile Age – James J. Fink. Published by Massachusetts Institute of Technology (MIT Press).

The Motor Car 1946-56 – Michael Sedgwick. Published by B T Batsford Ltd.

The Motor Makers – Martin Adeney, Published by Collins.

Post-War British Thoroughbreds – Bruce Hudson. Published by G.T. Foulis.

Rover, The First Ninety Years – Eric Dymock. Published by Dove Publishing.

Rover P4 D.I.Y. Hints and Tips – Published in association with *Overdrive*, journal of the P4 Drivers Guild.

The Classic Rovers, 1934-1977 – James Taylor. Published by Motor Racing Publications Ltd.

The Post-War Rover P4 and P5 – James Taylor. Published by P4 Spares.

Rover Anthology 1934-1949 – Compiled by Daniel Young and Published by P4 Spares.

Rover Anthology 1950-1967 – Compiled by Daniel Young and published by P4 Spares.

Advertising Rover 1904-1964 – Compiled by Daniel Young and published by P4 Spares.

Advertising Rover Volume II 1904-1984 – Complied by Daniel Young, and published by P4 Spares.

Sporting Rover Anthology 1930-1968 – Complied by Daniel Young and published by P4 Spares.

Practical Classics and Car Restorer Rover P4 Mechanics Briefing – published by Kelsey Publishing Limited.

Rover P4 1949-1959 – Brooklands Books.

Rover P4 1955-1964 – Brooklands Books.

Whittle, The True Story – John Golley. Published by Airlife.

Studebaker 1946-1966 – Richard M. Langworth. Published by Motorbooks International.

Haynes Guide to Postwar Collectors' Cars – Published by Haynes.

[The] Motor Magazine.

[The] Autocar Magazine.

Popular Classics Magazine.

Practical Classics Magazine.

Classic Cars Magazine.

Classic and Sportscar Magazine.

Motor Sport Magazine.

The Complete Encyclopedia Of The Motor Car – Edited by G.N.Georgano, Published by Ebury Press.

British Car Factories from 1896 – Collins and Stratton. Published by Veloce Publishing.

The Motor Men – Peter King – Published by Quiller Press.

Overdrive – The magazine of the Rover P4 Drivers Guild

Also from Veloce Publishing –

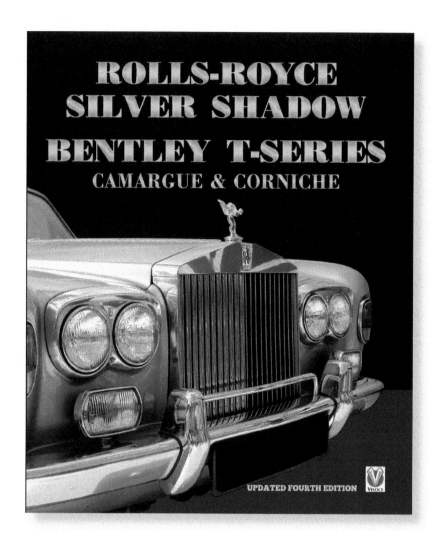

The Rolls-Royce Silver Shadow & Bentley T-Series were a revolutionary step forward when launched in 1965. Here's the full story, including related coachbuilt cars & the Silver Wraith ll, Corniche & Camargue, updated 4th Edition.

ISBN: 978-1-845843-01-4
Paperback • 25x20.7cm • £30* UK/$50* USA • 216 pages • 207 pictures

For more info on Veloce titles, visit our website at www.veloce.co.uk • email: info@veloce.co.uk
• Tel: +44(0)1305 260068
* prices subject to change, p&p extra

Definitive history of the MGA, the first British sports car to sell more than 100,000 units & be able to top 100mph. Includes Le Mans prototypes, the coupé, Twin Cam, 1600 & 1600 MkII models; competition history; 'secret MGAs;' USA success story; restoration notes, & much more.

ISBN: 978-1-845849-62-7
Paperback • 25x20.7cm • £25* UK/$39.95* USA • 160 pages • 145 pictures

For more info on Veloce titles, visit our website at www.veloce.co.uk • email: info@veloce.co.uk
• Tel: +44(0)1305 260068
* prices subject to change, p&p extra

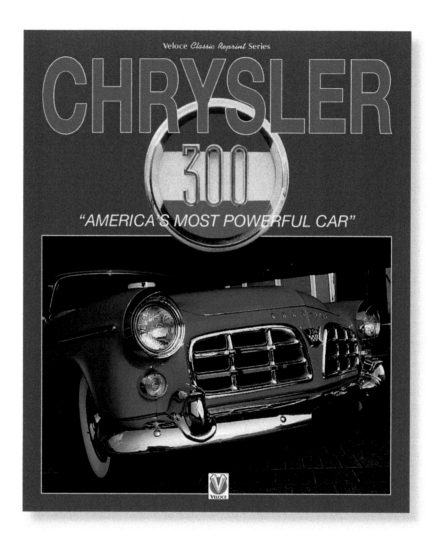

This highly illustrated book presents the history of one of America's greatest automobiles series, the Chrysler 300. Every model's specifications and role in Chrysler history is examined in detail. Includes sales and production records and a review of the new 300's close relative, the 2005 Dodge Magnum.

ISBN: 978-1-845849-61-0
Paperback • 25x20.7cm • £25* UK/$39.95* USA • 160 pages • 174 pictures

For more info on Veloce titles, visit our website at www.veloce.co.uk • email: info@veloce.co.uk
• Tel: +44(0)1305 260068
* prices subject to change, p&p extra

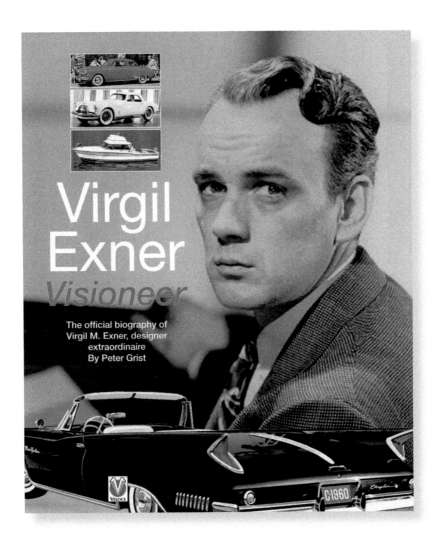

Gets inside the character of the man, his strengths and weaknesses, his personal tragedies and his vision of modern transport. Previously unseen works of art and family photos included. A unique and fascinating insight to a pivotal player in the development of the modern automobile.

ISBN: 978-1-845848-63-7
Paperback • 25x20.7cm • £25* UK/$40* USA • 176 pages • 388 pictures

For more info on Veloce titles, visit our website at www.veloce.co.uk • email: info@veloce.co.uk •
Tel: +44(0)1305 260068
* prices subject to change, p&p extra

INDEX

Dear Reader,
We hope you enjoyed this Veloce
production. If you have ideas for books
on Rover or other marques, please write
and tell us.
Meantime, Happy Motoring!

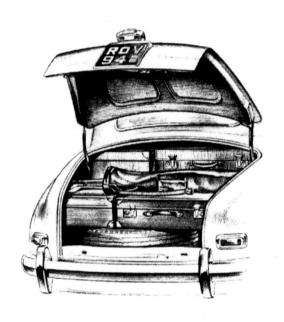

THE END